Management Development That Works

Management Development That Works

Editor
Patricia Hind

Copyright © Libri Publishing

First published in 2015 by Libri Publishing

ISBN 978-1-909818-67-5

Book design by Carnegie Publishing

Cover design by Carnegie Publishing

Printed in the UK by Halstan Printing

Libri Publishing
Brunel House
Volunteer Way
Faringdon
Oxfordshire
SN7 7YR

Tel: +44 (0)845 873 3837

www.libripublishing.co.uk

CONTENTS

SECTION 1
– INTRODUCTION

Introduction

Patricia Hind

If I asked you the question "What is management development for?" I'm sure you would all have an answer, based on your different experiences. I am equally sure there would be many different answers, representing a very broad range of objectives. Let me guess at a few:

- It's to develop executives or managers who want to do better or differently as a leader or manager

- It's to reward past good performance – high flyers receive the prize of a business-school programme or personal coaching

- It's to ensure that organisations score highly on 'best place to work' rankings – developing people is a good thing

- It's to help managers really drive business results

- It's to help organisational leaders to speak the same language at all levels of their organisation

- It's to fix or correct personal faults

- It's to broaden a manager's skill set.

There may be others I have missed out, so we have a huge breadth of scope and a pretty clear idea of what management development should deliver. I wonder if we are equally clear about how important it is to get it right.

Businesses are the life blood of our economy and our society. Both the developed and the developing world are societies of organisations. From businesses to hospitals, from governments to charities, organisations are the agencies of our mutual dependency. So societies are reliant on the success of their organisations. If they fail to offer meaningful employment, to pay living wages, and to produce goods and services for which people want to pay, then the results are far reaching. As a worst-case scenario, jobs, prosperity and optimism for the future will all disappear, with consequences ranging from low self-esteem to civil unrest. The relatively recent recession of 2008 has left scars, still painful, which speak eloquently to the effects of poor economic and organisational health. Management is the vehicle for delivering the success of organisations. Management creates and implements strategic plans, structures the organisation to operate efficiently and, perhaps most importantly, provides the leadership and motivation to keep employees engaged and productive. It is the critical coordinating function which underpins achievement.

This view was summed up by Santiago Inigues, the president of IE University in Spain, when he stated that:

> 'The best antidote to intolerance or the clash of cultures or poor foreign policies is to develop good managers, create new businesses, innovate and generate value and wealth at all levels of society.'[*]

So, for societies and organisations to function they must be able to fulfil their purpose, and to do that they need to be managed in ways that are effective, efficient and sustainable. With that 'frame' in mind, the task of helping managers and leaders to run their businesses in ways that create sustainable social, economic and human value is a significant responsibility, one that is shared by managers, organisations, business schools, faculty and consultants.

Given the breadth of management development objectives, and their importance, a third question springs to mind: how can organisations be sure they are getting real business value from the management development investments they choose to make? Or to rephrase that question, what actually works?

However, assessing the effectiveness of management development initiatives is not always easy. There are a myriad of different approaches and tools, from

---

[*]   Inigues S (2011) The Learning Curve: How Business Schools are Reinventing Education. *Palgrave Macmillan*

MOOCs to MBAs[*], to modular executive education programmes, through action learning, coaching and self-reflection, so it is impossible to find evaluation criteria applicable to all. Even more complicating are those many objectives we set out at the beginning of this introduction. Which to use? How many to choose? These are questions faced by learning and development professionals on a daily basis, often working within organisations that may be unsure about what they really want from management development – really different individual behaviours? More-motivated managers? More high-performing teams? All of the above? But obviously, all in the service of improved organisational performance.

The remit of this book is to offer an evidence-based view of the real world of management development both today and for the future. The authors and I are all professionals, involved in helping managers and organisations to be the best that they can be through different developmental processes. Each author offers a chapter which covers an aspect of management development about which he or she has deep experience, expertise and passion. This book is designed for you, the reader, to dip in and out, according to the issues interesting you at any particular time. Whilst it ranges across a breadth of approaches, content and contexts, we do not claim that this book is fully comprehensive. What we do claim is that the methods and approaches discussed are real and practical. This book will help you to understand what actually does work, under what conditions and why.

The book is divided into five sections. The first one is this introduction, which offers a brief summary of each chapter. In the second section, 'How Managers Learn', the authors examine the realities of professional adult-learning processes.

Lee Waller and Megan Reitz report a two-stage research process that has highlighted the role of neurobiology in interpreting and harnessing learning experiences. Firstly, they identify a number of critical incidents that form significant learning experiences for managers. Secondly, they find that the process of learning through these experiences induces a state of arousal and increased heart rate which appears to underpin the learning from the event through the development of 'muscle memory'. When this arousal is perceived as a challenge, rather than a threat, cognitive performance 'in the moment' may be improved.

---

[*]   MOOC: massive open online course; MBA: master of business administration (degree)

Such is the importance of this process to leadership development that Waller and Reitz argue that, for it to be truly impactful, really to help prepare leaders for the challenges of leadership, it must involve fairly hard-hitting experience. It needs to stretch participants, challenge them, take them out of their comfort zone, and present the possibility of failure. All of which require experienced, sensitive and responsible facilitation.

Kathleen King and Patricia Hind offer different examples of the value of action-research processes in organisational and leadership development. Action research is an approach that is specifically concerned with change and, more particularly, with effective, permanent and positive change, during which knowledge is produced in the service of action not theory. It has been extensively explored for both individual and organisational learning and found to be a successful and positive methodology for effecting change in organisations.

Kathleen King leads part-time degree programmes for professionals and explores the use of action research for individuals involved in bringing about change in organisations and communities. Patricia Hind leads a research project designed to bring about both organisational change and the development of responsible leadership in SMEs. Before offering their respective experiences of action research, the authors make a case for its relevance in contemporary management development and give a brief historical perspective.

The two examples of the use of the methodology are described in sufficient detail for readers to be able to consider how they might implement practically such processes in their own context. The results outlined in the chapter provide optimism that there is a new way forward, appropriate to the demands of the twenty-first-century organisational context.

James Moncrieff and Dev Mookherjee address the topical challenge of senior management development. As workforces age, the challenges of understanding how best to continue developing senior managers still in position beyond traditional retirement ages come increasingly to the fore. This chapter reports the results of research undertaken into exactly what capabilities are required of senior leaders and how to develop those capabilities effectively. The focus is on the key learning characteristics of the population and the approaches that seem to work best. Not only do the findings highlight the importance of emotional as well as intellectual stretch in the learning process, but they also indicate that, for senior managers, leadership development might be seen to hold some personal risk for participants.

The chapter makes specific recommendations about several aspects of senior management development, particularly with respect to the use of the 'live-case method', that must be addressed in order to ensure success with this challenging population.

To conclude this first section of the book, Roger Delves describes, again in detail, how an experiential approach to management development can meet the rigorous standards required for an MBA module regulated by the UK QAA requirements for postgraduate degrees. Received wisdom often assumes that 'soft' management skills, such as influencing and leadership, are almost impossible to develop and assess to the necessary standards, within a classroom context. Delves debunks this myth by explaining how an innovative and engaging experiential module, drawing on life and literature, provided robust and QAA-acceptable assessment.

Tackling the all-important but elusive concept of 'personal impact', the developmental aim was to help students to develop their thinking, behaviour and performance around their personal impact in order that they could 'be themselves more, with skill'. The use of novel ideas such as 'life canvasses' instead of case studies, blended with more traditional tools, created an environment in which students felt informed and motivated enough to engage experientially and enthusiastically with intensely personal and sophisticated inter-relational frameworks such as Transactional Analysis, Emotional Intelligence and Authenticity.

That fresh approach to management development concludes the second section of the book, and in Section 3 we next turn our attention to 'Where Managers Learn'. This section dips into the contexts and situations which are most conducive to management learning. These range from outdoor learning environments, classrooms, learning from home and actually learning by working with and in organisations.

Angela Jowitt opens for us with some reflections on her wide experience of working with a particular form of experiential learning – Outdoor Management Development (OMD). The fundamental idea, reinforced elsewhere, and often, in this book, is that management learning is facilitated most effectively through practical experiences and active reflection. As outdoor learning exercises are often novel and unusual for participants, the uniqueness of the activities provide a 'level playing field' to promote equality between participants in terms of skill and ability for the task, allowing individuals and groups to focus on the processes underpinning behaviours.

Jowitt argues that the success and impact of OMD, plus the overwhelmingly positive participant reviews of most OMD sessions, has led to their ubiquitous use on an enormous number of programmes or other learning interventions. However, the cultural background of participants is often not specifically acknowledged or addressed, and the research reported here indicates that this may be a critical factor in determining the experience each participant has, and therefore the learning he or she can take from it.

It appears that experiential learning demands a particular responsibility from facilitators and educational professionals. This is not simply about passing on information or 'teaching' new knowledge. Engaging with the subjectivity of experience and the holistic nature of 'being' that participants bring to experiential learning sessions means that these must be respected explicitly. A key part of this includes developing greater cultural awareness and remaining aware of the cultural diversity in the group. Cultural awareness is an important factor in working with *any* group, but particularly for effective OMD, as the novelty of the situations facing participants means that they are often unable to fall back on previous learning, so their default is to culturally defined behaviour patterns. It is critical that facilitators are mutually engaged in the learning space, being present and genuinely curious to hear the perspectives of all and slowing down the pace to allow everyone to have a voice, and to allow all to make sense of their own personal experience. Providing the opportunity for people to connect with the whole of themselves, including their personal and cultural history, is where OMD can prove a hugely powerful learning vehicle.

The next chapter, from Barbara Banda, picks up and develops this point. She turns our attention to what actually goes on within the learning environment that contributes to the effectiveness of management development. She focusses on the classroom, drawing on previous educational development work with migrant children in California. The collective 'third space' is a term coined to represent the operating environment within a classroom that can be generated to allow participants to be their 'true' selves. Whilst important for personal awareness and development, Banda finds that this strength can be offset by weak links between the programme environment and the participants' workplaces. Specific recommendations are made as to how these links can be strengthened by faculty being clearer about the activities participants must undertake before and after the programme to allow these connections to be improved.

Ilze Zandvoort moves on to offer a broad overview of the challenges that managers and companies face in introducing technology into their portfolio of development. This is an extremely topical area and, after a comprehensive introduction to the field of blended learning, Zandvoort identifies five areas that require careful thought for tailored, blended learning solutions. These are:

- Technology challenges
- Organisational challenges
- Design challenges
- Implementation challenges, and
- Engagement challenges.

The chapter argues that successful blended learning addresses all five categories and explicitly recognises that any approach to executive development must be aligned to strategic objectives as well as personal development plans, in order to deliver value to both the organisation and the individual. The links between technology and development are becoming ever more important as 'digital natives' join the workforce and the issue of blending technology with other learning interventions is a significant challenge, both for line managers and the L&D community. Intriguingly, the chapter concludes that any learning intervention designed to enhance management capability in today's business environment must mirror the complexity of that environment – another L&D challenge!

In the final chapter of this section, Vicki Culpin examines the use of 'live cases' in management development. The term is used to denote learning through a structured experience. Participants work on a real organisational concern to offer insights or solutions to help the business address the issue. Culpin offers a detailed critique of the different ways that live cases can be defined and used. She notes that, despite their differences, the approaches have two common characteristics: the involvement of the client organisation and the timely nature of the topic.

Her research examines whether managerial skills and abilities actually *do* improve or change as a result of utilising this methodology. Culpin goes on to demonstrate that live cases that are active, problem-based and 'just in time', involving real clients with real issues, indeed provide a rich atmosphere for learning. She demonstrates the ability of a live case study to develop and enhance a range of skills, tools and techniques for participants on executive education programmes and concludes that this is an excellent way to deepen the learning of classroom-based concepts and tools, describing how this expensive and time-consuming technique can actually deliver a valuable return on the investment required.

Moving forward, Section Four takes a look at what the management development profession needs to offer clients now, to equip them to deal with future challenges. Under the heading of 'What Managers Need to Learn for 2020', the concepts of risk, sustainability and artful knowing are considered in turn. These are topics that, whilst not always on business school agendas as a matter of course, should be there in the future.

The first of these, risk management, is of course not new. However, Jamie MacAlister offers a new take on the management of risk by aligning it with the concept of personal values. He argues that doing the right thing often means taking risk, but that taking risk is not always right. When faced with strategic and ethical dilemmas, leaders need to manage personal and organisational risk in making decisions effectively. Using a metaphor involving elephants, tigers, mice and honey badgers, MacAlister offers a tool to help managers understand the 'right' and 'not-right' aspects of the risks involved in the dilemmas they face.

From a learning perspective, and for true learning to take place, the chapter argues that we actually need to experience risk to reflect and learn from it, emotionally and intuitively. Business schools can shape participants' experiences in such a way that they can do this in a 'safe' environment, and leverage the paradox that safety is essential for learning to manage risk.

Matthew Gitsham develops concepts of risk by explaining the importance of the complex interconnected global challenges facing today's organisations. These challenges span national borders, have significant global consequences if not addressed, and require more than just action by national governments to tackle them. The so-called 'mega trends' include resource scarcity, urbanisation and population growth, amongst others.

Global strategies to tackle these interconnected challenges are increasingly organised under the heading 'sustainable development' – organising human society and activity in such ways as to enable people to meet their needs and lead fulfilling lives with dignity, at the same time as respecting planetary boundaries and enabling future generations to meet their own needs. There has been a radical shift in perceptions regarding which institutions in the world must play a role in responding to these kinds of challenges. There is now a widespread view that most of today's big interconnected global challenges are almost impossible for governments to address on their own, and that a much wider group of players needs to be at the table, which must include businesses.

The chapter relates real stories from senior leaders about their growing realisation of the importance of the sustainability agenda for the success of their businesses. They suggest that more is required than just briefings and lectures on global trends and their commercial implications. It seems that relationships and first-hand experiences are at the heart of what it takes for business leaders to build the emotional connection and commitment to put this agenda at the front and in the centre of their work. However, it is unlikely to be sufficient simply to offer frameworks and models within which to develop effective interpersonal relationships Therefore, to foster the right kind of leadership capability in organisations, a more radical approach to development is needed.

When designing development interventions, off-the-shelf solutions will no longer do. Unique and seminal experiences, elsewhere in this book described as 'crucible' experiences, must be created, offered and invested in, to bring about the sea change required in the leadership of those who must take their organisations forward to deal with ever more complicated, interrelated and acute challenges.

Building on this notion of the importance of personal experience, our next chapter, by Chris Nichols, explores a unique approach to management and leadership development. He describes the use of two techniques. The first is 'artful knowing', which means using artistic interpretation as a sense-making vehicle for personal and organisational development. The second demonstrates the craft of 'imagining' in the service of the same aim.

Nichols has an important message. He describes work that is about 'artful practice', not about 'being an artist' – but which still requires discipline and effort to develop the practice, to develop the ways of seeing and doing that go beyond the lazy shorthand of the commonplace.

He admits the work is risky – it isn't as predictable as using a formula or a template, and the results can vary because life varies. Organisations believing that they need certainty and predictability in the development of their managers find this approach challenging, although, he believes, ultimately liberating, catalytic and necessary. Working with these principles offers a journey in identity and purpose, and needs practitioners and clients to challenge and confront their uniqueness, as well as their sameness. By celebrating more of who we are and who we aspire to be, Nichols argues we can add huge value to organisational clients because becoming a successful leader is synonymous with becoming truly the whole of oneself. Artful knowing is a key part of that wholeness.

The final section of the book, 'Making It Work Now and for the Future', looks beyond what we are currently doing on the 'shop floor' of management development. The chapters consider, first of all, the translation and transfer of learning back to the work place, and finally the current and future position of management development on the world stage.

Ian Hayward addresses the challenge of evaluation, and acknowledges that this has both interested and frustrated management development professionals for many years. He argues that too little research has been undertaken to examine the link between leadership and management development and changed behaviour in the workplace, let alone the link with organisational performance.

After a thorough review of the literature, Hayward offers six practical and accessible principles for an effective evaluation strategy:

- Avoid evaluation 'afterthought'

- Cherry pick from the toolkit

- Check the 'fit' for 'purpose'

- Think multiplicity

- Weigh up perfection and practicality

- Communicate, communicate, communicate – and apply and monitor.

The principles outlined are offered, not to guarantee perfection, but in his words, hopefully to "help avoid expensive disasters!"

Moving on to our penultimate chapter, Lee Waller and Megan Reitz discuss the concept of 'sticky learning' – by which they mean learning that transfers effectively to the workplace. They notice that received wisdom holds that as little as 10-to-20 per cent of the learning gained from management development is actually applied on the job and acknowledge that this is a poor return on investment in anyone's book! This chapter explores exactly what influences the transfer of learning and what those involved in the process of learning, including the individual, the programme designers and organisations, can do to ensure that learning is applied in the workplace.

Reporting on an empirical research project, the chapter concludes that it is difficult to overstate the importance of ensuring that individuals arrive in the classroom with the necessary knowledge, skills and attitudes to learn. This indeed may be the key to ensuring subsequently that the learning is applied back at work. However, this exploration of all the factors in the transfer system showed that the development of these characteristics is very much a shared responsibility between individual learners, the programme designers and the organisations to which the individual returns. If one of these stakeholders fails to support transfer, the efforts of others may be negated and may have a serious impact on whether or not learning is applied.

The authors suggest that acknowledging and making explicit these inter-relationships could significantly increase the long-term impact of management and leadership development programmes – the holy grail of L&D!

To conclude, Kai Peters and Narendra Laljani take the bold but well-argued position that learning is the only viable competitive advantage for organisations. This, they suggest, explains why management development has been a growth industry over the last few decades. However, they advocate strongly that much closer attention needs to be paid to the relationship between the realities of the managerial world, which continue to change, and the management development industry, parts of which appears to be stuck in yesterday's paradigms.

Echoing Gitsham's chapter, the authors identify five key societal trends which they believe have become critical for organisations and their managers. The chapter offers a synthesis of these trends, each of which is significant in itself. However, they are also inter-related, creating what some have called a 'VUCA' world characterised by volatility, uncertainty, complexity and ambiguity. Those trends are both complex and complicated, but can be labelled:

- Disruptive technology

- Globalisation

- Demographic dynamics

- The knowledge economy

- The new social contract concerning the demands placed on businesses to operate sustainably and responsibly.

For successful development to take place, three significant developmental vehicles are discussed: stretch, or challenge experiences; developmental relationships; and critical reflection. The authors argue that the use of these three techniques together creates a developmental framework within which the dilemmas of leading in today's turbulent business landscape can be addressed.

The chapter concludes that, as the world is developing around us and new challenges are created, not only are our ways of working evolving, but also our entire lives. Coping with these developments, and effectively engaging with them, calls for the skills to accept ambiguity and complexity and to use humility and dialogue to guide judgement. An uncertain and volatile environment requires managers to perform a wide range of leadership functions. Developing these skills is not easy as one must balance a number of dilemmas without falling victim to indecision and inaction.

To sum up, and taking a 'helicopter view' of the work presented throughout this book, the key messages are that it is vitally important continually to experiment and review the techniques used to enable managers to lead their organisations successfully. To create the learning changes in knowledge, skills and attitudes that are fundamental to individual and organisational development, it is vital that the process is seen as a partnership between individual learners, their organisations and learning and development professionals. Many chapters in this book have highlighted the need for experienced, sensitive and skilled faculty to guide learners through the different experiences discussed here. The nature of those different experiences is also key. The added value of using different lenses, such as neuroscience, art, literature, action learning, live cases and outdoor experiences, has been demonstrated clearly.

There is no doubt that development processes can be influential, but they must go beyond traditional modes of delivery. Effective management development interventions can help create the individual skill sets and organisational capability needed to succeed in the decades ahead, and they will be a crucial driver of sustained success. However, the evidence presented in this book clearly shows that, to ensure that success, there are key issues that must be addressed. Not only must the techniques employed be relevant, accessible, credible and capable of driving the development agenda, they must move beyond simply responding to traditional perceptions and outdated ways of working.

In conclusion, the economies of the world, driven by managed organisations, are constantly changing and the management development industry needs to do more than react to those changes. The responsibility is to offer cutting-edge thinking and practice which feeds, nurtures, develops, cajoles, challenges and stimulates managers to be the best they can be, in order to create both social and economic value for the prosperity of communities everywhere.

Patricia Hind MSc., Ph.D., AFBPS
Director, Centre for Research in Executive Education
Ashridge Business School
Berkhamsted
Hertfordshire
HP4 1NS
UK

CHAPTER 1

The Neuroscience of Management Development

Lee Waller and Megan Reitz

Introduction

> Knowledge gained through experience is far superior and many times more useful than bookish knowledge.
>
> Mahatma Gandhi

The power, impact and value of experience as a vehicle for learning has long been understood. Lasting, transformational learning – learning that results in real change in attitudes, perspectives and behaviour – comes not through simply listening or observing, but through doing. This awareness is not unfamiliar to those of us who are engaged in the development of managers and leaders, who are employed in the task of aligning attitudes and behaviours with organisational objectives. But what is less understood is the role that our neurobiology plays in interpreting and harnessing that experience to facilitate its impact on those attitudes and behaviours.

Leaders today may operate in a highly sophisticated, modern world. But it could be argued that what drives them to action under pressure is the same innate need that drove their counterparts thousands of years ago – survival. What our brains are responding to, what it is that we must 'survive', has clearly changed beyond scope: we are now more concerned with losing our profits than losing our lives. However, when under threat, our neurological and physiological responses are precisely the same as those of our distant ancestors. These responses can have a decidedly detrimental impact on our behaviour, but if understood, can be manipulated to enhance performance and maximise learning.

This chapter reports on a research study which aimed to develop this understanding. The research results have provided insights into how and why learning through experience is such a powerful vehicle for developing leaders for the challenges of leadership. It begins with a consideration of what it is that these experiences need to teach the leaders of today: what is it that they need to learn to be truly effective leaders of the future?

Lessons in leadership

Many of us, past a certain age, will find ourselves claiming at some time or another that the youth of today do not know they are born. When we were young we didn't have avatars or iPads, we didn't have Skype, mobile phones or the Internet. And, for the most part, this is true. We do now live in a very different world from that in which many of us reached maturity. But whilst this modern world brings untold advantages, it also brings unprecedented demands on our organisational leaders.

Organisations today operate in what is often termed a 'VUCA' environment – a rapidly changing world which is volatile, uncertain, complex and ambiguous (Horney, Pasmore & O'Shea, 2010). Technological advances, widespread globalisation and increased diversity have resulted in a highly competitive climate which is fast moving and ever changing, and presents today's leaders with greater challenges than ever before (Adler & Kwon, 2002; Hogan, 2010; IBM, 2010). But are they – and the development opportunities afforded them – up to task? Most modern organisations have a talent programme designed to identify, develop and nurture the successors to the current board. But these leaders-in-waiting tend to be in a hurry and there is limited patience for the traditionally lengthy programmes and processes needed to develop them for leadership. Seasoned leaders are sought with 20/20 foresight, and they are wanted now, ready to 'hit the ground running'. The question arises, therefore: how can we accelerate this required development? What quick, innovative and effective fixes can we offer to prepare them for the challenges of leading in this complex, and often chaotic, world and get them job-ready now?

These are the questions that initiated an extensive and ongoing research project at a leading UK business school, designed to explore the possibilities of accelerating learning in a pragmatic manner. The objective was to design a programme which would really assist these future leaders to have immediate impact. The first step in this search was to develop two key questions that have now been asked to hundreds of senior leaders (Poole & Carr, 2005). The first of these questions is "what do you know now about leadership that you wish you'd known ten years ago?"

Before reading on, it would be useful if *you* could reflect on what you were doing ten years ago: what job were you in, where were you located, what were your family circumstances? Then consider what you know now that you wish you'd known then, in relation to leadership.

The original research returned a clear top answer: self-knowledge. Experienced leaders recognised that it would have been extremely helpful to their career progression and to their performance as leaders if they had known themselves better. They wished they could have recognised their strengths and their blind spots. They would have liked to have known how others *really* perceived them, and they wished they had had the confidence to understand that they were capable of more than they realised. So responses to the question included: "don't be so hard on yourself", "know your own weaknesses", "you can't be all things to all people", "you can't be right all the time – mistakes are ok" and "I didn't need to 'know' as much as I thought I did".

Learning from critical incidents

This then led to the second key question posed: "What were the critical incidents that taught you these valuable lessons?" Again, reader, you might like to consider your own path over the last ten years and ask yourself this question before you continue to the rest of this chapter.

Although respondents considered that 'classroom' based learning had an important influence, they felt overwhelmingly that learning through experience and on the job had the most impact. Some key incidents were referred to repeatedly (Poole & Carr, 2005) and they were found to be largely related to the following issues:

- Managing self

- Managing change

- Dealing with staff

- Dealing with peers

- Dealing with success

- Dealing with failure

- Delivering bad news.

The researchers found that the most common response to this question was a story involving respondents having to step up suddenly to leadership challenges. In these situations they realised there was no longer someone above them: the accountability was theirs; they now had to make the decisions. Such experiences were initiated either as a result of applying successfully for stretching roles such as setting up a new office internationally, or as a result of being 'forced' into taking leadership roles due, for example, to their boss being taken ill unexpectedly. Another common critical incident centred on having to undertake difficult conversations with team members, bosses, peers or customers. A third group of responses focused on experiences of having either very inspirational bosses or, on the other hand, very poor bosses. (The good news here is that even if a current boss is terrible, it would appear that their direct reports can still learn a great deal through working with them!)

Developing 'The Leadership Experience' programme

The original research thus indicated that seasoned leaders wish they had known more about themselves earlier and that there are a number of common critical incidents which prove to be particularly influential in developing leadership capability and in learning the lessons of leadership. Participants in the research reported that critical incident experiences built their confidence in relation to dealing with similar experiences later on: in other words, having done it once they felt more prepared to face the incident again and to tackle it more successfully. The researchers termed this learning process 'muscle memory' and refer to it further below.

These insights from the preliminary research led to the following hypotheses about the design of a management development programme:

- If a programme is designed with the overall aim of developing self-awareness and provides opportunities to experience the most common critical incidents uncovered in the research, leadership development will be accelerated and more pragmatic.

- Such a programme could help participants to develop the 'muscle memory' required to assist them in dealing with critical incidents back in the workplace when it really matters.

So the first iteration of 'The Leadership Experience: Leading on the Edge' (which was at first called 'The Future Leadership Experience') was designed and delivered in 2005. 'The Leadership Experience' (TLE) was a highly experiential programme lasting for two or two-and-a-half days. During the programme, essentially a simulation, participants are projected into the future to run an organisation in challenging circumstances. The process incorporated extensive peer and tutor feedback on the decisions participants took and the actions that resulted. Participants also received concurrent executive coaching which supported them before and after the residential element. These two elements of the programme were designed to help participants develop a deeper level of self-awareness. Together the participants navigated their way through a number of critical incidents and were facilitated throughout to enable deep reflection on their experience.

It became quickly apparent from anecdotal feedback that the programme was impactful. For example, one early participant stated:

> It opens up the way you can look at things and broadens your mind. When I look at some of the challenges I have faced in the past in the light of what I learned in the programme – well, there are some things I would do differently today.

Another stated:

> It's been a brilliant course – very intense and non-directional at times, which clearly provided the best learning opportunities. The context and content allow you to learn about yourself and about others so that you are able to take the best bits away and deploy them in real leadership situations.

Participants were reporting that their confidence had improved and that they felt better able to handle critical incidents when back in their workplace.

What the researchers were not so sure about were the processes which lay behind this impact. What was it about this development approach that led to such significant learning?

The neurology of effective learning

This chapter began with an uncompromising assertion that for learning to be truly effective and long-lasting, it needs to occur through experience. Corporate executives, entrepreneurs and senior leaders have all claimed to have learned more from real work and life experiences than from leadership development or MBA programmes (Thomas & Cheese, 2005). This is not to say that there is no place in leadership development for text books, for 'chalk and talk' or for MBAs. All contribute to the development of the competences required to operate as a leader, for developing skills in finance, marketing, strategy or change. But in order to prepare leaders for the challenges of leadership, to prepare them for the future and develop them as truly effective and credible 'leaders', learning is most impactful when it occurs through experience (Conger, 2004; Pye, 1994).

What also appears critical, however, is that these experiences are emotionally charged. Memories with emotional content tend to be longer lasting and more vivid (LeDoux, 2000). This has been illustrated by research exploring students' clearest memories, which found that vividness of memories correlated with rated importance, degree of surprise and emotionality (Rubin & Kozin, 1994). Think back to some of your earliest childhood memories and you'll likely find that those that you recall with the most clarity are those in which you were scared, happy, excited or sad. One of the reasons for this relationship can be found in the physical structure of the brain. The amygdala, which is involved in processing emotion, is located within the limbic system in close proximity to the hippocampus, which is involved in the access of memories (Phelps, 2006). So emotion provides an additional channel through which to access memory.

There is some debate, however, as to whether positive emotions or negative emotions are the most impactful. For example, research examining the critical incidents referred to by retired teachers when recalling their careers found that job difficulties and negative experiences were recalled three times more readily than positive experiences (Ben-Peretz, 2002). Conversely, research on memory of events has found that pleasant, positive and successful experiences are remembered better than negative ones (Matlin and Stang, 1978; Wagenaar, 1986). This ambiguity certainly appears to be the case for memory.

For learning rather than just recall, however, the evidence is a little clearer cut: negative experiences appear to out-perform the positive. One explanation for this effect is that failures, which can be construed as negative experiences, force us to revisit our experience in order to determine what went wrong and avoid making similar mistakes in the future. This pushes us to revise our mental models and reinforces our learning (Ellis & Davidi, 2005).

There may also be an evolutionary explanation for the power of negative emotions over positive, found in the rather sobering fact that, as a species, we are pre-programmed to notice the negative over the positive. Thousands of years ago our ability to spot the threatening predator would have proved more adaptive to our survival than our ability to spot a cool stream in which to take a dip.

Another important explanation for the impact of negative emotion on learning can be found in our bodies' response to stressful experiences. During such experiences, the body's stress hormones produce a state of arousal. This is our sympathetic nervous system response. When moderately aroused, our heart rate increases and pushes blood into the brain, improving our cognitive functioning and the formation of memories (Jamieson et al., 2010). We are alert, think clearly and make good decisions. If, however, we do not believe we have the resources to meet the challenge of the situation, we become over-aroused and our body, perceiving threat, sends blood away from the brain towards our limbs in order that we might fight or flee (Blascovich & Tomaka, 1996; Frankenhaeuser, 1986; Henry, 1980). The effect of this threat response is seriously to impede our cognitive processes, such as our ability to pay attention, to evaluate and appraise information, and to encode and retrieve memories (Lupien et al., 2007). It is responsible for those moments of panic when you can barely remember your own name let alone offer an articulate response to an unanticipated question.

Herein lies part of the power of experience in learning. Through immersing leaders in real-life, high-pressure experiences that simulate the stresses of leadership in a safe environment, those experiences can induce this stress reaction. For exercises which induce a moderate of level of stress, this is likely to result in a challenge being perceived and responded to. The blood supply to the brain will increase and the individual leader's cognitive performance in the moment will improve. However, very high-impact, emotional experiences while learning may result in a threat being perceived. The physiological response will send blood away from the brain, diminishing cognitive performance.

If encouraged to reflect on their experiences, this process itself should help participants to understand what their own individual trigger points are. Through reflection they can understand what, to them, constitutes a threat rather than a challenge, and can manage their responses, resulting in impactful learning from the experience.

This second stage of the research therefore hypothesised that:

- Moderate levels of stress during a learning experience will promote immediate and retained learning.

This proposition was tested with participants on 'The Leadership Experience' (TLE), the programme which had been developed to provide a high-impact and emotive leadership simulation. The researchers wanted to learn more about the participants' physiological responses to the experiential nature of the programme. A further research interest was to determine whether personality would have any impact on this physiological response to these stressful situations and, in turn, whether this might impact learning.

The research was designed so that two programmes, each lasting two days, were run with 14 participants attending each one. During their time on the programme, participants wore heart-rate variance monitors to analyse their physiological responses to a number of critical events. These monitors were more sophisticated than those worn regularly by gym users. Rather than just monitoring whether heart rate goes up or down, these devices monitored the *variance* in heart-rate changes, which provided an indication of activity in the individual's sympathetic nervous system and thus in essence monitored their neurological response to stress.

As well as the monitors, the participants also completed the following personality questionnaires:

- State-Trait Anxiety Inventory (STAI) (Spielberger et al., 1983) which measures both state and trait anxiety

- Life Orientation Test-Revised (LOT-R) (Scheier et al., 1994) which measures individual differences in generalised optimism versus pessimism

- Behavioural Approach Scale / Behavioural Inhibition Scale (BAS/BIS) (Carver & White, 1994) which measures individual differences in motivational systems. A behavioural approach system (BAS) is believed to regulate appetitive motives, in which the goal is to move toward something desired. A behavioural avoidance (or inhibition) system

(BIS) is said to regulate aversive motives, in which the goal is to move away from something unpleasant.

These measurements were completed immediately after the programme and again one month later. Participants also completed a learning questionnaire. This questionnaire was composed of 28 questions which, through a factor analysis, were reduced to four scales. The first scale was 'self as leader' and consisted of questions which explored the participants' perceptions of their strengths and confidence as a leader. The second scale, 'adapting to others', related to responses to others and the ability to adapt when dealing with others. The third scale, 'difficult situations', explored their abilities in handling difficult situations. The final scale, 'learning and development', explored more general aspects of personal learning and development during the programme. The research was looking for correlations between changes in heart rate, personality, and learning (Waller et al., 2014).

The analysis of the results focused on the response to two critical incidents which had been identified in the first stage of the study. First, an incident involving a difficult conversation with a stakeholder; and second, an incident involving a high-pressure communication event with staff. The findings were that participating in these did indeed result in an increase in participants' heart rates. This suggests that despite the fact the individuals knew the simulated situation was not 'real' they did actively engage in the scenario, and were concerned enough about their performance to induce a level of stress. One of the participants captured this by saying it was "very effective. I really didn't think that I would be able to be so effectively immersed in the scenario."

Importantly, the results also indicated that the increase in heart rate during the critical incidents was related to an increase in reported learning both immediately after the programme and a month later. This supports the hypothesis outlined above that moderate stress enhances learning. Interestingly, this was irrespective of personality variables, so it appears that whether you are motivated to achieve a goal or to avoid risk, whether you are pessimistic or optimistic in your outlook, or whether you are more or less anxious, if you engage in learning to the point that it raises your heart rate, you are likely to learn more and to retain the learning.

The researchers did, however, find that those with 'approach' personalities, as measured by the Behavioural Approach/Inhibition Scale, reported learning from a group activity, which – whilst being a fun, interactive and novel experience – wasn't expected to be related to learning. These types of individuals are driven to achieve goals and focus on reward (Gray, 1982) and so it could be that they were more engaged in the group activity than others and were more sensitive to the possibility of learning from the experience, and thus reported greater perceived learning.

Learning through experience that induces a state of arousal and increases heart rate does therefore appear to enhance learning from the event and, when perceived as a challenge, may also improve cognitive performance in the moment. However, this perception is a critical element. If we perceive a stressful situation as a challenge, we perform at our cognitive peak. If, however, we perceive a stressful situation as a threat, we essentially go into cognitive shut down in our preparation for fight or flight. So how do we ensure that we perceive stressful situations as challenging rather than threatening? Experiential learning has a vital role to play here too, thanks to its ability actually to change the physiology of the brain and ultimately alter our perception.

Building 'muscle memory'

This process occurs through neuroplasticity – changes in neural pathways that occur as a result of repeated behaviour, our environment, trauma and experience (Shatz, 1992). The process is well documented, but was once believed to halt in early childhood. And indeed, this is the stage of development during which the majority of our neural connections are laid down. Ask a five-year-old what she has done at school all day and her responses are likely to be vague, displaying little recollection of what she has actually learnt or done. Five-year-olds are good at remembering what they've eaten for lunch or who they played with in the playground, because they have had lots of experience in these activities and, as such, have laid down many neural connections through which to access their memories. They have, however, had little experience with sitting in a classroom and learning from their teacher, and therefore have few neural connections associated with this activity. As such, they will struggle to remember what they've learned.

It now appears, however, that this process of neuroplasticity continues throughout adulthood and that experience can change both the brain's physical structure and its network of connections. This means, from a neurological perspective, that each of us is entirely unique, with a unique pattern of neurological connections determined by our very own, unique set of experiences (Taupin, 2006).

It can be argued that the importance of this process to leadership development is that, by creating neural connections through experiential learning, leaders develop what has been dubbed 'muscle memory'. This term is most often used to describe how we remember how to ride a bike or drive a car – repeating the movements leads to physiological changes and brain muscle development, and the skill becomes stored in the brain as a memory (Lee & Schmidt, 2008). In the context of leadership, muscle memory is developed through practising with critical situations. Leaders' responses to these situations become stored as memories, leaving them feeling better resourced when they encounter them for real (Reitz, Carr & Blass, 2007). This resourcefulness in turn influences their *perception* of the situation. Feeling resourced, leaders perceive a stressful situation as a challenge rather than a threat, which pushes the blood towards rather than away from their brains, helping them to respond in the moment, at their cognitive peak.

Implications for executive leadership

Irrespective of status, level or experience, all leaders across all organisations will encounter novel, challenging situations which will test them in new ways, remove them from their comfort zone and challenge their capabilities. Given the growing complexity of modern organisational life, these encounters are even more inevitable. Being able to perform in these moments, to respond professionally, articulately and skilfully, is a mark of credible, effective leadership. But it's often at these times, these critical incidents, that leaders are most likely to feel under-resourced in terms of their skill or knowledge and will experience pressure, anxiety and panic. Then, as a result of their instinctive urge to fight or flee, they are likely to respond more poorly than they'd like.

It is therefore vital that leaders identify these incidents and find opportunities to practise for these challenging situations. This will build the neural connections and develop the muscle memory that will help them feel better resourced when they encounter such situations for real, and be better able to rise to the challenge and perform at their peak. As an insightful, but sadly unknown author once wrote: "The trouble with using experience as a guide is that the final exam often comes first and the lesson second." Through supported practice, however, leaders can transform the experience into the lesson that arms them for that final exam. What is also important is that leaders are helped to find ways actually to capture their learning from these moments. This means paying attention to who else may be involved that might offer feedback, building in time to reflect and consider what worked, what didn't, what has been learnt about the experience and about themselves.

These results can have wider organisational implications than just for individual development. As the line managers for their own people, leaders also have a responsibility to these direct reports and their teams to help them to identify what their critical incidents are, what might be their challenging moments, and present them with opportunities to practise, offer them feedback and give them time to reflect.

For leaders and their teams, simply being aware of how their brains and bodies respond under pressure and the impact this may have on their performance can also be really beneficial to their performance. For an individual to have an understanding of why their face is flushing, why their heart is pounding, and an appreciation that this is nothing more than a natural, adaptive response to a stressful situation, can in and of itself help individuals to regulate their physiological response and plant their feet firmly in 'challenge' rather than 'threat' territory.

Implications for learning and development practitioners

There are some clear and salient lessons here for business schools, for learning and development (L&D) practitioners, and all those involved in the development of leaders. The most critical is that, for leadership development interventions to be truly impactful, to really help prepare leaders for the challenges of leadership, they need to involve experience, and this experience needs to be hard-hitting. It needs to stretch participants, challenge them, take them out of their comfort zone and present the possibility of failure. By inducing their natural stress response, such experiential learning will improve perceived learning from the experience, and may build potential for improved cognitive performance in similar situations in the workplace.

It could also be argued that it is equally critical that these experiences occur in a safe and supportive environment, conducted by astute, experienced facilitators who pay attention to how the participants are responding and behaving, and provide appropriate and supportive feedback. As this chapter has reported, how individuals respond in these situations is determined, in large part, by their perceptions. People will all react differently and some may cross over into the 'threat' zone at different moments. It is the responsibility of the facilitator to be aware of behaviours that indicate this response, and to offer the support necessary to develop that individual's sense of resourcefulness and return them to 'challenge'.

Learning such as that described here need not only occur as part of formal development interventions. There are plenty of opportunities for on-the-job learning to incorporate these experiences. Stretch assignments and new responsibilities can challenge leaders, raise their heart rates and help to develop those vital neural connections that will help them deal effectively with future encounters.

There are also lessons to be learned in terms of how L&D departments evaluate the success of development interventions. Relying on the standard review sheet, which invariably assesses no more than participant's reactions to the experience, may well provide misleading information (Waller, 2012). Challenging experiences are unlikely to be always well received in the moment, and true learning can take time to embed. This slow-burn effect was demonstrated in 2009 on a 'The Leadership Experience' programme, where evaluation forms received up to four weeks after the programme was delivered were 50 per cent more positive than those received immediately after the event (Teckman, 2013). These figures found further support from the positive shift in qualitative feedback received after one and six months. Teckman warns "by fetishising the instant, semi-formed opinions delivered through the immediate post-programme evaluation forms, business schools risk promoting the safe and easy over the risky but transformative." (Ibid., p.99)

A more meaningful evaluation of embedded learning and real behavioural change is more likely to be achieved by assessments that are completed two-to-six months after a learning intervention and include opportunities for participants to share stories of success and failure in using what they've learned. Such measures provide a better understanding of whether learning is being applied and also offer the opportunity of exploring what might be helping or hindering leaders in implementing what they've learned.

Conclusion

The research in this area and an understanding of the neurobiological underpinnings of the processes involved in experiential learning provide powerful evidence for its value to practitioners of the development of leaders. Providing this type of learning can be more costly and more time consuming and, given its level of challenge, it can be a much harder sell to purchasing clients. However, it's not easy to argue with science, and the neuroscience here is clear: these methods work. They can improve cognitive performance in the moment, enhance learning from the experience and develop the 'muscle memory' necessary to ensure that our leaders feel resourced and equipped to deal with the challenges presented by this complex, dynamic and chaotic modern world.

References

Adler, P.S., & Kwon, S.W. (2002) Social capital: prospects for a new concept. *Academy of Management Review*, 27(1), pp.17–40.

Ben-Peretz, M. (2002) Retired Teachers Reflect on Learning from Experience. *Teachers and Teaching*, 8(3/4), pp.313–23.

Blascovich, J., & Tomaka, J. (1996) The biopsychosocial model of arousal regulation. In M.P. Zanna (ed.), *Advances in experimental social psychology*, 28 (San Diego, CA: Academic Press), pp.1–51.

Carver, C.S., & White, T.L. (1994) Behavioural inhibition, behavioural activation, and affective responses to impending reward and punishment: the BIS/BAS scales. *Journal of personality and social psychology*, 67, pp.319–33.

Conger, J.A. (2004) Developing leadership capability: what's inside the black box? *Academy of Management Executive*, 18(3), pp.136–9.

Ellis, S., & Davidi, I. (2005) After event reviews: Drawing lessons from successful and failed experience. *Journal of Applied Psychology*, 90, pp.857–71.

Frankenhaeuser, M. (1986) A psychobiological framework for research on humans' stress and coping. In M.H. Appley & R. Trumbull (eds), *Dynamics of Stress: Physiological, Psychological, and Social Perspectives* (New York: Plenum), pp.101–16.

Gray, J.A. (1982) *The Neuropsychology of Anxiety: An Enquiry into the Functions of the Septo-Hippocampal System* (New York: Oxford University Press).

Henry, J.P. (1980) Present concept of stress theory. In E. Usdin, R. Kvetnansky & I.J. Kopin (eds), *Catecholamines and Stress: Recent Advances* (New York: Elsevier/North-Holland), pp.557–71.

Hogan, T. (2010) Neuroscience provides tools to navigate the new business reality. *HR People and Strategy*, 33(4), pp.8–9.

Horney, N., Pasmore, B., & O'Shea, T. (2010) Leadership agility: A business imperative for a VUCA world. *People & Strategy*, 33, 4.

IBM (2010) Capitalizing on Complexity: insights from the Global Chief Executive Officer Study. Available at: http://www-304.ibm.com/businesscenter/cpe/download0/200422/ceostudy_2010.pdfn

Jamieson, J., Mendes, W.B., Backstock, E., & Schmader, T. (2010) Turning the knots in your stomach into bows: Reappraising arousal improves performance on the GRE. *Journal of Experimental Social Psychology*, 46(1), pp.208–12.

LeDoux, J. (2000) Emotion circuits in the brain. *Annual Review of Neuroscience*, 23, pp.155–84.

Lee, T.D., & Schmidt, R.A. (2008) Motor Learning and Memory. In H.L. Roediger, III (ed.), *Cognitive Psychology of Memory, Vol. 2* (Oxford: Elsevier).

Lupien, S.J., Maheu, F., Tu, M., Focco, A., & Schramek, T.E. (2007) The effects of stress and stress hormones on human cognition: Implications for the field of brain and cognition. *Brain and Cognition*, 65(3), pp.209–37.

Matlin, M., & Stang, D. (1978) *The Pollyanna Principle: Selectivity in Language, Memory and Thought* (Massachusetts: Schenckman).

Phelps, E.A. (2006) Emotion and cognition: Insights from the study of the human amygdala. *Annual Review of Psychology*, 57, pp.27–53.

Poole, E., & Carr, M. (2005) If I Knew Then What I Know Now!, *360° – The Ashridge Journal*, Spring, pp.46–50.

Pye, A. (1994) Past, present and possibility: An integrative appreciation of learning through experience. *Management Learning*, 25(1), pp.155–73.

Reitz, M., Carr, M., & Blass, E. (2007) Developing leaders: Innovative approaches for local government. *International Journal of Leadership in Public Services*, 3(14), pp.56–65.

Rubin, D.C., & Kozin, M. (1994) Vivid memories. *Cognition*, 16, pp.81–95.

Scheier, M.F., Carver, C.S., & Bridges, M.W. (1994) Distinguishing optimism from neuroticism (and trait anxiety, self-mastery, and self-esteem): A re-evaluation of the Life Orientation Test. *Journal of Personality and Social Psychology*, 67, pp.1,063–78.

Shatz, C.J. (1992) The developing brain. *Scientific American*, 26(9), pp.60–7.

Spielberger, C.D., Gorsuch, R.L., Lushene, R., Vagg, P.R., & Jacobs, G.A. (1983) *Manual for the State-Trait Anxiety Inventory*. Palo Alto, CA: Consulting Psychologists Press.

Taupin, P. (2006) Adult neurogenesis and neuroplasticity. *Restorative Neurology and Neuroscience*, 24, pp.9–15.

Teckman, J. (2013) The worst day of my life: The Future Leader's Experience. In E. Doyle, P. Buckley & C. Carroll (eds), *Innovative Business School Teaching: Engaging the Millennial Generation* (Abgindon: Routledge).

Thomas, R., & Cheese, P. (2005) Leadership: Experience is the best teacher. *Strategy and Leadership*, 33(3), pp.24–9.

Wagenaar, W.A. (1986) My memory: A study of autobiographical memory over six years. *Cognitive Psychology*, 18, pp.225–52.

Waller, L. (2012) Leadership development evaluation: An Ashridge market report. *Ashridge Business School Report*, August.

Waller, L., Reitz, M., Poole, E., & Muir, A. (2014) The neuroscience of leadership development: Preparing through experience. *Ashridge Business School Report*, April.

CHAPTER 2

Action Research: A Management Development Approach for Our Times

Kathleen King and Patricia Hind

Introduction

In this chapter, the authors argue that action research is a rich source of learning and development for everyone participating in organisational life. Simply put, action research is a process for uncovering new knowledge; however, it is a widely used term covering different meanings and approaches.

This is a chapter of two halves. It reports two quite differing approaches to using the principles of action research. Before offering their respective experiences, the authors make a case for its relevance in contemporary management development and give a brief historical perspective.

Why action research? And why now?

The financial crisis and the economic downturn at the beginning of the new millennium caused havoc in the world of business and organisations. The spectacular demise of once-admired giants in the corporate world, such as Enron and Lehman Brothers, raised widespread concern about business practices and the state of our corporations. Business schools were caught in the cross fire. Even the pearl in the management education crown, the MBA, came under attack (King, 2010). In an article entitled 'Making the Business School More Critical', Currie and colleagues (2010) pointed out that many of the business leaders implicated in the economic disaster are MBA graduates from some of the world's most reputable business schools. In the same special issue of the *British Journal of Management*, Ferlie and colleagues (2010) reviewed some of the criticisms levelled at business schools, including the typical pseudo-scientific, positivist approach to research which remains detached from managers' experience and day-to-day managerial practices. Moreover, the considerable pressure on business-school faculty to publish in peer-reviewed journals in pursuit of grants and much-coveted tenure, with far less kudos assigned to teaching, hasn't done much to generate interest in the practicalities of preparing leaders and managers for the challenges of our time.

Could it be that management education is stuck in a time warp? The business models developed and taught become ever more sophisticated, and yet the assumption upon which they are based appears basically unchanged – namely that given good enough tools we can predict, and even control, the future of our organisations. However, Antonacopoulou (2008) suggests that trying to simplify a complex reality is a lost cause and that management and organisational research needs to engage with practice and with the social complexity of organising. Similarly, we still put managers in classrooms where we teach them, despite the fact that one of the most essential management skills is to be able to think on your feet, in the reality of the business, with colleagues. In this chapter, we will argue that action research offers one way out of this dead-end street, because it starts from managers' daily experience in all its messiness and complexity, demands that they pay attention to their experience and take it seriously, and from there look at what theories and models have to offer that might be helpful, so that they can then go and try out a fresh look and approach.

We will explore action research as a discipline first and then offer two examples of how we have used it successfully as a management development tool.

A long and distinguished history

Before we consider some of the seminal work that has contributed to our understanding of action research, it is worth outlining its fundamental principles. It is an approach that is concerned specifically with change and, more particularly, with effective, permanent and positive social change. Lewin, the 'founding father' of action research, believed that the motivation to change was strongly related to action: if people are active in decisions affecting them, they are more likely to adopt new ways of behaving. "Rational social management", he said, "proceeds in a spiral of steps, each of which is composed of a circle of planning, action and fact-finding about the result of action" (Lewin, 1946). A key concept is experimentation, where individuals consciously try out different things and reflect upon anticipated and actual effects.

Lewin developed a systematic approach to a collaborative inquiry process, with the aim of enhancing learning and solving practical problems in organisations. Having first coined the term 'action research' in 1944, in 1946 he published a paper 'Action Research and Minority Problems', in which he described action research as a process of research into social action that in turn leads to further social action. The Tavistock Institute of Human Relations, influenced by Lewin, further developed AR, seeking solutions for practical problems of wartime situations in both Europe and America (Trist & Bamforth, 1951).

In action research, knowledge is produced in the service of action rather than theory and the approach has been explored extensively for both individual and organisational learning (Revans, 2011). Action research constitutes a rigorous and disciplined approach to knowledge and theory generation, intended to contribute both to the body of knowledge in social science and to social action in the service of addressing specific and real challenges.

Appropriately for today's global community, the development of action research has also been global. A significant contribution came from the liberationist practices of Paulo Freire (1970) in Chile. Freire was critical of traditional education models, which he considered oppressive and hierarchical, with the teacher imparting knowledge to passive recipients. Instead, he advocated a pedagogy that treats the learner as active co-creator of knowledge. His emancipatory, participatory approach influenced adult development models throughout Latin America. Fals-Borda (1997), a Columbian sociologist and activist, was one of the principal promoters of *participatory* action research. Heron and Reason (1997) further developed the principle of active involvement of all participants in research decisions as fully fledged co-researchers and proposed the term 'cooperative inquiry'.

In Scandinavia, Toulmin and Gustavsen set up work-place development projects in the service of social democracy (Toulmin & Gustavsen, 1996). In the US, Bill Torbert and colleagues coined the term 'developmental action inquiry' to denote a form of inquiry into practice which is "concerned with the development of effective action that may contribute to the transformation of our organizations and communities toward greater effectiveness and justice" (Torbert, 1991, p.219).

Schön (1983) argued that professional development that merely expects students to internalise knowledge, which they then need to transfer to their professional practice, bears little relation to how practitioners really 'think in action' and is wholly inappropriate in a complex, fast-changing world. He coined the phrase 'reflection-in-action', as distinct from reflection 'on action' – after the facts – and considered both essential in the process of continued learning.

Marshall and Reason (2007) consider action research to be more than a research methodology; rather, they consider 'an attitude of inquiry' a life discipline which informs and enriches every aspect of our lives – a perspective with which many action researchers would concur.

In this chapter we cannot begin to do justice to the wide range of contributions from across the globe that have made action research the powerful methodology that it is today. An excellent, comprehensive introduction to the various approaches can be found in *The SAGE Handbook of Action Research* (Reason & Bradbury, 2008) and in *The SAGE Encyclopedia of Action Research* (Coghlan and Brydon-Miller, 2014).

"There is nothing more practical than a good theory", Kurt Lewin (1952, p.169)

So 'action research' is an umbrella term, encompassing a range of perspectives and approaches, but whatever form it takes, the common purpose of the different schools is to bring sustainable improvement to a situation. Some action researchers concentrate specifically on work-related issues, whilst for others AR is a much broader discipline that involves all aspects of their life. Some action researchers take an instrumental approach. They are interested in improving their practice, without necessarily asking themselves broader questions about the impact of that practice on the wider human and other-than-human context in which it is situated. For others, critical reflection is an essential aspect of their research. Whatever the particular approach, all AR involves those cycles or spirals of action, reflection, experimenting and conceptualising.

In the following section we explore action research as an approach to the design, development and processes of two qualification programmes for organisational change and development practitioners. The programmes were an MSc qualification and a doctoral programme in Organisational Consulting, both designed to develop practitioners equipped to help organisations, and their people, to develop.

In the 1990s, when the master's programme was first conceived, much organisational consulting followed what Schein (1999) called the 'expert consultation' model. This was a process whereby consultants prescribe a course of action to the client, based on the client's or the consultant's diagnosis of the organisational issues. Schein argues convincingly that the assumptions underpinning this approach are problematic and restrictive, bringing potentially constraining or erroneous assumptions to the situation. He suggests an inquiry-based 'process consultation' alternative with an emphasis on inquiry.

The thinking underpinning the two programmes is that we work in a world that is heading for increasing uncertainty, complexity and ambiguity. In this context organisational leaders and change agents have to adopt an approach that is radically different from traditional, expert based, analytical and top down methods. Instead, those responsible for leading, managing or changing organisations need to look for patterns and interdependencies. They need to assume complex, non-linear relationships, to value curiosity, insight and intuition, and to work creatively with paradox, uncertainty and contradiction.

The philosophical home of this approach is a participatory paradigm, which assumes that our world does not consist of separate entities but of relationships, which we co-create actively and continuously. The methodology of choice is participatory action research. The 'frame' for this approach is driven by the desire to enable individuals, groups, communities and organisations to develop their own reflexive capacity and become less 'unthinking doers', whilst assisting researchers in embedding their research in the real works of actors and action. The outcome is to develop all those involved into being more like thoughtful, well-rounded actors (Wadsworth, 2008). This is complemented by an acceptance that tried and tested solutions no longer serve us and that today's expertise may be redundant for the issues we face tomorrow. What is needed is a potent blend of research, learning and practice that is accessible to practitioners and social scientist alike. Participatory action research offers this blend with its emphasis on reflective action.

Mirroring the iterative nature of action research, the academic programmes described here have evolved considerably since their inception. In response to persistent requests from leaders and managers in search of support in their difficult change work, both programmes are open to a broad range of professionals who are, in some form or other, supporting or leading change in organisations and communities. If anything, under the influence of a broad target group, and with input from alumni, the action-research stance has strengthened.

Although they share a common methodology and philosophy, the two programmes differ in somewhat in shape and purpose. The master's emphasises practice through reflection informed by theory. The doctorate focuses on making a contribution to our understanding of organisations and change through a sustained inquiry process.

Learning through a sustained process of inquiry[*]

Participants who join the programmes are typically successful leaders, managers or consultants at a mid-career stage. Many of them have come to a crossroads of sorts and are evaluating their lives and careers to date. Most of them are looking to deepen their understanding of their work and its impact on organisations and/or communities. To paraphrase Mintzberg (2014), they decide to study because they want to *do* a better job, not because they want to *get* a better job. In the course of their extensive experience, they have come to realise that reality is considerably more complex than even the most sophisticated management tools and models suggest, and they are keen to explore different ways of thinking about and working with change that are more true to their experience – and more effective.

In line with the philosophy and approach to organisational development outlined above, the programme focuses and develops three kinds of practices.

---

[*]   We use 'inquiry', rather than the more familiar 'enquiry', in line with the term 'action inquiry', which is commonly used in the US as an equivalent to 'action research'.

1. First-person inquiry

The approach taken considers consulting to people in organisations as a *craft*, a complex set of skills. Like other skills, such as riding a bicycle or playing a musical instrument, it can't be developed from merely studying text books. It requires practice. The term 'your practice' refers to participants' work. The term suggests the work to be 'in progress'. However, learning from experience requires both awareness and reflection. As humans, we have an extraordinary capacity to function without needing to pay close attention to our experience, with the obvious advantage that we are able to perform a range of complex tasks simultaneously. The shadow side of this ability is that we can function for long periods on automatic pilot. Awareness requires close attention to physical sensations as well as thoughts and feelings. We need to notice what is *actually* going on, rather than merely confirm our preconceived expectations of what *ought* to be happening. In our experience, this is one of the most difficult disciplines to develop, as humans are hard-wired to avoid discomfort and anxiety, which are an integral part of change work. The learning process on the master's programme therefore starts with paying attention to experience and developing the ability to stay aware in the moment, however challenging the experience. This process encompasses the first two stages, starting at the top, of Kolb's learning cycle (Kolb, 1984) (see Figure 1) and is known in the action-research field as first-person inquiry. Kolb's learning cycle is referenced elsewhere in this book, but is presented again here, not only for completeness, but also to emphasise its importance to first-person inquiry, which is considered an essential, but challenging, discipline for any organisational practitioner. Torbert (2004) suggests that individuals are not always comfortable with closely scrutinising their own experiences, relationships, organisations or their wider social conduct. Opening up one's behaviour to rigorous inquiry tends to be associated with situations of misconduct and trouble. The proliferation of literature following the collapse of corporate giants such as Enron and Lehman Brothers describes vividly the lack of accountability from leaders to themselves, their staff and their stakeholders, and the extent to which corporate behaviour has become immune to scrutiny or challenge.

The emphasis on first-person inquiry and self-reflection informs many of the design features of the programme. The theoretical territory, drawing on philosophy, sociology and psychology, is congruent with an emphasis on awareness and criticality. Participants are expected to bring different theoretical lenses to bear on their experience and demonstrate how they are illuminating their reflective practice and how the resulting insights inform practical experimentation – however modest – in their organisational practice.

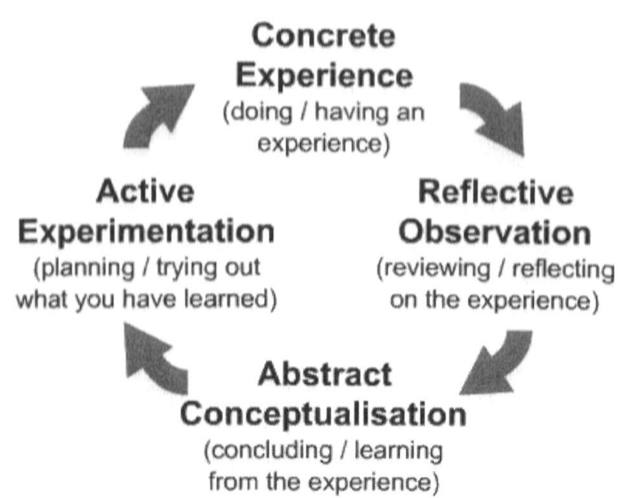

Figure 1 – Kolb Learning Cycle

Source: http://www.simplypsychology.org/learning-kolb.html

Uniquely, and powerfully, residential workshops are designed to facilitate the formation of the participant group as a temporary organisation. This provides participants with an opportunity to reflect and receive feedback on their habitual behaviour in organisations, and to consider the conscious and unconscious assumptions that inform their practice. Throughout the workshops, the emphasis is on experiential learning, dialogue and experimentation, rather than on teaching and 'knowledge transfer'.

Experimentation, self-reflection, mutual support and challenge are essential ingredients of what are termed 'practice groups'. Consisting of up to six participants and facilitated by faculty, these groups provide an opportunity to receive and deliver peer coaching on work-based issues. The emphasis of the process is on critical reflection and learning, rather than on mere problem solving. This concurs with Mintzberg's (2014) argument that: "people who practise management can benefit enormously by reflecting on their own experience and sharing the insights with each other. This kind of social learning has proved to be the most powerful pedagogical tool we have".

2. Second-person inquiry

Second-person inquiry has been described by Reason and Bradbury (2008) as the process of inquiring with others into issues of mutual concern. Although we have here a second subtitle to represent the second practice developed during the programme, it is somewhat artificial to separate the different action-research dimensions. As mentioned above, developing self-reflective, first-person practices involves the support and challenge of peers on the learning journey. True to the action-research tradition, this is research *with* rather than *on* others. Because it seeks to develop the collective abilities of inquiry partners as reflective practitioners, it reduces power differences which get in the way of honest and open communication and thus generates a more nuanced, mutually shared understanding from which to act effectively. Second-person inquiry seeks to foster mutuality by inquiring openly into the power play between agents, developing dialogic ways of conversing together, and jointly agreeing the value of what we are creating together (Torbert, 2004). Espoused by many managers, leaders, educators and researchers, it remains a challenging practice for all, including business-school faculty. In the role of educator, there is a responsibility not only for decisions concerning the curriculum and shape of the programme, but also for assessing and judging the work and progress of participants. In other words, the role has considerable position power. Holding this position in a way that is congruent with the principles of action research is full of the challenges, contradictions and paradoxes that participants also face in their practice at work.

To meet this challenge, faculty processes and judgements must be open to scrutiny, not only to external quality-assurance mechanisms, but also to participants. This is an essential part of the discipline of participatory action research. Participants typically appreciate the congruence – at least in aspiration – between practice and advocacy. However, there are occasions when they find faculty unwillingness to take the 'expert' position deeply frustrating. The peer-assessment element of the programme is but one example of participants reluctantly stepping into their power. "I have come here to learn, not to assess my peers" is a recurring mantra. And of course, participants have a valid point when they note that, although they are expected to assess each other's work, the criteria by which they are expected to do so are set by faculty. Despite the inevitable differences in role, and despite clear philosophy and advocacy about what constitutes good practice, faculty must continually seek to engage with participants in a process of dialogue and thinking together, rather than offering ready-made solutions, and must be persistently ready to meet this challenge.

3. Third-person inquiry

Finally, wherever practitioners find themselves working, their engagement with the world has an impact, and a legacy is left well beyond the boundaries of our human context. Our existence on this planet comes with responsibility for one another and for our social, cultural and natural context. In particular, it is the long-term impact on society and on our natural habitat that has been deeply and catastrophically neglected in organisational practices. Third-person inquiry – which involves daily attention to the consequences of our actions, in the short, medium and long term, on our immediate, wider and global contexts – is a discipline long overdue.

Attention to the ethics of all practice is critical. Participants must negotiate the often-precarious balance between, on the one hand, their personal ethics and sense of responsibility and accountability, and on the other, their membership of an organisation that may engage in questionable or downright unethical practices. It can be difficult to speak truth to power and challenge inappropriate or unethical behaviour, without being so confrontational that one is ejected by the system. The term 'tempered radicalism' has been coined by Meyerson and Scully (1995) to describe this precarious balance.

Learning is for life, not just for a qualification

How do participants experience reflective and participatory action research on the programmes we have been describing? How does it impact on their ability to bring about individual and organisational change? Here are some quotes from alumni and current participants:

> "I've finally got a grip on some of the habitual, problematic or painful patterns that were dogging my change work."

> "I have discovered how I was disempowering myself and how old and outdated habits got in the way of dealing with that was going on right here, right now. I feel I have liberated myself and found a new 'voice' in my work".

> "I have developed completely new ways of working with change. This approach to learning, grounded in my practice, has freed me

from my old mantra that I'm not a good learner. I have found new energy and excitement in my work in the process."

"As a result of my participation on the programme, I have made substantial changes to my personal life as well as my work. I do things differently at home now, and it's done my relationship with my kids no end of good. I've tackled some of the challenges I was facing head on. The support of my peers and the faculty has been invaluable in that process."

Clearly, action-research methodology has impact and influence from an individual perspective not only on professional practice but also on ways of living and being. The next section of this chapter describes an example of how action research has been used as a methodology to influence organisational processes and practices, and to bring about sustainable organisational change.

Enabling sustainability through action research

In much traditional management development, the use of research projects has been widespread. We know that work-based projects are absolutely the most valuable learning vehicle we can use. The 70–20–10 rule of thumb – which says that 10% of learning takes place in the classroom, 20% through networks, contacts and interactions with others, and 70% in the workplace – means that we must find an effective way of ensuring that learning takes place on the job. Projects are an ideal way to make this happen. However, the traditional way of using projects for development purposes is fraught with practical difficulties, as well as benefits.

The model is that senior managers from a company that is sending delegates to a management development programme will 'sponsor' projects considered to have strategic value for the company. The delegates will then usually be divided into small groups to work on the projects which will be delivered back to senior management at a later date.

A real plus for this approach is that it explicitly demonstrates the support of senior management for the development of its employees. Participants often feel valued and rewarded by being sent on an executive development programme – particularly if the title contains the words 'strategic' and 'leadership' – and attention shown to their development through the identification of projects, mentoring throughout the duration of the project and physical attendance for the presentation of results are hugely valuable.

Another advantage of this approach is that it very often does require participants to stretch themselves out of their comfort zone and operate cross-functionally. For example, an employee of a global electronics business, working in the European lighting sector, might be asked to conduct a project investigating the potential market for electric razors in India. Undoubtedly such experiences broaden participants' perspectives and enlarge networks, as well as providing exposure to senior executives which may well have career development potential.

However, many years' experience of facilitating such projects has highlighted some significant limitations. Firstly, as has been pointed out earlier in this chapter, today's business landscape is fast paced and volatile. After their development programme, participants return to their day jobs, and conducting their project for senior management is inevitably a part-time activity. Therefore, when the project is delivered several months later, it is often out of date. Senior management's attention may well have moved elsewhere and their involvement with the project might have been sporadic and difficult to access. So, very often the project presentations can feature indifference on the part of the sponsors and frustration on the part of the participants who have worked hard to deliver what was required.

In terms of actually delivering on the project, or the 'task', there are risks here too. The projects are often under-resourced – if there was budget to deal with the issue, it would not need to be a development project – and participants struggle to meet face to face, to access information or influencers, and to deliver the real insights required. For participants who see themselves being developed for bigger and better roles, the experience of offering a result which fails to meet the standards they normally set for themselves can be exasperating.

Then there are sometimes relationship issues around the way the project groups work together. As mentioned earlier, groups often have to work virtually. Although this is not in itself a bad thing in our globally connected world, it does bring an additional complication to juggling the project with the day job and with other people's day jobs, perhaps across several time zones. It is particularly difficult for these groups to calibrate for differences in skills, capacity and commitment. So whilst it is fair to say that, when such groups work well, it is hugely rewarding for all concerned and a great amount of learning takes place, when they don't, the disappointment can cloud any learning benefit from the programme.

An application of action-research principles to management-development projects reveals an opportunity to create a new learning vehicle: action-research projects. These are specific and stretching, but are developed by participants themselves and are relevant to participants' day jobs.

To conduct individual action-research projects as part of an executive development programme, participants need to be supported in scoping a project that is a real, current and live challenge – one that needs to be tackled in order to meet or exceed their own objectives. The objectives identified might be purely business related, such as deciding how to create more sustainable value, or more personal, such as looking at how to improve the effectiveness of their leadership practice.

They are guided through the process of identifying a question to which they would like an answer and planning 'experiments' or different ways to get the answers, always making explicit the other stakeholders with a place in these plans. The structure of the process then guides participants towards taking specific actions – their 'experiments' – to get the answers to the question identified, and then reflect on the consequences, either intended or unintended. The next step is, in the light of that reflection, to generate imaginative ideas of what to change and improve. New action plans can then be put in place.

The process is graphically shown in Figure 2.

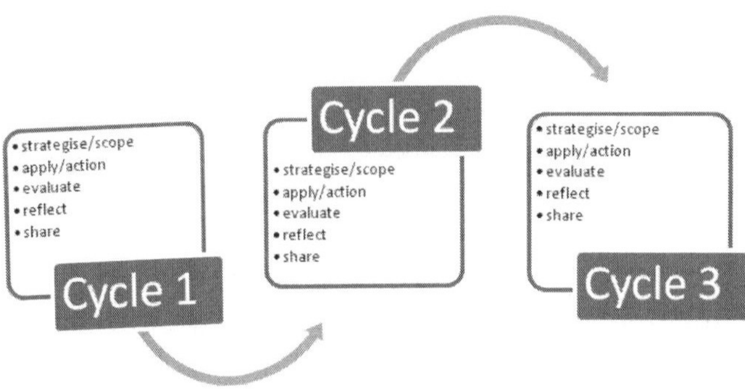

Figure 2 – Action Research Project Cycles

The advantages of using individual action-research projects are many. The project is real and relevant, so none of the effort is redundant. The individual has real motivation to deliver a quality result and can choose the project that s/he thinks will add most value either to the success of the organisation or to his/her leadership career development.

One example of this process being used was a research project undertaken by a cohort of the leaders of eight SMEs operating in the Western Cape Province of South Africa, in partnership with their local university's business school. The overall objective of the leaders was to embed sustainability practices into their business, but they also wanted to use the process to examine their own leadership practice and to develop themselves into fully 'responsible leaders'.

This project issued participants with a workbook which offered an opportunity for them to reflect on developments in their personal leadership journeys parallel to the sustainability agendas that were evolving in their businesses. The workbook created structured space for reflection on their business context, questions, plans, experiences, meaning, learning, sharing and further actions. This was followed by a round of personal interviews with participants.

The methodology was as follows:

- The cohort of eight companies came together for a one-and-a-half-day workshop designed to achieve three objectives. First, to create a communicative space for the project; second, to consider the nature of sustainability for each company; and third, to receive some 'training' on action-research methodology and to explore the workbook.

- There was a six-week period during which each company 'experimented' with their action-research projects in their own workplaces, supported by a dedicated member of the research team.

- The cohort reassembled for a final workshop at which they presented the results of their experiments, their own learning about embedding sustainability into their organisations and their future plans.

- The cohort agreed a shared understanding about the unique nature of sustainability in South African SMEs. Actions and processes to make progress along the journey to sustainability were identified.

Using the cycles of reflection and experimentation, each company developed a business-relevant concept of sustainability and implemented actions to embed specific practices within their business operations. Results of those actions determined future cycles of the research.

The results of the project showed that developmental changes occurred for all participants as they worked with the action-research methodology. The changes can be summarised as involving mindset, boundaries, skills, attitudes and constraints.

- **Mindset:** Participants reported that the project introduced a different way of thinking, processing and acting. Action research as a methodology, using the workbook as a vehicle, gave them an opportunity for guided and structured reflection. This brought mindfulness, focus, discipline and momentum to their journey of leading for sustainability.

- **Boundaries:** SMEs most often originate as owner–manager businesses and, as a result, their leaders are, from the beginning, used to resource scarcity and occupied with all aspects of the business. The leadership challenge was one of 'expanding boundaries' to include others in decision making, entrusting them with responsibilities, appreciating their ideas and so forth. Both the internal team and the external stakeholder networks grew in prominence and importance for these participants during the project. The lesson seems to be that true change towards sustainability demands a team approach that taps into the energy of relationships, the diversity of talent and value of social capital in stakeholder relationships.

- **Skills:** Participants reported being comfortable with using new vocabulary, a new emphasis in conversations, giving and taking feedback, self-reflection, importance of motivation and encouragement, influencing others, developing relationships, leading in the light of vision, and the ability to fight for what is right. Leading for sustainability seemed to have called these skills forward, focusing them on a common objective and honing them for greater effectiveness.

- **Attitude:** Participants recorded changes in themselves described by words such as 'structured', 'considerate', 'example', 'appreciation', 'patience', 'ethical' and 'responsible'. It seems that the project introduced a new mindfulness and awareness about self and others, about the present and the future, about society and the environment. The demand for profitability and success does not disappear in the face of sustainability, but the disposition of the business leader changes to one that deals with the ambiguity and tension in a different way, taking on the responsibility with an attitude of constructive involvement.

- **Constraints:** Time, money, people and information are commodities that can be low in supply for SMEs. The participants in the project still operated with these constraints but discovered the power of a supportive network and the encouragement provided by the stories of others.

It is clear that the action-research process facilitated planning, action, reflection and observation with regard to implementing sustainability practices in the participant companies. This finding clearly indicates the suitability of action research as a vehicle for organisational change. The process provided a discipline that ensured that changes were both realistic and focused on meeting business needs.

Conclusion

It is important to remember that whatever approach to using action research for individual or organisational development is taken, the methodology is a road map, a new approach to development that does not represent traditional capability building. Action research is about understanding in a systemic context and trying to ensure resilient learning. It is particularly relevant as a management development tool because action-research approaches:

- **Are more participatory:** The interactive and involving nature of action research makes it particularly suitable for use in organisational and individual development. New perspectives, information and feedback are crucial to expanding and deepening the knowledge base – this is a key element of learning.

- **Create space for learning and reflexivity:** Many organisations and individuals lack the space to reflect on their practices and experiences and to translate this thinking into learning, research and theory building. Action-research approaches are more likely to support these processes than conventional approaches.

- **Are more internally focussed:** Action research is not dependent on external expertise and the world of the known. It therefore has the potential to support ownership and retention of personal knowledge and learning

- **Support individual accountability:** Action-research approaches have the potential to facilitate accountability to all participants and organisational management. However, this does depend on the quality of participation. Participants must embrace action research with a true spirit of enquiry and a commitment to personal and/or organisational change for the better.

- **Can cope with complexity:** Action-research approaches are particularly suitable for coping with complexity. Development is often complex, involving realistic acknowledgement of the status quo, changing and turbulent contexts, and uncertainty with regard to the future. Action research can create a holding environment, a space in which interrelated issues can be explored so that action researchers can focus on specifics whilst maintaining an appreciation of their interconnected nature and the broader context within which they exist.

We began this chapter by recognising that traditional approaches to management development are no longer fit for purpose. The two examples of using action research for both individual and organisational development described here provide optimism that there is a new way forward, appropriate to the demands of the twenty-first-century organisational context. We need to continue to share stories and experiences to build the body of knowledge that will make the rich potential of action research available to all.

References

Antonacopoulou, E. (2008) On the Practise of Practice: In-tensions and Ex-tensions in the Ongoing Reconfiguration of Practices. In D. Barry & H. Hansen (eds), *The SAGE Handbook of New Approaches in Management and Organization* (Thousand Oaks, CA: Sage), pp.112–21.

Argyris, C., & Schön, D.A. (1996) *Organizational Learning II: Theory, Method and Practice* (Reading, MA: Addison-Wesley).

Coghlan, D., & Brydon-Miller, M. (2014) *The SAGE Encyclopedia of Action Research* (London: Sage).

Currie, G., Knights, D., & Starkey, K. (2010) Introduction: A Post-crisis Critical Reflection on Business Schools. *British Journal of Management*, Vol. 21, Special Issue 1, pp.1–5.

Fals Borda (1997) *The Challenge of Social Change* (London: SAGE) Series of International Sociology, 1986.

Ferlie, E., McGivern, G., & De Moraes, A. (2010) Developing a Public Interest School of Management. *British Journal of Management*, Vol. 21, Supplement 1, pp.60–70.

Freire, P. (1970) *Pedagogy of the Oppressed* (Harmondsworth, UK: Penguin Books).

Hall, B. (2008) I wish this were a poem of practices of participatory research. In P. Reason & H. Bradbury, *The SAGE Handbook of Action Research*, pp.171–8.

Heron, J., & Reason, P. (1997) A Participatory Inquiry Paradigm. *Qualitative. Inquiry,* 3(3), 274–294.

King, K. (2010) Introduction. In *Organisational Consulting @ the Edges of Possibility* (London: Libri Publishing).

Kolb, D.A. (1984) *Experiential Learning* (Englewood Cliffs, NJ: Prentice Hall).

Lewin, K. (1946) Action Research and Minority Problems. *Journal of Social Issues*, 2(4), pp.34–46.

Lewin, K. (1952) *Field theory in social science: Selected theoretical papers by Kurt Lewin* (London: Tavistock).

Marshall, J., & Reason, P. (2007) Quality in research as 'taking an attitude of inquiry'. *Management Research News*, 30, 5, pp.368–80.

Meyerson, D.E., & Scully, M.A. (1995) Tempered Radicalism and the Politics of Ambivalence and Change. *Organization Science*, 6(5), pp.585–600.

Mintzberg, H. (2014) http://www.mintzberg.org/blog/management-education

Pasmore, W., Stymne, B., Shani, A., Mohrman, S., & Adler, N. (2008) The Promise of Collaborative Management Research. In A. Shani, S. Mohrman, W. Pasmore, B. Stymne & N. Adler (eds), *Handbook of Collaborative Management Research*, 1st edn (Thousand Oaks, CA: Sage), pp.7–32.

Reason, P., & Bradbury, H. (2008) *The SAGE Handbook of Action Research: Participative Inquiry and Practice*, second edition (Thousand Oaks, CA: Sage).

Revans, R.W. (2011) *ABC of action learning* (Farnham: Gower).

Schein, E.H. (1999) *Process Consultation Revisited: Building the Helping Relationship* (Harlow, UK: Addison-Wesley).

Schön, D.A. (1983) *The Reflective Practitioner: How professionals think in action* (London: Temple Smith).

Torbert, W.R. (1991) *The Power of Balance: Transforming Self, Society and Scientific Inquiry* (London: Sage).

Torbert, W.R. (2004) *Action Inquiry: The Secret of Timely and Transforming Leadership* (San Francisco, CA: Berrett-Koehler).

Toulmin, S., & Gustavsen, B., (eds) (1996) *Beyond Theory: Changing organizations through participation* (Amsterdam: John Benjamins).

Trist, E., & Bamforth, K. (1951) *The Stress of Isolated Dependence: (1) The Filling Shift in the Semi-Mechanized Longwall Three-Shift Mining Cycle*.

Wadsworth, Y. (2008) Action Research for Living Human Systems. In B. Boog, J. Preece, M. Slagter & J. Zeelen (eds), *Towards Quality Improvement of Action Research* (Rotterdam: Sense Publishers), pp.45–60.

CHAPTER 3

Developing Senior Talent

James Moncrieff and Dev Mookherjee

This chapter focuses specifically on developing talent for the most senior of organisational roles. Talent management is a widely discussed topic in many organisations today, as human resources (HR) and learning and development (L&D) professionals are keen to invest in the development of high-potential people, to equip them to step up to senior leadership roles. It is here that executives hope to see the biggest return on their developmental investments. Organisations encourage this development in a variety of ways – through open enrolment programmes, tailored programmes, consulting assignments, and coaching and mentoring relationships. This chapter reports the results of research undertaken into exactly what capabilities are required of senior leaders and how to develop those capabilities effectively. The findings highlight the importance of emotional as well as intellectual stretch in the learning process.

Senior leader development

Whilst understanding that, in the words of Alexandre Dumas (1802–1870), "all generalisations are dangerous", it is possible to observe some relatively common characteristics of the senior management population and how they like to position and experience their own development.

- Managers at senior levels are likely to be strong intellectually, with sound functional and/or technical skills. Often it is those skills that have underpinned their organisational success. However, they sometimes lack the more subtle skills of managing relationships, leadership, engagement and influence that they need to participate effectively as a member of the top team.

- Managers moving from a functional or technical role can find it difficult to 'lift their heads' up and out of the day-to-day detail, to be able to delegate and to take a more strategic perspective.

- Functional and technical managers usually have well-developed analytical skills, dealing with data in logical, rational ways. As a result, they can find it difficult to make the transition to dealing with the uncertainty and ambiguity found at a strategic level, and to find the assurance to exercise the intuitive judgement often required.

- In other respects, they are usually highly self-confident and often strongly independent, having relied on their ability to get to where they are – often believing that they need no further development. So, as learners, they can be:
  - Reluctant to get involved in development activities
  - Sceptical about the value a training programme would provide for them
  - Wary of exhortations to lead, to be strategic, to be visionary, etc.
  - Wary of business school and consultancy speak
  - Nervous about exposure and self-disclosure, with well-formed defensive routines and skills to avoid difficult conversations
  - Stuck in 'yesterday's learning' because it got them to where they are today
  - Yet, quietly curious about psychometrics, self-analysis and feedback, and particularly about how they compare to others.

These characteristics must influence any approach to programme design for senior management. The following elements are important for any development intervention:

- Senior managers are usually intelligent and experienced enough to pick things up very quickly. So, not only is pace important but the emphasis needs to be on application – making sense of the learning and how to apply it in the workplace.

- The programme content and any work needing to be undertaken by participants at this level must be as relevant as possible. This holds true even when looking at other industries or fields such as sport or the arts. Time spent working on the real issues of the business or organisation is essential and is what will be valued and retained.

- This group of learners often wants the latest thinking – requiring evidence or research-based content delivered with confidence. However, they will also often reject what does not fit with their prior learning. So there is a challenge in resolving this tension, which involves changing and developing mindsets, challenging assumptions and questioning past experiences.

- It is important to challenge and stretch them intellectually and emotionally, to be rigorous with review and feedback on their work, and to be open to feedback from them, remaining robust and modelling personal resilience.

- It can help to involve more senior leaders, from their own or other organisations, particularly if these leaders talk about their own leadership journey in an informal setting. This can help the participants understand how others have developed into senior roles and how people and events have influenced their thinking and self-perception.

What do we know about how senior managers learn?

Research described in more detail elsewhere in this book has found that the most significant development moments for successful senior leaders have come in the form of critical incidents or role changes that took them outside their comfort zone and stretched them both intellectually and emotionally. These were often described as 'stomach churning' or 'crucible' moments (Laljani, 2009).

Laljani labelled these critical incidents "Mastery Experiences". He found that it was not professors or faculty who were instrumental in individuals learning from these experiences but mentors, coaches or colleagues who helped individuals to reflect critically on these experiences and to draw on their personal resources to cope while developing new ways of thinking and seeing the world.

This developmental support and critical reflection became an important ingredient in developing the core skills of senior leaders: self-awareness and emotional intelligence; strategic thinking and dialogue skills; contextual mastery of their field; and above all, judgement – what you do when the answer is not implicit in the data – drawing on your own experience, intuition and insights, and those of others, to take decisions and advocate a course of action in the face of complexity, uncertainty and ambiguity.

Laljani's findings are in support of those from Poole and Carr (2005) who found that the "salience [or valued relevance] of a development experience is increased if it is linked to future survival and invokes both intellectual and emotional challenge."

Poole and Carr posed this question to CEOs: "What do you know now that you wished you had known 10 years ago?" The overwhelming response was: "I wish I had known more about myself". They found that the most valuable learning experiences had come through tackling critical incidents that caused them to look deeply into themselves to find new personal resources that would enable them to cope.

The experiences reported by these studies include significant change assignments, important successes and failures, difficult staff issues and meaningful moments of self-awareness. The importance of the actual experience for learning is difficult to overstate.

However, these incidents and opportunities may be unpredictable, available only to a few and expensive to undertake. So, the difficulty for management development professionals wishing to facilitate effective learning is to be able to provide such events in a development environment. At some level, this can be done with experiential exercises, simulations and projects. These can stretch people and help them develop new skills and attitudes, but they are usually still perceived as 'training activities' and subject to the observations noted above. It can be difficult to transfer simulation learning from the training environment to the workplace; while the difficulty with 'projects' is to find an issue that is stretching enough to be developmental, yet not so urgent that it can wait six-to-twelve months for a solution.

In order to work with this dilemma, a number of approaches have been developed that can address this issue using the principles of action learning.

Action learning as both an organisational and individual development tool is addressed in this book in Chapter 2, by King and Hind. It is an important idea in management development generally and has long been recognised as a valuable method in the development of senior leaders. Reg Revans is widely regarded as the father of action learning and emphasises the personal engagement aspect of learning that the research described above has highlighted:

Action learning obliges subjects to become aware of their own value systems, by demanding that the real problems tackled carry some risk of personal failure.

(Revans, 1988)

Revans believed that leaders developed through being "confronted by risk, uncertainty and confusion". In these circumstances, prior accumulated knowledge cannot provide answers, only areas in which to ask fresh questions. So, unable to rely on professors or faculty for answers, learners must find their own individual and collective way forward by working to draw upon their individual experience and intuition, in order to create new solutions.

Further insights to the learning process have been offered by Pruyne (2009), who found that participants need to be able to 'bridge' the learning experiences to their own lived work experiences. She found that learning in context helped support later recall: "when participants are engaged in a memorable learning experience, they encode features of the learning environment as well as the learning, in the neural pathways of the brain."

Reitz (2009) suggested that traditional education methods may not help managers who expect their teachers to give them the answers – this can often give rise to a form of 'learned helplessness' in which the learner does not take responsibility for their own development. She describes this experience from a tutor's perspective as "a weighty expectation from participants that you will intervene, rescue them… while what we really need is to develop in participants an internal locus of control over their learning."

Summary of implications for senior management development

1. Traditional taught sessions are unlikely to engage or develop senior talent, unless extremely relevant, timely and well delivered by a respected expert.

2. Senior talent is most likely to be developed through experiences that stretch and challenge them both intellectually and emotionally.

3. These experiences need to contain elements of risk, uncertainty and ambiguity. They require some real exposure of the participant, with a risk of personal failure.

4.   They need to be able to draw on their own experience and intuition to find a way through, so that they become more aware of their own personal resources and don't fall into the trap of learned helplessness.

5.   Opportunities and support for critical reflection should be an integral part of any development activity, and should be enabled through the formation and continuation of sound developmental relationships.

So, what approach should be taken?

The choice of approaches begins with an understanding of the business or organisational outcomes being sought. Some development programmes may stand alone and focus only on the participants. However, more often, and particularly in the case of customised or tailored programmes, there is a need to harness the collective impact that one or more cohorts might have on the business or the organisation. This will influence both the nature of the experiences required, and the content and process of the intervention. Let's consider the options:

1. 'Out of comfort zone' exercises

At the simplest level, these 'out of comfort zone' experiences may be provided through exercises – interactive, participative activities – designed into a broader knowledge- or skills-oriented programme. These exercises will often involve metaphors for the equivalent experience in the work-place – such things as sport, music, art, working in unusual environments or undertaking unusual activities. These experiences can often raise self-awareness and a curiosity to learn more. As such, they can be useful at the beginning of a learning journey to 'hook' the participant, to engage them in their development and to increase their willingness to take on greater challenges.

2. Simulations

Simulations provide parallel experiences for real life, and can support further development if they are sufficiently stretching and supported by rigorous feedback and review. It is essential that participants recognise that while the context might be a simulation, what happens, what they do, what they say, what they think and how they feel will be entirely real – they are not 'role playing'.

One such simulation, used successfully at a business school on customised programmes with large corporate clients, confronts participants with a significant and realistic business opportunity with a global customer in the participants' own market (such as, for example, finance, insurance, manufacturing or IT). Working in functionally mixed groups, they must understand the opportunity, and interview a range of senior managers and functional/technical specialists in the customer organisation. Whilst participants are very much themselves, the roles of the interviewees are played by actors. Participants must then draw on their knowledge of their own organisation to formulate a solution, prepare a proposal and pitch for the global business on offer. (For example, if the corporate body is an insurance client, they might pitch for the global risk-management business of that customer; if a banking client, they might pitch for the global corporate finance business of that customer.) As well as the actors, the customer panel judging the proposals includes a number of real senior executives or directors from the business. This certainly ups the ante and increases the emotional stretch and makes very real the risk of personal failure.

Another twist on the simulation experience can provide this stretch in a different way. Because it begins as if it were a traditional competitive business simulation, participants are lulled into a false sense of security about the experience they are about to have. An unexpected and unrelated crisis is inserted into the simulation, taking them out of that context and placing them into an entirely new, complex and uncertain environment – one in which they are expected to work collaboratively to complete a number of difficult leadership tasks while dealing with an unfolding crisis.

The tasks require careful planning, sharing of information and collaboration in order to complete them successfully. Meanwhile, groups and individuals are constantly receiving other, even more stretching, demands on their time. Groups and individuals are observed throughout the simulation so that their real behaviours can be fed back and explored afterwards. They can be asked to keep a mood journal to capture feelings and thoughts through the day, to help raise their awareness of themselves and others and to help them begin to develop their critical reflection skills.

While complex and challenging simulations such as those described above can be stretching, they do not reach their full effectiveness when used in isolation, as stand-alone experiences. They need to be integrated into a full learning journey, as described in Case Box One.

CASE BOX ONE

A case study on a multi-modular method – from simulation to reality

The client

The client was a global group with interests in shipping, oil and gas, and renewable energy. The programme was designed over four modules, for a cadre of senior high potentials who were regarded as having the potential to rise two levels to the Group Executive Committee. The participants were all functional or technical managers who had had little management or leadership development and were uncomfortable when focusing on anything other than the task at hand or when working with issues outside their own field of expertise.

The learning journey

This was a modular programme in which the first module involved a fairly traditional business simulation whilst including a number of activities, such as working with musical and arts metaphors, to stretch and unsettle the group.

The second module involved a crisis-based simulation of the type described above. Although the context was a simulation, it moved them towards reality, as what they experienced intellectually, behaviourally and emotionally was real.

The third module focused on developing their coaching skills and took them closer towards reality as they both received coaching and coached others, on real issues that they brought to the module. The real stretch here was caused by the duration and intensity of the coaching sessions. Working in two groups of five, each person received coaching from another member of the team for 90 minutes; and each person coached another member of the team for 90 minutes. That's enough time for it to get real!

The observing members of the team were engaged through the following process: after an uninterrupted first 30 minutes, a time out was called and the process reviewed by coachee, coach, observers and facilitator. For the remaining 60 minutes, the observers were free to interrupt and redirect proceedings but they could only do this by coaching the coach – they could not address the coachee. As a result of this intensity and the opportunity to interrupt and contribute, people generally learnt more during the three occasions they were in the observer role than when they were coach or coachee.

The fourth module took them entirely into reality as it was designed around a live case, as described in more detail in Case Box Two below.

Outcomes

The participants grew significantly through the programme and acknowledged how differently they emerged from the learning experience from where they had started. Initially, they thought they had derived most value from the coaching module, returning to the work place and coaching their own direct reports. However, over time, as new issues and challenges unfolded in the workplace, they gradually began to value the real learning that came from the live-case module.

The organisation has since merged with a former competitor and most of the participants have moved into more senior jobs within the new entity.

3. The live-case method

The approach taken when working with real or 'live' activities can take several forms. Probably the most common form in development programmes is the project. This may be inter-modular or post programme, but it usually involves an individual or small group tackling an issue within their own organisation in parallel with their day job. To be effective, these projects must be real, must be important to the organisation and must have real outcomes. However, as noted earlier, it can be difficult at senior levels to find a project that is sufficiently stretching to be a vehicle for development but not so urgent that it can wait some time for a solution. The 'live case' provides a more urgent and time-constrained situation that increase both the intellectual and the emotional stretch. Approaches to the live case will vary depending on the nature of the client organisation providing the case.

Third-party client

This takes participants to a 'donor' third-party organisation which provides an important and usually urgent issue for participants to tackle. They typically have 36 to 48 hours in which to tackle the case and produce a well thought through and structured proposal to the client, with their analysis of the situation and their conclusions and recommendations. This approach stretches participants and raises the game, in that they are required to tackle an issue that is real and live to the client and, usually, outside the comfort-zone of their own day-to-day experiences. The experience meets the requirement for senior management learning of providing both a stretching emotional experience and a cognitive challenge.

A limiting aspect of the third-party case method is that the third-party project sponsor remains a client of the participants. The participants act as consultants to the third party and, as such, don't have the same 'skin in the game' as when they are working within their own organisations and performing in front of their own executives, who have career-influencing decision-making powers!

In-house client

Let's consider this approach in more depth. This is the more demanding form of live case as it has participants tackling a real and immediate issue within their own organisation. This means that they do have real 'skin in the game' because they will be performing in front of their own senior executives, with a real risk of real personal failure. It is important to make clear that the project is in no way part of an assessment process, yet it is difficult to isolate the impressions created during live-case performance from both senior management and peer perceptions of potential. So the stakes are high.

The live case is generally sponsored by a senior executive who is accountable for the resolution of the issue which is at the heart of the case, although it may involve multiple stakeholders as well. Participants work in a compressed timeframe (36–48 hours) to tackle this issue that is real, urgent and critical to their organisation. The aim of this form of live case is to provide a mastery experience that is contextually relevant. The contextual relevance will help them develop muscle memory for dealing with future critical incidents. During a taught section of the module or workshop, it is helpful to provide a number of frameworks which will help the group to develop their thinking and dialogue skills and take them through some exercises to practise using them. After that a hands-off approach is adopted in relation to the content. This is after all a real activity, with real business relevance, and the idea is to develop individuals to be able to handle these situations as leaders.

It is important that faculty adopt this hands-off approach during the case, as it is critical to overcome the tendency towards learned helplessness. This is a real activity, working on real issue in the real world. And in the real world, there are no facilitators to step in and rescue them from a tough problem or a difficult interpersonal situation. There is no-one to relieve the tension by giving them the answer or telling them what to do. This increases the discomfort, the emotional stretch and the risk of personal failure as it requires them to step up and be held accountable for their outputs.

A further stretch is introduced through the team working aspect of the case. Most senior managers are used to operating in competitive teams when working on cases and simulations in development programmes – and often they relish the competitive environment. The live-case approach requires them to work in teams, to pursue potentially different routes to solutions but to collaborate to present one consolidated set of conclusions and recommendations. This simulates people working across functional and organisational boundaries at senior levels and it means that they are not only relying on the quality of their own work but on that of the collective. The need for teams to work as a single interdependent group gives rise to significant emotions and behaviours: tensions, frustrations, confrontations, competition, opting out and blaming (usually the faculty). Case Box Two gives detail of an example of the use of the live-case method and Figure 1, below, indicates the flow of the development.

CASE BOX TWO

The programme

The client was a subsidiary national bank within a larger European bank. The participants were high potentials sitting two levels below Executive Committee level and regarded as having the potential to develop to the next two levels. The live-case module was part of a larger two-year development programme. It was preceded by a leadership module and was followed by in-company assignments, secondments, coaching and mentoring.

The module

The participants went through the programme in three cohorts of 24 with the first-module cohorts being mixed into three new cohorts for the second. This increased the networking opportunities and meant that they could not rely on previous relationships and behaviour patterns from Module 1. They had to learn how to integrate with, and work with, a new group of people.

A different live case was used for each cohort, so there could be no prior warning or pre-worked answers. This also engaged more executives in the programme as 'case sponsors' and gave the bank the opportunity to tackle three important challenges.

The structure and process

The initial case briefs were developed jointly with each sponsor. This was then sent to participants, with background reading, a few days ahead of the live-case module. Participants were able to do some initial thinking about the case and to tap into other sources of information within the bank.

After a taught session in which they were given some tools, and following a briefing from the sponsor, teams undertook the first task, which was to develop a deeper understanding of the issue and to ensure that they were addressing 'the right question'.

The sponsor returned the next day to take a "back brief" (Bungay, 2010), in which the teams presented their view of 'the right question'. This was defined as "the question which, when answered, would make the problem go away". All teams then worked together with the sponsor to agree on a form of words for a single question that they would all take forward.

Another taught session followed, in which participants learnt and practised a process and the behaviours needed to improve the quality of their dialogue. They were then asked to apply the process and behaviours for effective dialogue, while they worked on the case. This was a deliberate stretch in an attempt to encourage the managers to deal with both content and process simultaneously. It is a skill that most managers find difficult, yet it is one of the most important skills for successful senior leaders, because content and process occur simultaneously in the workplace. Most participants have difficulty with this and want to work on one or the other, so it becomes another source of frustration and blame – and a good source of material for personal reflection! A further source of learning came when participants had to integrate the work of several functions when working on cross-boundary issues. This proved another difficult process indicating a real need for skills development in this area.

After the presentations, the sponsor(s) gave their initial reactions to the recommendations and gave feedback on the quality of the work done and the presentation. The group reviewed the content of their work immediately, drawing lessons on how to tackle strategic issues and how to present success to their senior leaders. The following day, participants worked in their teams to give each other feedback and review their performance as a team. This was followed by a plenary review in which they reviewed how well the teams had interacted and performed as a collective. All this fed into personal reflection and development action planning. The teams later continued as action-learning sets to monitor, challenge and support each other in both applying their learning and tackling new real challenges.

The outcomes

The sponsors were pleased both with the quality of the recommendations and the quality of thinking that the groups had displayed in getting to them. They found the live case and the process helpful in developing their own thinking and understanding of the issue. The sponsors invited each cohort to join their own senior teams (on a virtual or part-time basis) in further studies and ultimately the implementation of the final solutions. This enabled the Executive Committee members to tap into some of the best talent in the business to think about their issues. It also enabled them to get to know the talented people outside their own part of the business, whilst giving the participants more exposure at senior levels, and to Executive Committee members other than their own.

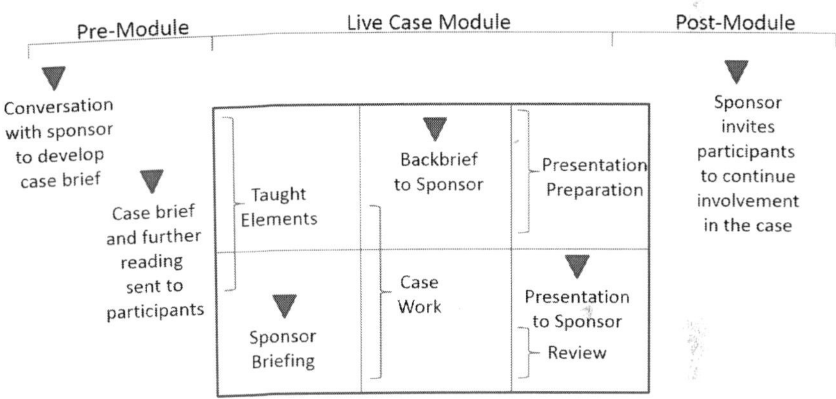

Figure 1 – Schedule of Development Using the Live-case Method

Conclusions

Analysis of case studies such as this suggests that the ability to work with content and process simultaneously – i.e. Strategic thinking and strategic dialogue – might be one of the most significant skills for senior leaders. Earlier researchers have suggested similar concepts. Laljani (2009) identified them as contextual mastery with cognitive and behavioural complexity. Revans (1988) described it as wisdom – the ability to ask insightful questions, in the face of risk, uncertainty and confusion, as well as the ability to act appropriately.

Given the challenges in developing senior talent that were identified earlier in this chapter, the authors believe that the live-case method can be an extremely effective approach in senior management development. Within a learning environment, it can probably approximate more closely to those workplace 'stomach churning' moments, than any other development method. As a developmental experience, it appears to tick all the boxes when it comes to senior management development as it is:

- Relevant and real

- Timely and urgent

- An intellectual stretch

- Outside of the comfort zone

- It requires working with content and process simultaneously

- Provides demanding interpersonal situations

- Exposure and risk of real personal failure

- An emotional stretch

- Free from teacher dependence and learned helplessness

- Fosters deeper self-awareness and awareness of others.

However, success cannot be guaranteed. There are several aspects of the management of a live case that must be addressed before embarking on an experience that might hold personal risk for participants:

- *Contracting*
  There are several aspects to the contracting process around a live case. The first is to consider how the live case (module) is integrated into any development programme and the client's ongoing talent-development process. Whilst the live case is a great vehicle for applying the learning from earlier modules, it is essential that the skills developed through the live case are harnessed and applied as soon as possible afterwards.

  Contracting in this instance involve a four-way relationship between the live-case sponsors, the learning and development (L&D) programme sponsor, the participants and the faculty. Both the L&D sponsor and the faculty need to be able to interact credibly with the 'C-suite' executives to engage them in the programme and in sponsoring a live case. The L&D sponsor needs to contract clearly with the participants about the role and relevance of the experience and its integration with ongoing development activities. Faculty need to manage the expectations of the L&D sponsor who may get nervous when participants get frustrated or dissatisfied with the process.

- *The relationship with participants*

Facilitators need to contract very clearly and very early with partici-pants and need to reinforce the message throughout the process. If they are to trust the faculty and the process, and be prepared to ride the emotional rollercoaster that a live case can set in motion, partici-pants need to understand the background research and rationale for the method.

The method may to be at odds with the mental model that senior managers have of development programmes. The hands-off nature of the faculty role is crucial for effective development, so it is essen-tial that the participants understand the part faculty will play – and in particular, that participants appreciate the value added by faculty holding the discipline of the method.

- *The facilitator role*

The importance of the hands-off stance cannot be overestimated. There are three key issues:

  - The need to 'hold the line' on the discipline of the method and the frameworks. If participants are allowed to stray from the method-ology, they find it difficult to make progress.
  - A core skill for senior leaders is the ability to work with content and process simultaneously. It is essential that the facilitators hold this tension by requiring participants to deliver against each of these elements at each stage of the case. In this way, they will develop and apply both their strategic thinking and their strategic dialogue skills simultaneously.
  - The need for more explicit and adequate support from faculty for participants to experience real critical reflection. Faculty must adopt a hands-on stance when it comes to critical reflection but keep their hands-off when it comes to the content or process of the live case itself. Participants often miss key opportunities to learn because they just do not see the relevance of a particular behaviour or incident. This is usually because they are so task focused but can occasionally be the result of insensitivity or a lack of perception. Some participants simply do not know how to reflect critically.

The capacity for self-generated critical reflection is a core skill of the successful senior leader. Faculty need to work actively on developing this skill alongside a hands-off approach to the live case itself, whilst resisting the urge to leap in and offer solutions to their problems.

Business schools must examine closely the capability of their faculty to work expertly with live-case methodology in order to be at the forefront of the development of 'C-suite' talent. This is an area that is complex and challenging, but the rewards for individuals and organisations will be great.

References

Bungay, S. (2010) *The Art of Action: How Leaders Close the Gaps Between Plans, Actions and Results* (London: Nicholas Brealey Publishing).

Laljani, N. (2009) *Making strategic leaders* (London: Palgrave Macmillan).

Poole, E., & Carr, M. (2005) If I knew then what I know now. *360°: The Ashridge Journal*, Spring 2005, pp.46–50.

Pruyne, E. (2009) Designing high-impact learning environments: Translating academic research into learning practice. *360°: The Ashridge Journal*, Winter 2009, pp.4–9.

Reitz, M. (2009) Experiencing Leadership. *360°: The Ashridge Journal*, Winter 2009, pp.10–13.

Revans, R. (1988) *Action Learning: ABC of Action Learning* (Farnham: Gower).

CHAPTER 4

Developing Personal Impact by Blending Learning, Life and Literature

Roger Delves

A common aim of much executive development is to increase the personal impact of participants. This chapter describes how, as part of a redesign of a traditional face-to-face MBA, a module on personal impact was created which used a highly innovative blend of virtual learning material and experiential face-to-face workshops. The real innovation was to combine a new and fresh use of canvasses drawn from real life and, unusually, from literature. This created an environment in which students felt informed and motivated enough to engage experientially and enthusiastically with intensely personal behavioural inter-relational frameworks such as Transactional Analysis, Emotional Intelligence and Authenticity. The objective was to stimulate students to open up and engage with their own authenticity and emotional intelligence, thereby experiencing the power of the tools for themselves.

The result was a two-day workshop within a wider 100-hour module which had impact, memorability and applicability for a demanding group of MBA and EMBA students.

The brief for the project was to design all elements of an entirely new MBA module that was innovative, engaging, impactful and blended. The stakeholders were a complex web that included the MBA management team, the student themselves, the tutor team and the wider business-school community which was watching, in real time, an experiment in creative techniques. The outcome was a module of 100 hours notional learning, split 32:68 in favour of the virtual space. This first face-to-face experiential learning element was 16 hours long, supported by 34 hours of prior virtual learning.

The chapter will include an overview of the module's learning objectives as they related to this part of the module. There are two key features of this chapter:

- First, to identify what was compelling about the transfer of knowledge via material in the virtual space.

- Second, interrogating the experiential learning in the face-to-face environment, the chapter will identify what went well, where the surprises were and when and why students responded especially powerfully to the creative techniques that the module deployed.

So, the overarching aim was to help students to develop their thinking, behaviour and performance in order that they could 'be themselves more, with skill'. The face-to-face elements of the module referenced Shakespeare's *Othello* to harness the power of storytelling and used the metaphor and parallel of climbing Mount Everest to draw on the unique achievements of individuals who had faced and overcome huge challenges.

The two canvasses which formed the bulk of the face-to-face time of the module were used to illustrate and examine the frameworks offered to the participants; the materials and processes developed to serve this purpose will be reviewed later in this chapter. The first canvas was the story of the disaster on Everest in 1996, narrated live by Rebecca Stephens, OBE, an associate fellow at Ashridge, the first British woman to summit Everest and the first British woman to summit the Seven Summits. The second canvas or framework was the equally compelling tragedy of Othello, Desdemona and Iago as captured by Oliver Parker's 1995 film with Kenneth Brannagh as Iago and Lawrence Fishbourne as Iago.

The virtual learning elements of the module offered a number of media-rich ways to assimilate and understand the underlying academic theory which was to be explored experientially in the classroom. We created a series of media objects – pieces to camera in which the teaching team explored and explained the various models and theories which we needed the students to understand *before* the face-to-face elements of the programme. A particular challenge for this module in 2012, when the redesigned MBA was to be launched with much new content, was that this module was the very first module experienced by the first cohort, meaning that neither students nor faculty had prior experience of this blended approach within the framework of the new MBA.

The media objects were a mix of 'talking head' pieces to camera and focussed PowerPoint presentations with voiced commentaries, along with interviews to camera in which one faculty member quizzed another on their particular areas of expertise. The Everest case was also captured on camera, with the case narrated by this chapter's author and with expert input provided by Rebecca Stephens. In addition, required and recommended reading was identified which needed to be completed in advance of the face-to-face element, and a number of links were offered to external sources such as YouTube, where useful additive content was found from which students would benefit.

An important and transferable learning for faculty was how time consuming and challenged it was to create these media-rich objects. This was not just because the material required a lot of preparation but also because faculty who were very well used to working in a classroom context found that dealing with the same material with just a camera or a microphone for company was more daunting than expected.

We quickly realised that, to develop this learning experience for our students, time management was critical; but we also needed to bring into the team someone able to produce performance as well as set the technology up correctly. It was no mean feat to find someone with the confidence and credentials to tell experienced faculty with years of classroom experience behind them that they sound or look wooden or flat; but when we did, it offered a huge advantage. The media objects produced needed to be compelling and, where possible, compellingly different in order to capture and keep the attention of students whose normal on-line experiences are full of encounters with highly polished, highly interactive, highly professional and expensively produced material.

By incorporating material to be watched, to be read and to be listened to, the module architecture was designed to reflect all stages of the learning cycle and the different learning styles to found among a diverse student group (Honey & Mumford, 1982). In addition, in light of how experiential and personal the face-to-face element was to be, it was vital to the credibility of the module that it was underpinned by robust applied research firmly grounded in a real business-world context.

On the 'risk register' for the development of the module was the obvious one that the necessary transfer of knowledge would not take place successfully in advance of the experiential face-to-face elements. Contributory factors here could be a lack of willingness among students to do the pre-work (we deemed this to be a low risk, as this was the students' first module and we assumed high engagement and motivation). More worrying would be the students' potential inability to master the required material from the stimuli we provided. To mitigate this risk, the faculty team discussed the possibility of 'testing for understanding' in advance of the face-to-face element of the module, thereby giving students who lacked in-depth understanding an opportunity to master the material better before meeting the experiential workshops. The idea was to create a self-completion questionnaire, which would not be an assessed element of the module, but which would allow students to see what progress towards understanding the material they had made. In the end, the design team felt that this did not constitute treating the students as responsible adults and we decided against it.

However, in the event, students arrived for this module at least well-prepared, with a firm understanding of the theory around the content the frameworks offered (Emotional Intelligence, Authenticity and Transactional Analysis).

Before describing how the two elements of virtual and face-to-face learning were experienced, it is necessary to review the learning objectives. The entire MBA programme has the overall objective of contributing to the creation of self-aware, self-confident graduates, grounded in reality. This Personal Impact module is regarded as a central contributor to this overall programme objective and so, on completion of this entire module, the successful participant should have specific knowledge and understanding of the role of his or her 'personal impact' in meeting this objective.

The Personal Impact module's specific objectives were:

- First, on completion, successful students would able to use the frameworks of Emotional Intelligence, Authenticity and Transactional Analysis to develop a sound and sophisticated personal awareness.

- Second, successful students should be able to use this personal awareness in the use of a set of professional practice skills which would increase their personal impact. They should be able to apply the concepts, frameworks and models offered within the module when working in complex, unpredictable and/or specialised contexts, and should be able to exercise personal responsibility in professional practice, and to adapt skills and design or develop new skills and/or procedures for new situations.

The first element of the module, personal awareness, was to be explored through the lenses of Emotional Intelligence, Transactional Analysis and Authenticity. The choice of these particular frameworks for inclusion in the module was supported by the need to highlight the role that emotions play in forming our relationships, in navigating through the politics of work environments to maintain successful and fulfilling employment, in making good decisions in life, understanding the drivers of social behaviours, and being successful.

Emotional Intelligence (Goleman, 1996) has emerged as a way to capture the abilities and skills that enable individuals to maximise their own social and organisational performance and success using emotional awareness of self, and offering emotional management techniques. Transactional Analysis (Harris, 1967) offers a 'frame' for relationships with others using concepts of maturity and relational expectations, whilst Authenticity helps people to explore their relationship with integrity, with principles and with values, and helps individuals to see the extent to which the nature and quality of these relationships inform their approach to the workplace and to the interdependent interactions needed to manage within it.

There were some key principles underlying the design and delivery of the module which it will be useful to make explicit. Everything that the students needed to do was laid out within the digital learning zone, in a variety of forms including a piece delivered to camera, a written explanation of how things were designed to work and a number of announcements reminding students in advance of our expectations:

- Prior to the face-to-face element, faculty constantly stressed the need for adequate preparation for that element.

- Faculty stressed that the available face-to-face time was to be used to explore concepts, not to transfer knowledge and understanding about these concepts.

- Faculty stressed that it was the students' responsibility to undertake and complete the necessary preparation during the time they spent in the digital learning zone. To embody this principle, it was made clear that for students properly to prepare themselves for this journey, they would need to undertake some quite demanding self-managed learning before they arrived for the face-to-face session.

To meet the needs of the QAA and Higher Education Academy in the UK, MBA learning must be demonstrably assessed. Faculty wanted the assessed elements to do two things: one was take the students back to the underpinning theory to ensure that it had been absorbed and understood, especially since they had by the point of assessment also experimented with the theory in the experiential workshops. The second was to create an opportunity for reflection on the module and in particular to encourage the application of theory after reflection and to help in the identification of transferrable learning. The intent was that this module, however experiential, would also be practical, pragmatic and of real applicable value to students.

Individual student grades were determined by assessment of individual presentations (20 minutes duration) on the final day of face-to-face sessions (weighting of 50%) and by assessment of the written assignment (1,500 words, weighting of 50%) submitted at the end of the module. Both assessed elements needed to demonstrate application of the key theories, concepts or experiences. The assessed presentations were also filmed, with copies made available to participants after grade publication to reinforce their learning and feedback.

To ensure rigour and consistency, faculty involved in assessment and grading were provided with a detailed set of assessment criteria (a generic example of which was included in the Assessment section of the student handbook for student reference – the students were pointed to it and it was also available separately on the digital learning zone). This ensured that common understanding was shared by all markers and all students, particularly about what was required from the individual presentations.

Students were explicitly encouraged to understand what was expected of them to achieve the different grades.

Firstly, an assessed presentation of a minimum of 15 minutes and a maximum of 20 minutes was required, entitled *My Leadership Story*. For success on this assessment, students needed to offer an engaging account of their personal-impact praxis in a professional context, without the use of PowerPoint slides. They were expected to evidence a number of models, frameworks and ideas using the lenses and skills provided over the three elements of the Personal Impact module. A key criterion was that a central, clear and distilled message should be communicated to the audience by the end of the presentation.

The audience for the presentation was the student's peer group and the assessing faculty member; no time was allowed for questions. The presentation offered students the opportunity to reflect upon, experiment with and deepen their understanding of the theory introduced in the pre-reading. In this relatively 'safe' environment, students were asked to examine their own performance when applying the theories and to experiment with them to understand how best they could develop their own personal impact.

There was also an individual written assignment which provided an opportunity for students to reflect on what they had explored within the module and to identify those elements which had particular resonance for them personally. They were encouraged to identify particular learning which was transferable to their own workplace or their planned future careers. They were encouraged to continue to ground their reflections in the models, theories and sense-making tools they had explored. When grading these assignments, faculty were looking for evidence that the students had understood and could apply the models.

The assessed paper carried 50% of the overall score and was a 1,500-word paper (+/- 10%) with this title:

> *Using your selection of appropriate models and frameworks from the Personal Impact module, critically evaluate the personal impact skills and behaviours of two leaders you know or have known.*

Marking criteria included:

1. Evidence of aspects of the chosen leaders' personal impact which were well developed and those which needed some further development, along with reasoning for these choices.

2. Consideration of how aspects of personal impact influence how others perceive a leader.

3. The assessment needed to include critical reflection of the student's own experiences.

4. The identification of transferable learning which would improve their own personal impact skills and behaviours.

Personal awareness: preparation

Three significant areas of academic theory and two canvasses had been identified through which the concepts of personal awareness and personal impact were to be explored.

The preparation required for this first face-to-face element encompasses the following theories:

1. **Emotional Intelligence (EI)**
   Media-rich material was developed by module faculty. This offered a broad introduction to EI and its relevance to the workplace. In addition, core reading was identified and recommended including material created by the generally accepted father of EI, American academic Daniel Goleman. The vehicle used to work with emotional intelligence was the MSCEIT model (Identify/use/understand/manage emotions) developed by Mayer, Salovey and Caruso, which was referenced and illustrated, along with the Plutchik (1994) Circumplex Wheel of Emotions.

2. **Authenticity**
   Again, media-rich material was generated, this time by the module leader, a subject expert in the field. The material offered an overview of Authenticity and authentic leadership plus an interview of the module leader by a faculty colleague. The interview further explored the use and validity of authentic principles in the workplace. In addition, core readings from the works of leading Authenticity academics Luthans and Avolio (2003), Bass and Steidlmeier (1999), J.C. Thoms (2008), and Michie and Gooty (2005) were identified and recommended, alongside work from the lead faculty and author of this chapter. This material explored the subjects of values, trust and personal integrity.

3. **Transactional Analysis**
   To support this concept, an audio-supported PowerPoint slide set was developed to introduce the concepts of parent, adult and child and the concept of hidden drivers. Self-completion questionnaires were included in the pre-workshop material, allowing students to arrive with an understanding of their own personal 'egogram' and the presence or absence of hidden drivers in their own psychological make-up.

The audio material was supported by helpful articles and by links to external sites which carried TA material of value.

The Canvasses

1. **Everest**: The learning vehicles for the use of this canvas can be described as 'metaphor' and 'parallel'. A portfolio of compelling material was created around this canvas. Rebecca Stevens was the first British woman to summit on Everest, which she did in 1993. The following year she became the first British woman to complete the Seven Summits challenge – scaling the highest peak in each of the world's continents. A 'living case' has been created by Roger and Rebecca around events on Everest in 1996 (these events are captured elsewhere in books by two of the protagonists: Jon Krakauer's *Into Thin Air* (1997) and Alexander Boukreev's *The Climb: Tragic Ambitions on Everest* (1997)). This case is delivered within the module as a piece to camera and was made available to students prior to the first face-to-face element. Embedded in the case are the questions students were required to consider before the face-to-face element.

   Students were also required to listen to and absorb the story of Rebecca's own summit climb, which took place in 1993, and which Rebecca had committed to camera. Prior to the 1993 climbing season, fewer than forty people had ever reached the summit of Everest. Like the case itself, an examination of this climb was used to shed useful light on emotional intelligence and on authenticity.

2. *Othello* is a timeless Shakespearian tragedy. The story was used to offer students a common canvas on which to examine emotional intelligence and authenticity in action. Students were asked to absorb two learning items before the face-to-face part of the module. The first was a short, accessible synopsis of the storyline. Students were not expected to read the play in the Shakespearian original vernacular as not all were native English speakers. Instead, they were asked to watch the 1995 film production – directed by Oliver Parker and starring Kenneth Branagh, Laurence Fishburne and Michael Sheen – and to make notes on their impressions of it before the first face-to-face workshop. They were required to consider:

   - What the action told them about the different relationships of the key characters with these concepts, and
   - What transferable learning could be taken from the play to the workplace.

The following paragraph identifies five examples of the thirty questions posed to students to stimulate exploration of these fundamental questions:

- Is Iago's hatred of Othello based in anything authentic? Can hatred or dislike ever be either authentic or emotionally intelligent? In what Transactional Analysis state is Iago predominantly, as revealed by his own early description of his relationship with Othello and his future plans?

- If hatred/dislike can be authentic or emotionally intelligent, how does that line up with living by appropriate principles and values?

- Othello himself is described as both strong hearted and noble, yet also innocent. Is it likely that he could have lived as a warrior leader and remained innocent?

- How authentic are Othello's actions regarding his secret marriage to Desdemona? Is it an Adult action and approach? Is he justified or, by circumventing her father's likely withholding of permission, has he acted in an emotionally unintelligent way, in an inauthentic, self-directed way, in a way likely to generate trouble for the future? What about Desdemona? How do you judge her actions with regard both to the development of her relationship with Othello and to the way she decided to keep the relationship, and the secret marriage, from her father? Which ego state appears to be in the ascendancy with her?

- Why is Othello's view of Iago ("A man he is of honesty and trust") so inaccurate? What does this view tell us about Othello as a leader, if anything? What does it tell us about Iago's management of his own personal impact?

Students were not required to undertake the pre-work in any particular order. The way they approached the material was a matter of personal choice and responsibility. However, they were aware that they needed to arrive for the module confident that they could address the questions posed about the events on Everest and able to examine the events captured in the Othello storyline through the lenses of EI, TA and Authenticity.

The experiential workshop: Day One

The face-to-face workshop designed to explore personal awareness (the first of the three elements of personal impact examined within the overall module) took place over two days. Prior to this, students had spent an orientation weekend together and thus knew each other, but did not know the faculty. A surprise result of the virtual pre-work was that almost every one of the twenty-eight students commented that they already felt familiarity with faculty through the media-rich pre-work sessions. This was an interesting learning for those involved in the development of the material: in a blended-learning programme, astute use of media objects featuring the teaching faculty can generate a relationship even before the faculty meet the students in real time.

The pre-work was reviewed and refreshed through a 30-minute Q&A session. This was a relatively traditional session with large laminated versions of the key models and important slides from the pre-work displayed on the walls around the room for quick reference (a system which worked very well throughout the three days). Faculty were quickly able to point to pertinent models and, perhaps more importantly, to show links between models and ideas as the days passed. There were also flip charts available to capture ideas and to throw out other models if these came to mind and were deemed useful. Many students personally updated this approach by simply photographing the materials using smartphones – a useful application of technology in the moment.

During this session, some feedback was also provided on the TA scores and driver scores from the pre-work, as well as responses to questions on the theories. In essence, this was a useful session to ensure that students had ongoing awareness of the learning content. Most, although not all, students did contribute and those contributions suggested that material had been consumed and understood, which was encouraging. However, for future iterations of the module it will be useful to consider if there may be other ways of feeling confidence in the learning of non-contributing students.

Finally, in this section, we asked the table groups (5 tables of 6 seats each, set out in café style) to identify three learning objectives they would like to have delivered over the two days. The time we made available was thirty minutes. Three faculty members provided support for this process. The learning objectives were captured on a flip chart and committed to the wall.

After a short break, the students were invited to browse at three 'drop-in centres' set up in the teaching room. One was established for Rebecca to talk about the Everest case. A second was for Kerrie Fleming to talk about Emotional Intelligence and SDI (the Strengths Deployment Inventory, a self-awareness tool administered during the induction weekend just passed, and favoured by the faculty team because of its use of language around our individual Motivating

Values System and Values Relating Style). At the third, Roger Delves was available to talk about TA and Authenticity. Students could drop in on any table at any time to ask questions of understanding and clarification, or to listen to the member of faculty exploring elements and aspects of their particular areas of knowledge and understanding. Although this exercise was allotted 45 minutes in the timetable, the exercise found its own natural length at around 75 minutes, due to student interest and engagement.

Next we moved into a specific exploration of the Everest canvasses. The exercise was in three parts and this filled the rest of Day One.

Part one: Everest case questions

1. Given the circumstances which pertain on Everest – ambiguity and uncertainty, stress and high ambition – is there a best approach to take to leadership there?

2. Were the events on Everest in 1996 due to leader failings? If so, what were they? Could they have been avoided?

Working in groups of six, students prepared a 15–20 minute presentation of their answers to both questions after which a short plenary discussion took place. The students displayed a real ability to interpret the actions of individuals through the lenses of the models. The discussions focussed particularly on motivation and decision making. The personal knowledge provided by Rebecca of the mountain, and also of some of the key characters involved in these dramatic and deadly events, greatly enhanced this session.

Part two: the fishbowl

Rebecca was invited to sit in a fishbowl to field questions on the story of her personal climb on Everest and on the Everest case generally. The students sat on chairs in a large circle and Rebecca sat on a chair in the middle of the circle, with two empty chairs facing her. When a student had a question to ask, he or she would come forward, sit, pose the question, hear the answer and then be replaced by a fresh questioner. The second empty chair was for the following questioner, meaning that a questioner could occupy the chair during the preceding question, increasing the spontaneity of the session. This was a compelling session, which again lasted longer that the time allocated to it. The questions, being the fruits of the pre-work, were informed and challenging. Rebecca's style of quiet, authentic yet authoritative commitment was well suited to the format and levels of attention were very high throughout the session.

Part three: reviewing the learning

Students worked in groups of three to consider what transferrable learning had emerged from the day's activity. The day concluded with a plenary session to examine and share some of the transferrable learning. The view of the facilitators at the end of this first day was that:

- The students had spent a lot of time mastering material in the learning zone before the module

- The students were entirely competent at using the lenses introduced in advance of the face-to-face session

- The experiential nature of the day was well received by students

- The quality of the learning was excellent.

In the evening, students were asked to re-visit the *Othello* synopsis and/or watch the film again and/or consider and reflect on the questions ready for Day Two.

The experiential workshop: Day Two

Day Two was designed to allow students to continue to explore the application of the same models and theories – Emotional Intelligence, Authenticity and Transactional Analysis – but this time using the canvas of the *Othello* material. A learning review was conducted by Kerrie to ensure reconnection with the Day One learning using the wall-mounted material. This was to continue to establish the models and their application in the minds of the students.

Exercise One

Questions about *Othello*, taken from the pre-event learning material, were posed and, in newly created small groups of six, students:

1. Identified the TA ego states and the ego state changes that took place, and analysed the communication transactions that they observed

2. Considered the level and nature of emotional intelligence displayed, and

3. Considered whether the characters were acting authentically within the academic definitions.

In plenary, we asked the group to choose for classroom discussion two or three specific questions that had been offered in the pre-work. This exercise was very well received, and the understanding of the plot and the actions of the key protagonists was clearly good.

Exercise Two

Each group was asked to rewrite the plot line and create a brief synopsis for a new version of *Othello*; and then each group was allocated a different theoretical 'lens' through which to view its work.

For example, one group was asked to make use of Transactional Analysis and to assume that each character could remain with their 'Adult in the Executive' throughout the play. Another group was instructed to assume that every character was authentic in their behaviours throughout the play, and were asked to consider the plot implications for this change. A third group were to assume that each character had well-developed emotional intelligence throughout the play.

In plenary, each group shared its new plot and synopsis and there followed a whole group discussion on how the changes in behaviour that had been imposed on the key characters had changed what happened to each of them. This exercise helped individuals to work together to understand the real impact on events of increased emotional intelligence and the importance of key actors maintaining authenticity and retaining their adult in the executive.

It's fair to say that the new plots that emerged as a result of this engaging exercise were not as compelling as Shakespeare's original; but they were also significantly less catastrophic. The learning emerged clearly here that when we take the dramatic out of our thoughts and actions, we are left with the adult: the thought-through words and actions of considerate, emotionally intelligent, authentic people.

Exercise Three

Each student was asked individually to reflect on a key scene or plotline from the film or play of their own life. Using the same technique as in Exercise Two, they were asked to re-write the scene or plotline to create a better outcome, using the lenses of the frameworks from the module to support and validate the "new actions and decisions" of the players involved in the scene or plotline.

The intended learning outcome here was for students to see that each individual has a responsibility to behave in an appropriate way, and when individuals fail to do so, things often do not develop as hoped.

Exercise Four

Individual students volunteered to explain briefly what had in fact happened and what could/should have happened if they and others had behaved differently. This involved a maximum of three volunteers.

Exercise Five

This comprised a paired 'walk and talk' exercise and asked students to rehearse and dry run (not role play unless both wanted to do so) one or two of the new conversations that might be created by the rewritten scene or plotline. The pair conclude by sharing what each felt went well, badly or as expected during the conversations. There were two iterations, allowing for one new scene from each student.

A final plenary session was held to review the two days of activity and to reflect on what had been explored which had potential to be transferred to the workplace. We also considered the usefulness of the models in the context of a high-pressure MBA/EMBA environment and discussed how the application of the models might enhance the MBA/EMBA experience, and the degree to which that experience might be expected to be a microcosm of the working world.

Conclusions

The positive module reviews indicated that at each stage of the process the students had experienced a valuable learning intervention. Some of the key learnings for the faculty team included:

- Well-designed, well-produced media-rich content will be readily consumed in advance of any face-to-face sessions as long as the quantity of material broadly matches the published study-time requirements. It is therefore important realistically to manage student expectations in this regard. However, the production of these materials to the required standard is both time and resource intensive for faculty and must be 'budgeted' for.

- In our experience, students' own motivation levels can be trusted to ensure that they complete the study requirements: no pre-event testing was required to encourage or guarantee compliance. The MBA programme represents considerable investment of time and money for these students, and maximising their return on that investment may be a powerful incentive to put effort into the programme.

- When experiential sessions require students and faculty to use exploratory frameworks at a level of personal depth that is meaningful, the sessions are demanding of energy and emotions, so time allowed must be generous and breaks should be more frequent than for more traditional classroom learning.

- More traditional classroom stimuli, such as flipcharts and posters which capture the key models, are a vital component in energising group discussions and should be retained in effective blended learning. However, rather than a channel for new content, they serve a role of support and reinforcement.

- The use of 'life canvasses' rather than more traditional 'case studies' was a well-received and successful innovation. The intrinsic interest of the subject matter both stimulated and held attention. Both the live canvasses represented versions of storytelling, which is proving to be a powerful conduit for adult learning.

Throughout the entire module, students were encouraged and equipped to develop the skills and attitudes of mind that would enable them to undertake further critical study in the field of personal awareness, and the related fields of resilience and personal impact, that could be of value in later (lifelong) learning.

As with all executive education, or management development, the proof of the pudding is in the relevance to participants' working lives. Further work to track the long-term effectiveness of the learning that took place during this module is underway.

References

Bass, B.M., & Steidlmeier, P. (1999) Ethics, character and authentic transformational leadership behaviour. *Leadership Quarterly*, 10(2), pp.181–218.

Boukreev, A., & Weston De Walt, G. (1998) *The Climb: Tragic Ambitions on Everest* (Pan Books).

Caruso, D.R., & Salovey, P. (2004) *The Emotionally Intelligent Manager* (San Francisco, CA: Jossey Bass).

Delves, R. (2007) The importance of exploring and validating personal values in creating a sustainable, authentic leadership style. *Sixth International Studying Leadership Conference*, Warwick University, pp.1–38.

Goleman, D. (1996) *Emotional Intelligence: Why it can matter more than IQ* (Bloomsbury).

Goleman, D. (1998) *Working with Emotional Intelligence* (New York, NY: Bantam).

Harris, T.A. (1967) *I'm OK – You're OK* (Random House).

Honey, P., & Mumford, A. (1982) *The Manual of Learning Styles* (Maidenhead: Peter Honey Publications).

Krakauer, J. (1998) *Into Thin Air* (Anchor Books).

Luthans, F., & Avolio, B.J. (2003) Authentic leadership: A positive development approach. In K.S. Cameron, J.E. Dutton & R.E. Quinn (eds), *Positive Organizational Scholarship: Foundations of a New Discipline* (San Francisco, CA: Berrett-Koehler), pp.241–58.

Mayer, J., & Salovey, P. (1990) Emotional intelligence and imagination. *Cognition and Personality*, 9, pp.185–211.

Michie, S., & Gooty, J. (2005) Values, emotions and authenticity: will the real leader please stand up? *Leadership Quarterly*, 16 (2005), pp.441–57.

Plutchik, R. (1994) *The Psychology and Biology of Emotion* (New York: Harper Collins).

Thoms, J. (2008) Ethical integrity in leadership and Organizational Moral Culture. *Leadership*, 4(4), pp.419–42.

SECTION 3 –
WHERE MANAGERS LEARN

CHAPTER 5

OMD! Cultural Impact on Experiential Learning

Angela Jowitt

This chapter will focus on the role of experiential learning in management development and in particular the aspect of experiential learning known as OMD (Outdoor Management Development).

The chapter will share the body of knowledge and the insights that have been accumulated not only from an academic perspective but, equally importantly, from a practitioner point of view.

First of all, the chapter will outline the knowledge gleaned from practitioners of OMD over the last 20 years, in particular emphasising cultural differences that may influence the learning that participants can take from such learning interventions. Drawing upon culture models, the links between theory and practicality in the field of experiential learning. In conclusion, the chapter will offer some 'top tips' for facilitating multicultural groups on experiential learning exercises.

This approach to learning has its roots in models of learning that will no doubt be familiar to experienced learning professionals. Most influential was that proposed by Kolb, who outlined a four-stage model. The stages of the model are as follows: firstly that the learner starts by having a concrete experience; he or she reflects upon it; then derives some conclusions from that reflection; and, finally, makes a decision to try a different behaviour as a result (Kolb, 1984, in Merriman et al., 2007, p.165).

Kolb's model is difficult to challenge and has been (and still is) still widely used, although it is not without its critics, who claim that it is overly rational (e.g. Michelson, 1996) and that it takes people out of their holistic context (e.g. Beard, 2008).

In response to these criticisms, other authors have taken a more situational approach, arguing that different learning will occur in different contexts (Boud et al., 1993, in Merriman et al., 2007, p.169); and some consider the influence of emotion in learning, addressing how both positive and negative emotions can occur during the learning process, and the impact this may have on the learner's experience (Beard & Wilson, 2002; Heron, 1992). Illeris emphasises the subjectivity of the learner, stating that learning facts does not result in personal development. For personal development to occur, the learner must subjectively experience the learning, making personal meanings that are of interest and importance to that individual (Illeris, 1999).

However, despite these different flavours within the literature, there is general agreement that experiential learning is a constructive process in which learning is unique to the individual (Illeris, 1999; Usher & Edwards, 1994, in Moon 2004). It is both an internal and external process and can be said to observe the dualisms of reflection and experience, knowledge and skills, and theory and practice.

Each individual taking part in the learning will construct his or her own internal experience and meaning. The external experience is of equal importance – both environmental and societal (Beard & Wilson, 2002; Boud et al., 2000, in Moon, 2004; Heron, 1992; Illeris, 1999, 2007) – and the individual must be self-aware and engaged. In experiential learning, one has to take part actively in the exercise to derive any true learning. The experience must be externalised before it can be internalised. Finally, a critical element of experiential learning is to reflect upon and review the experience in order for the learner to draw conclusions, something which is often captured in the form of a group debrief held at the end of an activity, where people share their reflections and learning.

So, let's focus now on OMD in particular. What do we mean by the phrase? In a nutshell, Outdoor Management Development (OMD) involves a metaphor for learning. Participants are taken out of the classroom and presented with challenges or problems that, typically, cannot be addressed or solved by individuals working alone. Group engagement is often the key to success with challenges that may be physical or conceptual (McEvoy & Buller, 1997; Williams et al., 2003). The common features are that it is a specific development technique; the challenges are conducted in the outdoors, facilitated and debriefed using skilled facilitators; and that transferable learning will be drawn from the exercises to the workplace.

Some background – the evolution of OMD

The fundamental idea, outlined earlier, is that that management learning can be facilitated through practical experiences and active reflection (Beard & Wilson, 2002; Hamilton & Cooper, 2001; Kolb, 1984; Saunders, 1997, in Meyer, 2003). As outdoor learning exercises are often novel and unusual for participants, the uniqueness of the activities provides a level playing field to promote equality between participants in terms of skill and ability for the task (Irvine & Wilson, 1994). This permits individuals and groups to focus on the processes underpinning behaviours – and becoming able to identify these is in fact a recognised learning outcome for this sort of learning intervention (McEvoy & Buller, 1997). Outdoor Management Development has proved to be a powerful method of developing an awareness of the self and others, as one's behaviour is clearly visible, lacking the cover of the organisational norms and systems (Dainty & Lucas, 1992).

The early literature heralded OMD for offering value in two key areas:

- Its "uniqueness" (Boud et al., 1993; Irvine & Wilson, 1994; Krouwel & Goodwill, 1994)

- The power and impact of that unique experience (Dainty & Lucas, 1992; Krouwel & Goodwill 1994).

These ringing endorsements, plus the overwhelmingly positive participant reviews of most OMD sessions, have led to the ubiquitous use of OMD sessions on an enormous number of programmes and learning interventions.

More recently, and quite rightly, a more questioning approach has been adopted to the use and effectiveness of OMD. Whilst there was general recognition that it was successful and popular, there was a concurrent overriding concern that nobody knew why. There was (and still is) a lack of solid empirical evidence (Badger et al., 1997; Burnett & James, 1994; Eikenberry in Silberman, 2007; Ibbetson & Newell, 1996; Irvine & Wilson, 1994; Worrall & Cooper, 2001 in Williams et al., 2003; Ekenberry, Ch. 15 in Siberman 2007) that OMD experiences provide an acceptable return on investment in terms of participant learning.

More recent trends in the literature have taken a learner-centred approach with a greater emphasis on reflection (Beard & Wilson, 2002; Boniface, 2000; Moon, 2004), whole-person development (Leberman & Martin, 2004; Meyer, 2003), holistic approaches to learning (Beard & Wilson, 2002; Desmond & Jowitt, 2011; Le Cornu, 2005) and meaningful learning experiences (Taniguchi et al., 2005). Over time, this learner-centred approach has replaced the experience-centred approach.

Fundamental to the success of experiential learning is an understanding of how different development becomes when working with adult learners. Adults come to learning not only with capabilities and potential but also with histories and constraints. **"Experience is remoulding us every moment and our mental reaction of every given thing is really a resultant of our experience of the whole world up to that date"** (James, 1950, in Stevens, 2006, p.155).

Working with adult learners experientially lends itself to the philosophy of 'andragogy', which translates from the Greek as 'adult learning' ('andra' meaning 'man' and 'gogy' meaning 'learning'). Knowles (1968) developed the andragogy framework, which focuses on the life experience of the adult as a source of learning, positing that adults define themselves by their experiences and the positions they hold in life, such as marital status, hierarchical position, parent and political activist (Knowles, in Merriman et al., 2007; Caffarella & Baumgartner 2007). Andragogy has an action orientation and stresses the need for the personal motivation of the learner. It is a self-directed process defined by Knowles as "freedom of the learner" (in Illeris, 1999). This process is greatly aided when the purpose for learning is clear. Given that life experience has already shaped adult learners, they also bring their own set of assumptions and prejudices, and so a motivation to learn is not always something which can be assumed. Equally, the learner may be trapped in their lived experience, creating barriers to learning based on the assumptions they hold about themselves, others and the cultures in which they operate.

The importance of this lived experience for management development is clear. Adult learners have established ways of being, habits and rituals. Patterns of behaviour may emerge – if I behave in a certain way, I receive a reward (e.g. a promotion), which serves to reinforce the behaviour. But within this, adults may also learn bad habits and behaviours which need to be unlearned. Learners will construct their own internal meanings based on the experience they bring with them to the learning situation. Experiential learning is as much about unlearning old ways as it is about learning new ways (Anderson in Moon, 2004). Adult learners may struggle to accept or change their existing beliefs, and the key to unlocking this dilemma lies in peer feedback, delivered within the moment. Negt neatly describes this as "capturing reality" (in Illeris, 1999, p.128). There are implications for the questions "how do I get on in this organisation?", "how do I add value here?" and "how do I need to be different?" As organisations become more internationally mixed, learners have to interact with others from different cultural backgrounds. Experiential learning has much to offer in the way of answers to these questions as it involves direct interaction with the environment, although the learning is not necessarily immediate. There may be a period of "cognitive dissonance" (Illeris, 1999) if the learning is closed down too early, giving the learner a sense of unfinished business. It is therefore considered important to give learners some time and space to reflect and resume debriefing discussions once reflection has occurred. In addition to sufficient reflection time, adequate connections relevant to the world of the learner (sense making and transfer) must be made (Illeris, 1999).

Outdoor Management Development as a significant learning intervention first gained ground in the 1970s with ideas emerging from, notably, John Adair and his work on Action Centred Leadership and similar concepts suggested by the Leadership Trust (Krouwel & Goodwill, 1994).

John Adair's (1973) Action Centred Leadership Model (see Figure 1) relies on the leader to apply him- or herself in three main areas: managing the task; managing the team; and effective leadership of the individual according to the situation in which the leader finds his or herself.

Figure 1 – John Adair's (1973) Action Centred Leadership Model TM. p.38

It has been extremely relevant for OMD in that it offers a particularly simple yet useful framework for the all-important debrief and reflection at both the mid and endpoint of the exercises. The formula for most OMD experiences often follows a predictable sequence:

- Groups or teams are formed and asked to consider how they intend to work together

- A group problem-solving exercise is briefed

- The exercise is performed

- Facilitator-led group and individual reviews are conducted.

There may be variations on this formula – for example, particular leaders may be nominated for a specific exercise, and the focus may be on identified competences such as influencing – but generally, most OMD experiences are shaped in this way.

Learning across culture – what we have seen

Whilst OMD is widely used and has proved effective across the globe, the cultural background of participants is often not specifically acknowledged or addressed. Many of the effectiveness studies involve younger groups of managers such as those on a pre-experience MBA. The rest of this chapter will offer insights from the experience of working intensively with experiential learning over many years. The sample of several hundred participants has been made up of both homogeneous and heterogeneous culture groups from all over the globe, and includes a wide span of age groups from graduate intake to older 'C-suite' participants. The analysis here will offer a breakdown into three 'rough' categories:

- Participants from Western developed countries, largely from Europe and the USA

- Participants from the Middle East, largely UAE, Qatar, Saudi Arabia and Egypt

- Participants from the Far East, largely China.

Anecdotally, there are some obvious headline differences that it is worth noting first. For example, if a group of managers largely from Western developed cultures are asked the question "What is the most important aspect of team working: task, process or relationship?" they will typically and unanimously respond "Task!" In contrast, if a comparable group of managers from the Middle East are asked the same question, they may respond unanimously but with the answer "Relationships". The importance of connections and interpersonal bonds comes through much more strongly in Eastern cultures than they do in the West, at least in terms of espoused values.

However, there are headline similarities as well. What we see, irrespective of culture, is that when presented with a task they must actually perform, most managers are extremely task focused, goal focused and competitive, and concentrate on achieving results. In all cultures, the euphoria experienced upon successful completion, and the deflation when a task hasn't gone well, is similar. Nevertheless, we notice significant yet subtle differences between cultures in the degree to which these responses are displayed and in the manner in which the task is approached (i.e. the *process*).

In groups with more Northern European participants, we often see a clarity of rules, more rational discussion and less display of emotion. The task focus is generally dominant throughout the process, action often starts almost immediately and the dialogue is focussed on that action. We may see the leadership shift around the group in response to identified expertise, so leadership may move to individuals displaying the skills needed at a particular time. In service of this task focus, conflict is sometimes avoided altogether or it is discussed with a degree of discomfort.

In contrast, in the case of groups from the Middle East, the task is completed, but there is much more conversation along the way. We notice circles of people having lengthy discussions about the nature of the task and expressing opinions on the options available before any action is contemplated.

Moving further east, working with groups from China presents a different picture altogether. Chinese culture tends to be more accepting of the rules of the game, unlike European groups, whose members will challenge the rules and ask detailed questions. Again, the group tends to be highly task focused, engaging in hearty dialogue where everyone talks at once. To the untrained European eye, where turn taking in conversation tends to be more the norm, this feels chaotic and confusing. However, amid this maelstrom of noise comes incredible efficiency and speed. Chinese groups are often really good at achieving success despite the process seeming unclear and muddled to an observer.

Reviewing the learning with Chinese groups can be much more challenging than with relatively open European groups. In Chinese culture, it is important to ensure that participants never experience 'loss of face' and this can make it difficult for groups to offer critical reviews of their own performance, or that of others. The difference here with European groups is stark. Westerners will often start a review by talking about what went *wrong* regarding the learning from the review to serve a 'fault fixing' purpose. In Chinese groups, the feedback often centres on the leader during the activity and how their expert leadership led to the group's success. There is a tendency towards 'report talk' where the group will repeat at length what actually happened in quite a factual way, and it can be challenging and difficult to encourage the group to take the review to a deeper level around processes, personal feelings and relationships. Reviews with Chinese groups are, however, rich in content, and each person does value having an opportunity to speak. The group will listen with respect as each person shares in turn. It is wise, therefore, to factor in plenty of time for reviews with homogenous Chinese groups.

When reflecting on the validity of these anecdotal observations, it is apparent that they fit well into the Cultural Types model proposed by Lewis (2012), and also to Hofstede, Hofstede and Minkov's (2010) model of cultural dimensions.

The Lewis model suggests that there are three basic approaches to problem solving:

- Linear active

- Multi active

- Reactive.

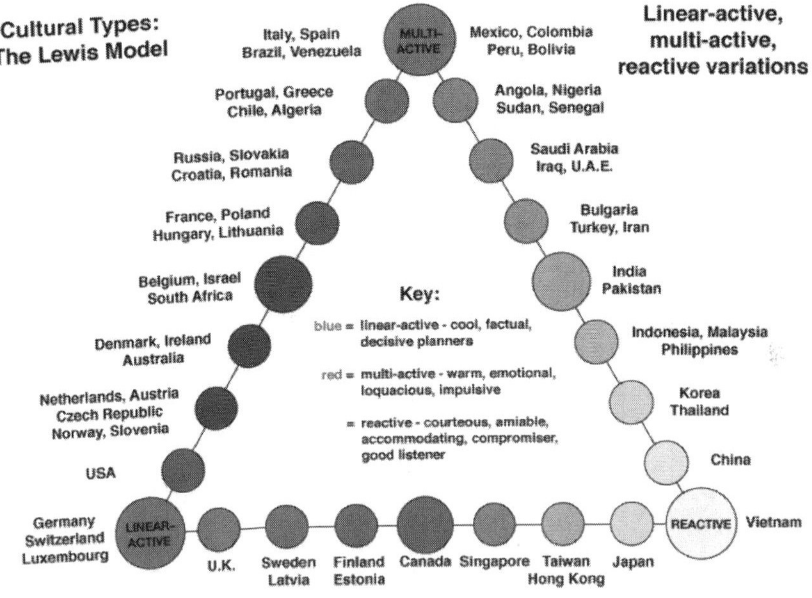

Figure 2 – The Lewis Model (Lewis, 2006)

The Lewis model suggests that US and European groups, particularly Northern European, tend towards a more linear-active orientation when working in teams. This means that these groups display a need for real clarity around the rules. This is not necessarily indicative of a rule-following mentality: the clarity is sometimes required in order that they can break the rules, or at least push back on the boundaries set!

Another indication of this tendency is the response to metaphor. Much outdoor learning relies on the use of metaphor. Pieces of guttering become 'cliff edges', areas of woodchip become 'ravines' and buckets containing tennis balls become 'toxic waste' containers. However, one will often hear European groups cut through the metaphor with a more literal interpretation of the rules. It is hard to know whether this is because European groups are more prone than, say, Chinese groups to reject the notion of metaphor, or whether cultural norms of politeness often associated with Chinese culture prevent them from voicing what they are thinking.

There are also differences in how groups react to ambiguity in the task brief. Where a European group may be more prone to show frustration during the planning phase, suggesting a preference for a more linear approach, in contrast, a recent group from Egypt became highly collaborative during the planning phase in order to make sense out of the ambiguity. Perhaps this is indicative of a more flexible way of accepting ambiguity. When presented with an ambiguous brief, the Egyptian group split into smaller groups and sat in a circle while one person briefed the group on their understanding of the task.

Table 1 maps the behaviours indicated from the Lewis model against observations from faculty experienced in experiential learning facilitation.

Table 1

Linear Active	Practitioner Observations of Western Groups
Talks half the time	Contained emotion, not comfortable talking about it
Does one thing at a time	
Plans ahead step by step	Dislikes metaphor
Polite but direct	Task oriented
Partly conceals feelings	Individualistic
Confronts with logic	Strong opinions, may not listen
Dislikes losing face	May notice disengagement of team members
Rarely interrupts	
Job oriented	Leadership rotates around the group
Uses mainly facts	May be more prone to avoiding conflict
Truth before diplomacy	More rule bound, wanting clarity of the rules and boundaries
Sometimes impatient	
Limited body language	Will tend to be very bound by time and will show discomfort, tension or frustration when a deadline looms
Respects officialdom	
Separates the social and professional	

Multi-Active	Practitioner Observations of Middle Eastern Groups
Talks most of the time	Relational, will talk through ambiguity together
Does several things at once	Task oriented but will rely on strong relationships during the process
Plans grand outline only	Communication seems chaotic and noisy but lots of interaction and engagement by all
Emotional, displays feelings	Hard to pull them together to have a review, need to have a clear structure in place
Confronts emotionally	Take a pride in their group membership
Has good excuses	Seem to deal with conflict in the moment
Often interrupts	Get a general flavour of the task to be done and go about it in a seemingly haphazard manner
People oriented	Time may not be so high on the agenda
Feelings before facts	
Flexible truth	
Impatient	
Unlimited body language	
Seeks out key person	
Interweaves the social and professional	

Reactive	Practitioner Observations of Far Eastern Groups
Listens most of the time	Strong respect for hierarchy
Reacts to partner's action	May not see lots of challenge
Looks at general principles	Usually a clear leader is appointed and they are respected
Polite, indirect	Highly reluctant to talk about negative emotions
Conceals feelings	Will tend to play back a verbal account of what happened in the review but unlikely to dig below the surface
Never confronts	High value on praise
Must not lose face	Sound like they are in conflict to the Western ear but it is often just an open discussion at volume
Doesn't interrupt	Mixed response to time management – may depend on the leader and how they view time; the others will defer to the preference of the leader
Very people oriented	
Statements are promises	
Diplomacy over truth	
Patient	
Subtle body language	
Uses connections	
Connects the social and professional	

Similarities seen across all groups	All competitive – wanting to be the best/fastest
	All task focused
	Rarely resist the experience, but all may resist the debrief
	The women are stronger across all cultures than a decade ago
	Don't assume gender is an issue – women of all cultures will interact, though it may require some discussion about how to do that to fit cultural needs
	The use of psychometrics is useful as it can help distinguish differences and similarities within the cultures – an 'SDI Red' from UK may look different to an 'SDI Red' from China, but the internal processes they go through may be similar
	Really need to slow the process down when debriefing

Whilst the Lewis model offers an interesting descriptive analysis, Hofstede's theory of cultural values looks at how these values relate to behaviour and is a useful framework within which to consider experiential learning. Hofstede's research based model proposes a number of dimensions as detailed below. Hofstede warns against the dangers of cultural stereotyping. However, if viewing groups using experiential learning through this lens we can see some trends appearing that can help us structure our learning interventions more carefully.

Hofstede's scales are:

Power distance – The extent to which people accept power and hierarchy.

Collectivism/individualism – the extent to which a culture views its circle of responsibility. Individual societies are loosely connected and collective societies are more tightly connected to one another.

Masculinity/femininity – Highly masculine cultures will be seen as highly competitive, valuing achievement and success. Feminine cultures value work–life balance, will involve others and value consensus and involvement.

Uncertainty avoidance – Weak uncertainty avoidance means that there is not a high dependence on structure and predictability, the culture thrives on change and curiosity is encouraged. Here rules are not so highly regarded, a more flexible approach is valued. Strong scores show the opposite: rules are needed and security is a high priority.

Long-term Orientation - Low scores suggest a norming culture which focus on the 'here and now' of quick wins, tending not to focus so heavily on long term strategy. High scores will tolerate thrift and perseverance in order to get results in the long term. There is a strong culture of 'don't give up'.

Practitioner anecdotal observations have been mapped against Hofstede's work.

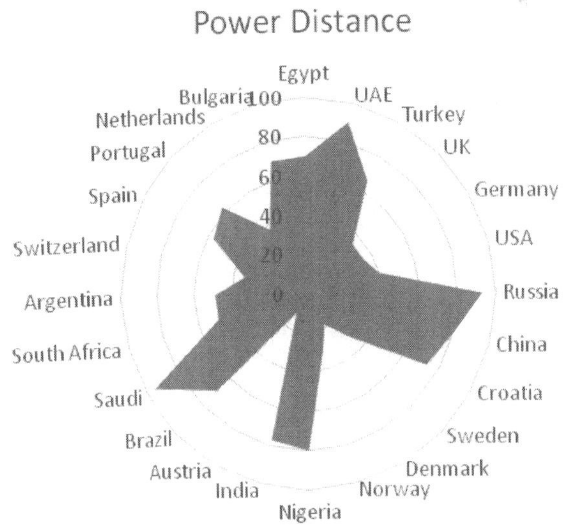

Figure 3 – Power Distance

Hofstede's research results here suggest that Saudi, Chinese, Russian, UAE, Croatian and Indian groups will be more mindful of the power relationship. This is noticeable in the classroom, where there is often a greater need for the facilitator to state their credentials in order to establish their position in the hierarchy. For credibility to be established these groups do tend to require greater emphasis on status. We observed that there does tend to be a clear leader assigned and that there was a greater amount of 'tell' style leadership demonstrated in experiential tasks. Lower scoring groups, notably from Scandinavia, Northern Europe and the USA, show less emphasis placed on power, and a more informal relationship between facilitator and learner. In these groups we do see a tendency for greater levels of collaboration in groups, less emphasis on appointing leaders and for group members to share responsibility throughout a task.

Figure 4 – Individual - Collective

Again, the trend sees European, Scandinavian, US and South African groups showing a greater level of individual preference over collectivism. They tend to operate from the position of 'self'. Individuals are more willing to propose and act upon their own ideas during the task, possibly not checking with the team first. They are also more likely to share their point of view in the debrief and there is more willingness to be controversial. Collective cultures demonstrate greater interdependence in the task and are less prone to speak up and disrupt group harmony so there is less to 'work with' in the debrief as people

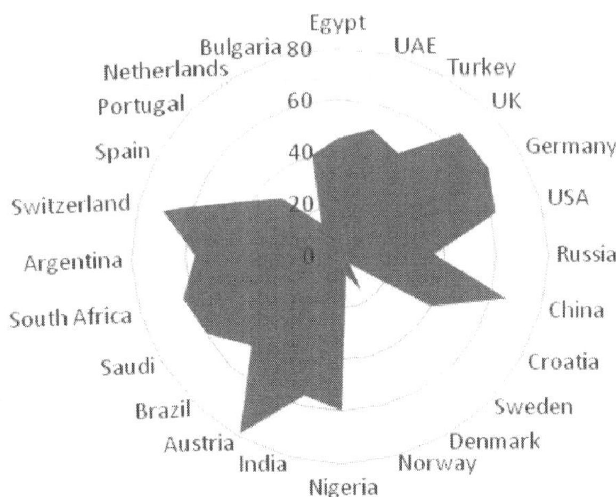

Figure 5 – Masculine - Feminine

Lower scores here include those of Portugal, the Netherlands, Scandinavia and Russia. This suggests that opportunities for dialogue and discussion will be important elements of any learning intervention. Frequent break-out groups where collaboration can take place will be well received. The higher-scoring nations on the masculine–feminine scale will be less easy to engage in dialogue unless it is clear to them how it will impact on the 'bottom line'. Groups scoring high in this area do correlate with greater evidence of a competitive element to their activities. This in our experience should be used with caution as the enthusiasm to win may overshadow the quality of learning.

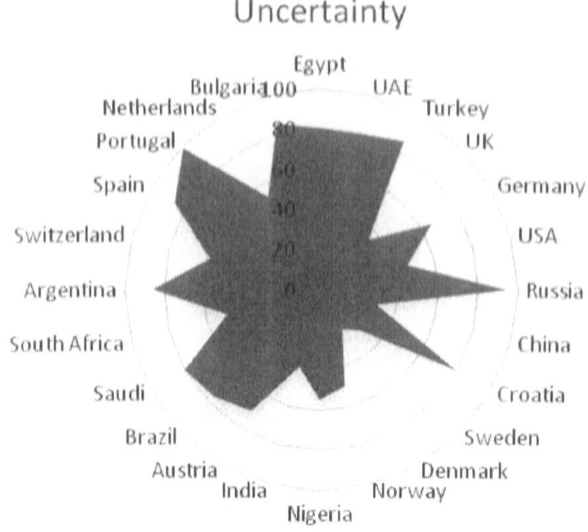

Figure 6 – Uncertainty Avoidance

Not to be confused with risk aversion, this is about how willing groups are to bend the rules gain greater clarity NL, UK and Scandinavia all score low in this area. There is greater likelihood of these groups questioning the rules of the task, looking for alternative ways to interpret the rules and outright bending of the rules. On the other hand countries such as Spain and Portugal, the Middle East, Brazil and Russia all demonstrate high scores. Groups scoring higher will interpret the rules literally and not stray from the instructions given. If the facilitator offers these groups the opportunity to break the rules, there is either much surprise, or even resistance. Our experience with these groups has shown that there is more value placed on experiential learning if it is supported with more theoretical underpinning

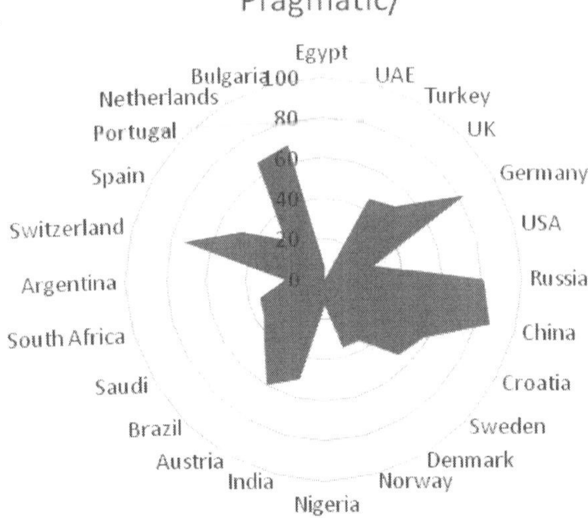

Figure 7 – Long-term Orientation

Low scoring groups which have been observed include UAE, USA and South Africa where it is true to say there is value placed on getting quick wins. Groups observed from Germany, NL, UK and Austria groups observed have demonstrated a tenacity and unwillingness to give up. However, the data is less conclusive on this scale based on observed behaviour.

The lesson to be learned by aligning practitioner experience with theoretical models is simple. No matter which framework we use, it is easy to demonstrate differences in behaviour and learning style that seem to have cultural correlations and therefore awareness of these must be factored in to effective facilitation of experiential learning. Some obvious areas to address are how to ensure that all group members 'have a voice' and can be heard. Will a Chinese person be comfortable speaking up in a group of mixed nationality? Often (although of course not always) we notice that people from the Far East are quieter in their approach and tend to contribute less in the debrief. How can cultural awareness help to get round this dilemma?

Top tips for successful facilitation of experiential learning

- **Plan ahead.** If you know the cultural mix of the group in advance it may help to structure the programme design to suit all.

- **Include variety in the exercise mix.** Allow for rationality, relationality and reflection. Not everybody will learn the same things from the same exercises, so a good mix to allow for different preferences is vital.

- **Be curious.** Everything that happens is data. If a facilitator fully engages with curiosity they can ask challenging questions that really make the group stop and think about what is going on.

- **Respect the participants' learning space.** Allow them to experience it from their own perspective, whilst acknowledging that of others.

- **Constantly challenge your own, and the participants', assumptions.** Real learning brings about real change, even if it means there may be a little discomfort along the way.

Conclusion

Experiential learning requires a particular responsibility on the part of facilitators and educational professionals. It is not simply about passing on information or 'teaching' new knowledge. Engaging with the subjectivity of experience and the holistic nature of 'being' that participants bring to experiential learning sessions means that these must be explicitly respected. Practitioners need to be questioning constantly and must be fully present for their learners, engaging with them at a personal level. Part of this might include developing greater cultural awareness, remaining aware of the cultural differences in the group and – because individuals differ in their lived experiences – remembering to avoid stereotyping. Cultural awareness is an important factor in working with *any* group – for example, a UK group with members from different parts of the country will still reveal cultural differences. The important thing is to be mutually engaged in the learning space, being present and genuinely curious to hear the perspectives of all and slowing down the pace to allow everyone to have a voice. The value of the experience can be huge and therefore time allowed for experiential learning on a curriculum is time well spent – as long as even more time for sense making and reflection is also allowed. The opportunity for people to connect with the whole of themselves, including their personal and cultural history, as they make sense of the here and now, in order that they may shape their yet-to-be-experienced future is a powerful learning vehicle.

References

Adair, J. (1973) *Action-Centred Leadership* (London: McGraw Hill).

Badger, B., Sadler-Smith, E., Mitchie, E. (1997) Outdoor Management Development: Use and Evaluation. *Journal of European and Industrial Training*, 21(9), pp.318–25.

Beard, C. (2008) Experiential Learning: The Development of a Pedagogic Framework for Effective Practice. Doctoral Thesis, PhD by publication, Sheffield Hallam University.

Beard, C., & Wilson, J.P. (2002) *The Power of Experiential Learning: A Handbook for Trainers and Educators* (London: Kogan Page).

Boniface, M.R. (2000) Towards an Understanding of Flow and other Positive Experience Phenomena within Outdoor Adventurous Activities. *Journal of Adult Education and Outdoor Learning*, 1(1), pp.55–68.

Boud, D., Cohen, R., & Walker, D. (1993) *Using Experience for Learning* (Bury St. Edmonds: St. Edmondsbury Press Ltd.).

Burnett, D., & James, K. (1994) Using the Outdoors to Facilitate Personal Change in Managers. *Journal of Management Development*, Vol. 13, No. 9 (MCB University Press).

Dainty, P., & Lucas, D. (1992) Clarifying the Confusion: A Practical Framework for Evaluating Outdoor Development Programmes for Managers. *Management Education and Development*, Vol. 23, Part 2, pp.106–22.

Desmond, B., & Jowitt, A. (2011) Stepping into the unknown: dialogical experiential learning. *Journal of Management Development*, Vol. 31, No. 3, pp.221–30 (Emerald Group Publishing Limited).

Hamilton, T.A., & Cooper, C. (2001) The Impact of Outdoor Management Development (OMD) Programmes. *Leadership and Organization Development Journal*, 22/7, pp.330–40.

Heron, J. (1992) *Feeling and Personhood: Psychology in Another Key* (London: Sage).

Hofstede, G., Hofstede, G.J., & Minkov, M. (2010) *Cultures and Organizations: Software of the Mind*. Revised and expanded 3rd edition (New York: McGraw-Hill USA).

Ibbetson, A., & Newell, S. (1996) Winner Takes All: An Evaluation of Adventure Based Learning. *Management Learning*, 27: 163.

Illeris, K. (1999) *How We Learn: Learning and Non-Learning in School and Beyond*, 4th edition, 2007 (Abingdon: Routledge).

Illeris, K. (2007) What Do We Actually Mean by Experiential Learning? *Human Resources Development Review*, 6, 84.

Irvine, D., & Wilson, J.P. (1994) Outdoor Management Development: Reality or Illusion? *Journal of Management Development*, Vol. 13, No. 5, pp.25–37.

Knowles, M.S. (1968) Andragogy, Not Pedagogy. *Adult Leadership*, 16(10), pp.350–86.

Kolb, D.A. (1984) *Experiential Learning: Experience as the Source of Learning and Development* (New Jersey: Prentice-Hall).

Krouwel, B., & Goodwill, S. (1994) *Management Development Outdoors: A Practical Guide to Getting the Best Results* (London: Kogan Page).

Leberman, S.I., & Martin, A.J. (2004) Enhancing Transfer of Learning through Post Course Reflection. *Journal of Adventure Education and Outdoor Learning*, 4:2, pp.173–84.

LeCornu, A. (2005) Building on Jarvis: Towards a Holistic Model of the Processes of Experiential Learning. *Studies in the Education of Adults*, Vol. 37, No.2, Autumn 2005.

Lewis , R.D. (2006) *When Cultures Collide (3rd Ed.)*, Nicholas Brealey Publishing International. London. P42

McEvoy, G., & Buller, P.F. (1997) The Power of Outdoor Management Development. *Journal of Management Development*, Vol. 16, No. 3, pp.208–17.

Merriman, S.B., Caffarella, R.S., & Baumgartner, L.M. (2007) *Learning in Adulthood: A Comprehensive Guide* (San Fransisco, CA: John Wiley & Sons).

Meyer, J.P. (2003) Four Territories of Experience: A Developmental Action Inquiry Approach to Outdoor-Adventure Experiential Learning. *Academy of Management Learning & Education*, Vol. 2, Issue 3 (December), pp.352–63.

Michelson, E. (1996) Usual Suspects: Experience, Reflection and the (En)gendering of Knowledge. *International Journal of Lifelong Education*, Vol. 15, No. 6 (November–December), pp.438–54.

Michelson, E. (1998) Re-membering: The Return of the Body to Experiential Learning. *Studies in Continuing Education*, 20:2, pp.217–33.

Moon, J. (2004) *A Handbook of Reflective and Experiential Learning: Theory and Practice* (London: Routledge/Falmer).

Silberman, M. (2007) *The Handbook of Experiential Learning* (San Fransisco, CA: Pfeiffer).

Stevens, R. (2006) *Social Psychology: Understanding the Self* (London: Sage Publications).

Taniguchi, S.T., Freeman, P.A., & Legrand-Richards, A. (2005) Attributes of Meaningful Learning Experiences in an Outdoor Education Program. *Journal of Adult Education and Outdoor Learning*, Vol. 5(2), pp.131–44.

Tuckman, B. (1965) Developmental Sequence Small Groups. *Psychological Bulletin*, Vol. 63, pp.384–9.

Usher, R., & Edwards, R. (1994) *Post-modernism and Education* (London: Routledge).

Williams, S.D., Scott Graham, T., & Baker, B. (2003) Evaluating Outdoor Experiential Training for Leadership and Team Building. *Journal of Management Development*, 22(1), pp.45–59.

CHAPTER 6

Working in the Collective 'Third Space': Creating a Classroom Experience that Contributes to Learning Transfer

Barbara Banda

Each year, organisations spend millions of pounds in developing management capability through off-the-job management development programmes (OMDPs) (Chartered Management Institute, 2005). Researchers have focussed much attention on organisational ROI – trying to understand how learning is transferred from purposefully created programmes to participants' workplaces. However, there has been little or no focus on trying to understand exactly what happens within the actual delivery or classroom space of the programme to contribute to this transfer.

This chapter uses the concept of the collective 'third space' (Gutierrez, 2008) as a lens for examining the activities within the OMDP, as well as for understanding how these activities contribute to participants' learning whilst on the programme and also to the continuation and consolidation of that learning when back in the workplace. The chapter will also explore how this third space can be enriched to further enhance learning. The 'third space' is a term coined to represent a place where individuals let their real selves show, as opposed to the 'first space' of the domestic sphere, the family and the home, or the 'second space' which is the sphere of civic engagement including school, work and other forms of public participation.

We will begin with an overview of the origins of the collective third space and then report the results of a study carried out to explore how this third space can be created and used in business schools to contribute to participants' learning. Finally, we will identify what more can be done by business-school faculty, in the classroom environment, to maximise the benefits of OMDPs. This is an important issue as many organisations find that providing the time and resources to release their managers to attend business-school programmes is a challenge that they often feel unable to rise to. This chapter will suggest that the investment can be extremely worthwhile.

Gutierrez developed the concept of the collective third space in the context of her educational development work with migrant children in California. The theoretical underpinnings of her work sit within the Vygotskian-based socio-cultural, cultural–historical activity theory (e.g. Beach, 1999, 2003; Daniels, 2006; Edwards, 2005)

Gutierrez's construct originated in her classroom research of migrant Spanish-speaking children and adolescents in California. Like the class-room space of the management development programme, her classrooms were designed to enable her to introduce her pupils to new concepts and knowledge that could cross boundaries. At first, the relevant boundary was between her teaching of the new ideas she was introducing and the wider reality of the children's lives. Whist working with teenagers, she and her co-authors (Gutierrez et al., 1995; Gutierrez et al., 1999) showed how power is constructed between teachers and students in most class-rooms. They identified that classroom teachers used a 'monologic' script[*] which represents their own dominant cultural values. This one-track and one-directional form of communication clearly had the potential to stifle dialogue. Consequently, students who did not act in accordance with the teachers' perception of acceptable behaviour formed counter-scripts. An example of this would be a teacher talking to student about the landmark Brown vs Board of Education case which ended legal segregation in public schools. Students would start to talk about the music artist, James Brown.

---

[*]   Scripts are defined as the normative patterns of life within a classroom. It is an "orientation that members come to expect after repeated interactions in contexts constructed both locally and over time." (Gutierrez et al., 1995, p.449)

The teachers would then pick up on the students' discussion and develop a conversation so the two scripts would meet. Where the scripts of the teachers and the counter-scripts of students occasionally intersected, new meanings would be created which went beyond the apparent boundaries of both scripts. In this third space, the competing discussions and views would meet to produce new interactions and rich zones of collaboration and learning.

In her later research, Gutierrez worked with high-school students from migrant-farmworker backgrounds who were participating in a summer residential programme designed to encourage them to go on to higher education. This study demonstrated how a third space could be purposefully designed, defining it as a particular social environment wherein "students begin to reconceive who they are and what they might be able to achieve academically and beyond" (Gutierrez, 2008, p.48). Gutierrez argues that the collective third space is a "transformative one where the potential for an expanded form of learning and the development of new knowledge are heightened" (Gutierrez, 2008, p.152).

Gutierrez identified two key building blocks that are necessary to create the third space:

- First, it needs to be a space in which students can connect their pasts with the present and the future. To facilitate this, she allowed students to use hybrid (English and Spanish) language practices, so students could use both their mother tongue and their more recently adopted language. She also introduced the 'testimonio', a reflective autobiography that the students wrote to reflect on and imagine their lives. The environment created allowed the students' past, present and future to be connected and encouraged them to become conscious actors. The idea is that students "invoke the past in order to reframe it so that it becomes a resource for current and future action" (Gutierrez, 2008, p.154). The effect is to produce a curriculum grounded in the historical and current particulars of students' everyday lives, while at the same time oriented toward an imagined, but possible, future:

> A curriculum that fuses social, critical, and sociocultural theory with the local, the historical, the present, and the future of migrant communities. In this rich ecology, the learning of new concepts and skills, as well as the development of a collective identity, is facilitated through a range of language, reading,

writing, and performative practices that embody or enact key concepts, emotions, and theories."

(Gutierrez, 2008, p.153)

- The second building block is termed a 'sociocritical literacy' (Gutierrez, 2002). Simply put, this is the articulation of the students' cumulative experience – their history. Students are encouraged to notice the tensions between texts, institutions, their society and the cultural practices they experience. So for Gutierrez, creating a collective third space means paying attention to the multiple voices and histories in the classroom, and in particular attending to the contradictions and tensions existing within the classroom and using them as the basis for change and learning.

Using these ideas, a study was carried out to understand how the activities of faculty and participants could contribute to the creation of a collective third space in management education. The research aimed at understanding whether attention to a third space would have an impact on participants' learning, either during the programme, post-programme or both. The study treated each participating manager as a single case and followed their progress as he or she made the transition from the management development programme and the workplace. Managers attending a mix of five middle and senior open-enrolment off-the-job management development programmes (OMDPs) were interviewed before, during (at the close of the programme) and approximately six weeks after their attendance on the programme. Each of the three interview phases of the study expanded on the previous one. As well as the interviews, participants were asked to write a reflective diary during the programme and faculty observations of participants were carried out in the classroom environment throughout the entire period of the OMDP, and in the workplace at three- and six-month intervals after the programme. Further semi-structured interviews were conducted with participants at the end of these visits.

The results of the study showed that the methods used by the faculty to interact with the participants on the management development programme did indeed allow the creation of the collective third space for thinking and questioning. This had had aspects in common with the space created by Gutierrez in her work with the teenagers from the farming community (Gutierrez, 2008; Gutierrez et al., 1995; Gutierrez et al., 1999). This environment did appear to contribute to participants' ability to gain new understandings and insights. However, there were some important differences between the space created in Gutierrez's classrooms and that created on the management development programme. In addition, there appeared to be limitations as to the learning that was achieved by the participants and to the possibilities for learning transfer.

Key Elements in the Creation of a Third Space within the Classroom of the OMDP

Exploration and discussion of participants' personal and work histories was actively encouraged, bringing the past into the present.

Specific tools were used to allow disclosure of participant histories e.g. psycho-metrics, role-play.

New constructs were provided which allowed participants to understand their past actions and develop different actions in future.

The engagement of competing discourses was encouraged and emergent new meanings were facilitated.

Faculty adopted a 'facilitative' rather than an 'expert' position.

The space of the development programme allowed for the discussion of each participant's past, present and future. The personal histories that participants brought to the classroom were critical in mediating this process. There was a recognition that participants' histories-in-person (Holland and Lave, 2001) meant that they had established ways of approaching problems and viewing situations. Indeed, a key method for linking the past to the present and the future was by inviting participants to consider and bring experiences from their workplaces into the OMDP. For example, in a discussion on working with difficult people, participants were invited to talk about difficult people they had worked with in the past and how they dealt with any problems in those relationships. Thus, faculty encouraged participants to use their knowledge and experience as a springboard for creating innovative solutions to prob-lems. Furthermore, there were also points during the programmes when the participants were challenged to consider what type of person they wished to become and, in so doing, were encouraged to rethink who they are and what they could become.

Faculty also used tools which encouraged disclosure of participants' histo-ries. These included the use of psychometric questionnaires, role-plays, multimedia, group discussions and peer coaching groups. The processes encouraged a reframing of the past, as participants were able to reflect on why they had responded to a situation in a particular way. For example, through using personality questionnaires with feedback, participants could understand the self they were communicating on the OMDP and reflect on how this might relate to the self they communicated in the workplace.

They were encouraged to question how they might wish to change these perceptions.

The programmes offered tools to participants, including new visual concepts to allow them to develop different terminology for describing both familiar things and for understanding 'new-to-them' constructs. This new language was intended to act as a means of enabling participants to see how past actions can be understood and future activities developed. For example, the Thomas–Kilmann Conflict Mode Instrument (Kilmann and Thomas, 1977) was used. This is a self-assessment questionnaire describing responses to conflict and it allowed participants to identify the style they may have used in the past (for example, avoidance) and see why, if similar incidents were to arise in future, an alternative approach (such as collaboration) might be appropriate.

During the course of the programmes, the engagement of competing discourses was encouraged. Individual programme sessions, lasting between two and four hours, were interactive and participants were encouraged to put forward their personal views on the issues being discussed. As participants came from a variety of organisations, they frequently had different perspectives. Their ideas were challenged, both by other participants and by faculty. The competing discourses did, on occasion, create new meanings and they allowed participants to recognise that there may be multiple standpoints on a given issue. For example, on one occasion, the participants and faculty were engaged in a discussion about the relevance of psychometric instruments. Some participants argued that such instruments simply put people in boxes and that they found this unhelpful. Others said they found such categorisation useful as they could use the categories to understand others and then adapt their behaviour towards them. After a heated discussion, facilitated by the business-school faculty, the group agreed that such categorisation was neither right nor wrong, but offered a different set of lenses through which to look at others. For the group, this concept of lenses represented new meaning.

Finally, participants and faculty actively engaged in interactions that facilitated activities in the space created by the OMDP. Multiple voices were ever-present as participants shared their viewpoints and issues, and offered challenges to faculty. Different perspectives were respected and faculty did not adopt an 'expert' position, making it clear that they did not possess all the answers to the situations the participants described and retold. This process took place in small coaching groups, where participants shared personal stories. Different perspectives were offered by other group members and participants were encouraged to consider alternative views on their issues. Through this process, fresh ways forward emerged that individuals had not considered before.

There were, however, important differences between the nature of the managers' experiences and those of the youngsters reported earlier in this chapter. Since the students in Gutierrez's (2008) research had a shared history of being poor migrants, the curriculum could be carefully designed around the needs of that community. However, the managers in this study came from multiple contexts, making the grounding of the curriculum in their past, present and future lives more problematic. Like the students, the managers were encouraged to recognise the tensions between the ideas to which they were introduced and the activities and practices they were used to. The students left their particular third space feeling empowered and looking forward to achieving their dream of attending university. They could be said to have made an aspirational transition. However, the managers returned to their (probably) unchanged workplaces, where they had to deal with the transition of repositioning themselves within established working practices.

Like the students who left Gutierrez's classrooms, the intention was that managers would have learnt new ways to navigate the outside world. However, the participants returned to the familiar settings and entrenched practices of their workplaces as individual actors needing to negotiate how to use these tools to accomplish the form of selfhood that they had been encouraged to envisage while on the OMDP.

The study also attempted to identify the participants' key learning and how their experience of the collective third space had contributed to it. The learning in the collective fell broadly into three areas:

- There was a change participants' self-awareness. Group members gained a deeper understanding of their sense of self. Participants reported that this allowed them to return to work with renewed confidence.

- They gained an appreciation of new concepts which allowed them to reinterpret and reframe what was happening in the workplace.

- Participants often realised that they had to let go of things which they had previously perceived to be important if they were to progress in their organisations.

It was notable that both during and after the OMDP, participants expressed their concerns about how they could use their new insights to overcome opposition they might encounter. A key finding was that it was felt that the OMDP did not always prepare them adequately for negotiating resistance. Participants reported feeling the need to be provided with strategies for dealing with this issue.

Much of the discussion and the exercises on the programmes studied focussed on promoting a deeper understanding of the individuals' professional identities. Participants were encouraged and challenged by faculty to see themselves from the perspective of the other. The data from the study reveal that for both middle as well as for more senior managers these insights enhanced and validated their sense of professional self and that this validation caused them to change their behaviour on their return to work.

An example of this was Stefan, who had recently taken on responsibility for a team of female administrative staff. He described how he felt they were not responding favourably to his direct management style. During the programme, he struggled to decide what would be required to change the situation but, by the end of the programme, he came to understand their viewpoint:

> I can now understand why when I got the admin department there were a couple of girls who were really worried especially about some of the things I might do and I think the reason they were worried, looking back on what I have just done for the last week, is that I would just have stood there and told them what to do and how good it was going to be and just do it. Now I am going to have to do a complete 180 and go back on everything I said prior to joining the course and I think we will start with some coaching and some brain-storming sessions listening to their ideas.

> *Stefan, end-of-programme interview*

On return to the workplace, he used the ideas he had encountered on the programme. Specifically, he used a coaching technique he had learned and offered the team the opportunity to set their own personal objectives and have some say in what their roles and responsibilities should be. The effect was that he reported developing a totally different relationship with his female staff. They began to take the initiative for getting things done. This allowed Stefan time to focus on other "more managerial" tasks. He initially found this very difficult to adapt to because, in his organisation, the men told the women what to do and they did it. Now he was having to allow the women to think for themselves.

For Mary, the behaviour of others in the third space of the classroom changed her perception of the value of her contributions to a group. In her work environment, she reported fearing interactions with other managers because of her self-perceived inadequacies. In the third space of the classroom, she experienced others paying attention to her, which improved her sense of self greatly.

> You don't realise until you go on a course… that you have certain skills you didn't realise you had. People listen to you when you are sitting in a group situation and you can contribute to that situation.

> *Mary, end-of-programme interview*

Like Stefan, she reported that, once back at work, this realisation gave her the confidence to try out new behaviours with her line manager. Although she was experienced, her manager was still charged with final approval for most of her projects and continued to question the way she was working. She had felt unable to challenge or criticise him. However, after the programme she felt more able to take control. For example, when recruiting a new team member she made it clear that she would be in charge:

> When the trainee position came up, Dave was like "I'll draw up the advert". I said "No you won't, Dave". I said "I'm doing the recruitment, I've been asked to do the recruitment. I'm going to do it."

> *Mary, interview at the end of field visit 2*

The space of the OMDP also provided participants with new concepts, which did not focus specifically on self-awareness or on relationships with others. For example, James, a participant on a Strategic Decisions Programme, explained how, following the programme, he was able to put the tools to immediate use allowing him to engage with a client in a different way than was possible prior to the OMDP.

> I was working with a company a couple of weeks ago reviewing their branding strategy. They're working with an agency on marketing and reviewing their branding strategy. So I said… I'm starting to do some work on strategy, is there an opportunity that

> I could help you with around strategy? I could have a conversation around strategy with him. Ok, I couldn't maybe advise him on anything but certainly I could ask the right questions, I felt, and [it gave] me a very good insight into what they're doing and why they're doing it.
>
> *Joseph, post-six-weeks interview*

Finally, the study showed that most of the participants arrived at the OMDP with a clear view of what mattered to them as individuals and they were motivated to become more expert in these areas. However, the programme encouraged them to realise that that focus might not assist them in progressing within the organisation. For example, what mattered to Laura (a junior manager) was protecting her employees' jobs. She was therefore concerned about being placed in a position where she was required to discipline and dismiss people for what she regarded as "unfair" reasons:

> I'm not a ruthless manager and if I had to be I would have to move jobs because instinctively [I feel that treating people unfairly is] not right.
>
> *Laura, end-of-programme interview*

She wanted to ensure that she could continue to protect staff as she made the transition to a more senior role. Following the programme, she looked afresh at this preoccupation, adopting the role of senior management. She realised that she could not protect all jobs, and that she would have to let people go. However, during a major restructuring, she was able to articulate the management position regarding redundancies in difficult conversations with the people she managed. Her confidence came from her experience on the programme, which gave her the assurance to follow through with the requirements of her new role:

> I don't think that's been easy, but I've managed it.
>
> *Laura, interview at the end of field visit 2*

Participants sometimes failed to appreciate the importance of clarifying whether what mattered to them was also important in the context of achieving organisational goals or outcomes (Engeström, 2001). Thus, Laura did not understand that being a "fair and supportive" manager would be less emphasised in her new role.

Whilst offering evidence that participants' experience of the collective third space contributed to them being able to make positive changes once back at work, there were limitations within the development programme. These made it difficult for the participants to implement some of the changes that they wanted. One area of strength, which was also a limitation, was that much of the focus of the course was on participants' self-understanding and thus, whilst they often developed a deeper understanding of themselves, they were not always clear how to use this understanding to change their behaviour. So the link between present and future was not always firmly established and it was sometimes difficult for them to use their new understanding effectively as a source for future action. Furthermore, the focus on self-understanding led to insufficient attention being paid to how participants could focus less inwardly, but also on what was important externally in the context of their organisations.

A second limitation was that many of the participants were new to their roles and hoped that the programme would provide them with tools to negotiate these new positions. The expertise they possessed in their previous roles was not sufficient to enable them to transition successfully to their new positions. This meant that they frequently did not know what 'good' looked like in these new roles, although they were clear about their desire to do things differently from their predecessors. As the OMDP was happening away from the workplace, with the participant often the only person from their company on the programme, it was hard for them to find the answer to what 'good' looked like in their organisations.

A third limiting factor was that participants often reported being unclear about what should be important to them at work and exactly what their organisations expected from them on their return. They were often unsure which activities they should focus on changing, or indeed, whether they were permitted to change organisational practices. Joseph, for example, was uncertain how far his line manager wanted him to go with focussing his role on becoming more of a strategic than an operational consultant. So it seemed that participants had not always recognised the need to identify and prioritise the issues they needed to work on.

Indeed, participants' lack of clarity regarding what was important in their practices at their level of their organisations (Hedegaard, 2008) meant that it was difficult for them to align what was important to them with the organisational objectives. These findings suggest that there may be a need for participants explicitly to analyse what is important to the organisation both before and during the OMDP. As a consequence of this not occurring, participants failed to arrive at the OMDP with an understanding of the scope of their responsibilities and, consequently, were unable to use the time to work on areas that were important to the organisation. On return to work it was thus difficult for them to integrate what they had internalised into their workplace activities. Unlike Gutierrez's (2008) students, the courses were not comprised of homogenous groups, nor were they anticipating future practices of which they had no past experience. It was therefore critical that they understood the specific needs of their organisations and how these could be met. Indeed, participants' uncertainty regarding organisational expectations seemed to account for their inability to develop expertise in their ability to read and effectively navigate their organisations, despite exploring their sense of self and discussing real-life issues during the OMDP.

Thus, participants' ability to transform their workplaces was restricted because of the OMDP's intense focus on each of them as a person, rather than as a participant in their workplace activities and practices; and because of the failure to align their objectives and goals with those of their organisation.

Whilst recognising the limitations of the collective third space, it is still worth considering the aspects of faculty behaviour which contribute to its successful design.

- Key amongst these is the skill of the facilitator in creating a dialogue between him- or herself and the participants in a way which creates new knowledge. Working in a highly interactive and participative way, facilitators must connect concepts and theories to create something that is real for participants. During this process, the participants' experiences must be given equal validity with those of the facilitator. In this study, the participants' experiences were encouraged, discussed and worked with in the moment. In this way, the facilitator and the participants were able to engage in a conversation which, through linking theory to practice, became something that the participants felt they could connect to their daily lives. Within the classroom context, there was openness and honesty from the facilitators whereby they often shared their (not always positive) experiences of the workplace and life in general with participants. Their style was not one of a guru or expert talking to students but rather of a conversation of equals.

- When the faculty positioned the programme as part of a learning journey – not as a silver bullet which would solve all their problems – participants had realistic learning expectations. They were then able to consider a future in which a few realisable things needed to change.

- Additionally, within the programmes, where real reflective time was offered, this was impactful with participants who used the time to reflect on who they were and who they wanted to be.

- Finally, where the programme focussed on the participants within their practices, rather than on the participant alone, there were indications that participants could better connect what they were doing on the programme to their daily work.

So what more could faculty do to create an effective collective third space? The findings indicate that this requires a close connection between management education and the workplace.

A key weakness in the programmes that featured in this research appeared to be that the links between the participants' workplaces and what was happening on the programme were often not strong enough. This could be strengthened by faculty being clearer about the activities participants must undertake before and after the programme to allow these connections to be improved.

Pre-work should include participants exploring:

- What is important in their organisation

- What is important to their manager and their work colleagues

- How the manager currently contributes to those practices

- Their desired contribution to those practices

- Who or what might assist or constrain their ability to act differently following the programme.

Having gained these understandings ahead of the programme, the third-space time can focus on the manager in his/her practices.

To summarise, to be maximally effective and really contribute to management learning, the third space needs to allow sufficient time to explore participants' histories and real issues. It must use a blended approach to teaching and learning, in particular including a greater use of dialogue. Other interactive learning vehicles include action-learning sets, coaching and workplace interventions to follow up on the programme. The post-programme focus should then be on how individuals can negotiate their own contribution into practice.

The third space is expensive for organisations and their managers, in terms both of money and time – it is vital that it provides an adequate return on these investments.

References

Beach, K. (1999) Consequential transitions: A sociocultural expedition beyond transfer in education. *Review of Research in Education*, 42(1), pp.101–39.

Beach, K. (2003) Consequential transitions: A developmental view of knowledge propagation through social organisations. In T. Tuomi-Grèohn & Y. Engestrèom (eds), *Between School and Work: New Perspectives on Transfer and Boundary-Crossing* (Amsterdam, London: Pergamon), pp.39–61.

Daniels, H. (2006) *Vygotsky and Pedagogy* (London: Routledge/Falmer).

Edwards, A. (2005) Let's get beyond community and practice: the many meanings of learning by participating. *Curriculum Journal,* 16(1), pp.49–65.

Engeström, Y. (2001) Expansive learning at work: toward an activity theoretical reconceptualization. *Journal of Education and Work,* 14(1), pp.133–56.

Gutierrez, K.D. (2002) Rethinking critical literacy in hard times: Critical Literacy as a transformative social practice. Paper presented at the annual meeting of the National Council of Teachers of English, Atlanta, GA.

Gutierrez, K.D. (2008) Developing a Sociocritical Literacy in the Third Space. *Reading Research Quarterly,* 43(2), pp.148–64.

Gutierrez, K.D., Rymes, B., & Larson, J. (1995) Script, counterscript, and underlife in the classroom: James Brown versus Brown v. Board of Education. *Harvard Educational Review,* 65, pp.445–71.

Gutierrez, K.D., Tejeda, C., & Baquedano-Lopez, P. (1999) Rethinking Diversity: Hybridity and Hybrid Language Practices in the Third Space. *Mind, Culture and Activity,* 6(4), pp.286–303.

Hedegaard, M. (2008) A Cultural-historical theory of children's development. In M. Hedegaard & M. Fleer (eds), *Studying Children* (Maidenhead: Open University Press), pp.10–29.

Holland, D.C., & Lave, J. (eds) (2001) *History in Person: Enduring Struggles, Contentious Practice, Intimate Identities* (Santa Fe, NM: School of American Research Press).

Kilmann, R.H., & Thomas, K.W. (1977) Developing a forced-choice measure of conflict-handling behavior: The 'MODE' instrument. *Educational and Psychological Measurement,* 37, pp.309–25.

Mabey, C. (2005) *Management development works: The Evidence* (Chartered Management Institute).

Nelson, K. (1986) *Event Knowledge: Structure and Function in Development* (Hillsdale, NJ: Erlbaum).

CHAPTER 7

Blended Learning: Harnessing Technology to Build Leadership Capability

Ilze Zandvoort

Technology has significantly changed the way organisations operate and so it is not surprising that technological advances are impacting the way we develop managerial capabilities. Management learning has long included a blend of technologies, from the more formal original CD-ROM formats, replaced later by web-based e-learning and 'massive online open course' (MOOC) platforms, to the more organic formats, such as YouTube, TED talks, Wikis and the Internet in general. Despite many organisations realising the benefits and indeed the necessity of introducing the use of technology into their L&D activities, few have been able successfully to navigate the challenges associated with designing and delivering the combination of technology with other forms of learning methods that is the hallmark of blended learning. That they need to do so is driven by the fact that many organisations have people working in globally dispersed virtual teams, involving remote management, decision making and problem solving, so modern-day leadership skills must be developed in those places where the leadership occurs.

The aim of this chapter is to explore some of these challenges that companies face in introducing technology into their corporate L&D initiatives, and to offer some solutions based on research and experience. Broadly speaking, there are five areas that require careful thought for tailored solutions:

- Technological challenges

- Organisational challenges

- Design challenges

- Implementation challenges

- Engagement challenges.

Successful blended learning addresses all five categories and recognises explicitly that any approach to executive development must be aligned to strategic objectives as well as personal development plans, and should thus deliver value to both the organisation and the individual. We will address each of these areas in turn later in this chapter.

What exactly is blended learning?

Let's start by being clear about what we mean by 'blended learning'. The term was coined following the emergence of e-learning, the purely online form of course delivery made popular during the rise of the Internet. Despite the fact that the corporate e-learning market has experienced rapid growth since the 1990s (Bucciarelli et al., 2010), with many organisations using e-learning as their preferred method for management development (Mansour, 2009), the jury remained out on the effectiveness and efficiency of the purely online approach. This lead to experimentation with combining online learning solutions and traditional face-to-face teaching solutions – the basis of the blended learning approach.

Many attempts have been made to define the concept of blended learning ranging from: "A distributed, hybrid, flexible, or multimodal form of learning" (Duhaney, 2004) to "using the best delivery methodology (-ies) available for a specific objective, including online, classroom-based instruction, electronic performance support, paper-based, and formalised or informal on-the-job solutions" (Hofmann, 2014a).

Distilling ideas from the literature, we will define blended learning as any combination of different modes of delivery, models of teaching and styles of learning which are used to create a meaningful learning environment. This generally means that a combination of online and face-to-face learning activities is used, in a classroom, at work or in a self-study environment, in order to meet learning objectives.

Why use blended learning?

The most common reason that organisations use blended learning to develop their managers is simple pragmatism. Not only are the people scattered geographically, but the pace of their work has increased to such an extent that organisations and individuals struggle to free up sufficient time to attend intensive face-to-face development events. This, often in combination with a crunch on HR and L&D budgets, has forced many organisations to look for practical solutions offering a global reach that is flexible, adaptable to local and global needs, less time consuming and more affordable.

There are three key dimensions to consider when designing a successful blended learning intervention. First of all, *where* the learning takes place. Blended learning allows for learning in a variety of settings, in and out of the classroom. Ideally, actual knowledge transfer either to or from the learner should take place outside the classroom. Knowledge transfer to the learner includes new information, frameworks, models and perspectives. Examples of knowledge transfer from the learner could include sharing information with colleagues, or exploring new behaviours and skills. Both these forms of learning transfer can take place in either in the virtual space or the workplace. Classroom-based learning events preferably are used to create an experiential learning environment which allows managers to practise new behaviours and to make sense of their contextual challenges in a safe and supported environment.

The second dimension is timing. Blended learning can be either synchronous or asynchronous. Virtual synchronous interactions are live-time interactions involving participants, preferably in an interactive manner. Asynchronous interactions usually take the form of online discussion, or reviewing a recorded synchronous session. Both formats can encourage managers to discuss with peers how to make the best use of frameworks and models, which builds shared understanding, trust and collaboration. They also gain added benefit from being encouraged and motivated by those sharing tips for successful adaptation of theoretical concepts, whether in live-time or with a delay. Asynchronous learning means that individuals can learn at their own pace, at times convenient to them, allowing for self-pacing, minimising the stress of either fast or slow learners otherwise frustrated with the pace of delivery associated with traditional classroom-based management development programmes.

The third important dimension of blended learning is the *range* of learning activities that can be offered, which includes simple information transfer, group discussions, demonstrations, simulations, 'role play' and 'real play', meaning that a design can cater for a range of different learning styles and for different learning content.

So, as organisations increasingly search for learning that 'sticks', they search for solutions that are continuous, collaborative and connected beyond the classroom. Blended learning offers great opportunities to meet these needs. However, delivering what organisations need in terms of speed, scale, reach, cost, learning transfer, application, relevance and rigour is a big ask for any learning intervention. Given the flexibility of the concept, it is tempting to think that 'a little bit of this' and 'a little bit of that', applied in good faith, will do the trick. This strategy is unlikely to deliver learning. An effective strategy can only be achieved when the specific needs of the organisation and the managers within it are the focus for the design of the blended approach. This involves thoughtful exploration of the culture and the context of the audience, understanding their challenges, opportunities and developmental needs, in order effectively to combine learning resources to achieve successful blended learning solutions. Therefore, a blended learning development programme aimed at improving organisational and individual performance cannot be treated as a one-size-fit-all approach, nor as a one-off event, nor even as a smorgasbord of learning offerings. Instead, it needs to be seen as a tailored process of carefully combining relevant learning activities, in the most appropriate sequence and relevance for the audience. Learning has to 'land' in an organisation if it is to make a difference.

The first step is to understand the purpose of the learning journey. Before embarking on the practical task-orientated process of creating a blended learning solution, it's important to take a step back and get a really clear idea of the purpose of the blended learning: to understand the business goals and be clear about related content that will need to underpin strategic and personal objectives. The target audience must be understood. Do they need to develop knowledge, skills, attitudes, new behaviours or a combination of all of the above? How receptive are they to change, to learning new things, to using technology, to sitting in a classroom, to trying out new things? Do they need to learn and work independently or collaboratively, locally or dispersed? When that context is fully understood, design work can begin.

So, how can we ensure the success of a blended learning approach?

In order to answer this, we need to ask a couple of supplementary questions. First of all, what do learners look for in order to value their learning? This will be a key determinant of perceived success. And secondly, what might get in the way of successful learning? Let's consider these questions in turn.

What do learners look for in order to value their learning?

Research looking at student benchmarks in online learning specifically suggests that learner satisfaction comprises five key factors (Alavi & Gallupe, 2003; Endres et al., 2009):

- Satisfaction with faculty practices and delivery, including responsiveness and contact

- Course materials, including support materials to help with learning concepts

- Learning practices, including learning from others

- Student-to-student interaction, and

- Online tools, effective technical support and efficient administration processes.

In addition, the perceived relevance to the learners' workplace is paramount (Bocchi et al., 2004):

- Learning concepts that can be applied on the job

- Learning that is relevant to current or future position/industry

- Working with facilitators and/or faculty members experienced in working in companies or as consultants.

In addition, most managers need to see how each programme element contributes to their specific learning and development objectives. They require their learning to be accessible, yet challenging, relevant yet rigorous – and all-importantly, it must be applicable.

What might get in the way of successful learning?

Let's now return to those key challenges identified at the start of this chapter. We'll consider each, then offer some recommendations for best practice in design and delivery.

The five categories are:

- Technological challenges

- Organisational challenges

- Design challenges

- Implementation challenges

- Engagement challenges.

1. Technological challenges

Technology is what has made blended learning possible, so it's great to use it to deliver engaging new content and to overcome physical presentation problems. However, we are all familiar with the frustrations associated with technology that does not quite deliver what we want, so there are some useful rules that should be followed. It goes without saying that it's always a good idea to involve the technology experts early on in your design and scoping conversations.

This section highlights four pitfalls to avoid and reviews best practices (Hofmann, 2014b; Kaur, 2013) to overcome technology challenges in blended environments.

- **Don't get seduced by technology or the latest technology fads**

Just because your organisation has access to specific technologies, such as video conferencing, WebEx, Lynch, Yammer or even an LMS and e-Learning platform, does not mean you need to include it all in your blended learning design. Ensure that if you include the latest technology such as gamification, simulations, mobile apps or avatars and animations in your blended learning design it is actually meeting the learning needs, and that your technology experts can support you.

- **Do check out the technology landscape of your audience group**

One of the key reasons blended learning has become popular is because it allows for greater global reach and scale. However, the dispersal of the geographical locations of your audience group brings with it specific difficulties to overcome. For example, not all sites offer participants the same technological landscape. Some countries do not offer a bandwidth that support live video streaming; some offices do not have computer cameras to enable video calls; others may only offer open-plan office space with no opportunity for a quiet room in which to join a virtual meeting; and security settings and firewalls in some of your locations may not allow managers to access your online content or discussion forums. Understand where your participants will be when they need to access the virtual elements of your programme: will they be working from an open-plan office, a hot desk, a cubicle, a hospital, a factory, their home – or might they be on the road?

Ensure that you understand not only your audience's technological landscape, but also their level of technical proficiency. Have they got previous experience of using the technologies you are considering? To what extent have they adopted the use of technology? Do they predominantly work on mobile devices?

Before you commit to a specific blend of technologies, conduct a 'technological landscape audit' and create a profile of target participants. This should include technology available, specific geographical or site challenges to be dealt with, access to technical support, learning environment and languages spoken – and don't forget the technical capability of your potential participants.

> **Food for thought**
>
> How many of your managers have received training in scheduling and hosting effective virtual meetings across multiple time zones? How many of your line managers have received training on how to have difficult but productive conversations on the telephone, or how to conduct effective developmental or performance management reviews remotely?
>
> Blended learning has the potential to have a dramatic positive impact on day-to-day management.

- **Don't consider technology in isolation from content and desired learning outcomes**

The selection of the appropriate technology is just one piece of an integrated puzzle. There are some basic building blocks that need to be in place in order to help you select the most appropriate technology blend. First, as we said earlier, be clear on the purpose of the blended learning programme and then be sure to know what the target audience needs.

Here's the tricky bit. You need to review the content of your programme. Look at the learning objectives of each chunk of content and select the most appropriate technology for effective transmission of learning. If that's a straightforward information transfer, perhaps a PowerPoint pack is appropriate. If it's a skill-based element, maybe you need a simulation. Whatever is needed, you must ensure that there is excellent technical support for each technology you select. Of course, you also need to ensure that all participants receive timely and relevant technology support to help them to access and utilise the technologies effectively. They hate not knowing! Put in place a mechanism to gather feedback on how participants are experiencing the technology and ensure that reported problems are addressed. Finally, make sure that the facilitators are proficient with the technology and able to deal with the most common problems experienced by users – this is often an overlooked challenge!

- **Don't forget to budget and plan for technical support**

This is another element of blended learning that can sour the experience of participants and derail the overall effectiveness of the learning if it is not addressed properly. Making sure that all participants can access all the relevant elements prior to the start of the programme, in particular before any synchronous component, is key. This almost always requires a dedicated technical resource to offer individual support prior to and during a programme. Because blended learning is flexible and allows participants to access asynchronous learning activities 24/7 in any time zone, it is imperative to consider how ongoing technical support will be provided, and to budget for this upfront. As discussed in a later section, should you wish to deliver blended learning solutions totally in house, you may also need to invest both time and money to ensure your internal facilitators are technically skilled and supported.

2. Organisational challenges

In general, most organisations tend to 'get' blended learning. Many organisations are even enthusiastic in embracing it in a variety of L&D initiatives. However, very few organisations fully comprehend the complexity of the processes that need to be considered in order to make sure it really delivers value. A common pitfall is to consider specific learning elements in isolation (Hofmann, 2011) and thus not give sufficient thought to a corporate blended learning strategy, guidelines and governance.

This section builds on research and experience to highlight specific organisational challenges that can be overcome.

- **Position blended learning as having <u>at least</u> equal value with more traditional classroom-based activities**

For many organisations and managers, virtual and blended learning solutions are a cost-saving necessity and may be perceived as providing a second-rate learning experience. We know that the introduction of technology into corporate L&D initiatives can save money but we also know from research that online learning activities, whether self-directed or facilitated, synchronous or asynchronous, can be a very positive learning experience for learners (Čonková, 2013). In blended learning, peers play a particularly important role in shaping satisfaction with the online activities as cohorts tend to discuss and compare the ease of use, accessibility and general usefulness of the technology during the face-to-face activities (Arbaugh, 2014).

Therefore, it is essential in blended learning to ensure a smooth launch and a consistently efficient roll-out experience within the organisation. A well-planned launch event is a key part of the blended learning experience where participants (and their managers) receive a comprehensive introduction to the entire structure of the learning programme, including clarifying expectations about how to install and use technology, and participation and attendance/completion requirements (Hofmann, 2014a).

- **Prepare the groundwork for embedding the learning back into the organisation**

It is essential for the champions of blended learning (i.e. senior leaders, HR, L&D, facilitators and technology support members) all to adopt and display a positive attitude towards the technology selected in order to reinforce the mind-set that blended learning is not a second-rate solution compared to traditional classroom-based executive education. As blended learning often involves periods of application and reflection interspersed with delivery of theoretical input, it is imperative that the organisation is prepared for participants to experiment with new behaviours and new ideas in the workplace. This means that line managers need to be aware of their employees' learning experiences and to be able to support participants' experimentation with new behaviours and attitudes, in order to embed the learning. This is no different from any other forms of development, but because of the possible 'cheap option' perception, it needs to be addressed more keenly.

- **Select and prepare the right facilitators for blended learning**

Research has suggested that there are three main factors that contribute to a positive attitude towards the adoption of technology in blended learning. Not surprisingly, the most influential is the perceived usefulness of the technology (Padilla-Melendez et al., 2008), followed closely by peer encouragement and the positive attitudes of online facilitators or instructors (Martins & Kellermanns, 2004). This is why we're suggesting that in the early stages of introducing blended learning into organisations, facilitators should be selected for their commitment and enthusiasm towards online activities, almost above their subject expertise (Hofmann, 2014a).

Because blended learning constitutes a variety of elements and experiences, it is best delivered with a team of well-prepared facilitators who themselves have been immersed in blended learning and who understand the journey that participants will experience. They must treat each individual element of the blended learning as equally valuable and relevant to the learning outcomes.

- **Manage and monitor the participants' blended learning journey**

In blended learning, there will always be some elements of self-managed learning and, indeed, this is part of the allure of the approach. However, should the self-managed learning activities be positioned or seen as optional, chances are high that they will not be completed by all. One way of overcoming this problem is to introduce some sort of assessment. This is often seen as contrary to the ethos of management development and, in an case, is not always practical or possible within an organisational setting. But it makes a huge difference if you can ensure that participants are clear about attendance and completion expectations. Remember, "what gets measured, gets done" so these need to be monitored. The two things that work in maintaining engagement are staying in touch with participants throughout their blended learning experience and ensuring that the programme design has a clear structure and development purpose (Hofmann, 2014a).

3. Design challenges

Not all management development needs are most effectively met in a blended learning design. Again, we're back to asking some questions. The first is "what do you need to develop and why?" and the second is "How will success be measured?"

- **Ensure the intended development is suited to a blended learning design: the 'what' and the 'how' question**

Designing good blended learning is not simply about grafting technology onto existing development programmes. As we mentioned earlier, before the actual design process can start, a needs and technology analysis has to be completed. Once you have clarity around the content needed to fulfil the overall training objective, it's a good idea to divide the content into smaller chunks. For each chunk, ensure that you have specific learning objectives, then determine which delivery method (face-to-face or technology-based) will most effectively convey the learning to the target audience. Ensure that the sequence of activities supports the overall learning objective as well, and try not to force a blended approach onto something that is more naturally suited to either face-to-face or purely online.

Food for thought

How does learning get measured in your organisation? How is learning valued, shared and demonstrated? What would it take for your organisation to be acknowledged as a 'leader in learning'?

Considering the whole value chain of your blended learning programme offers the opportunity to be really clear about the ROI you need.

- **Know your target audience and cater for their needs**

One advantage of blended learning is that it caters for the needs of very disparate groups. When designing your blend, identify a number of typical participants, each with different learning styles and backgrounds (for example, an activist or a theorist, a novice or a very experienced participant) and create a learning persona or pen portrait for each of them. Encourage your subject experts to consider what teaching styles and technologies might be needed to meet the needs of all these groups, and to challenge some of their preconceived notions about how effective learning may be delivered in a particular context and culture (City & Guilds Kineo, 2014).

- **Match the most suitable delivery option to specific performance objectives**

Think about which of your learning outcomes are related to transferring knowledge-based or skill-based performance objectives – there will probably be a bit of a mix. Then select the best delivery option for each. For example, skill-based performance is suited to participative and experiential activities, often done in collaboration with others, virtually or face-to-face to harness peer sharing and feedback. In contrast, knowledge or information-based performance can often be best developed individually in a self-directed environment. Before selecting a specific technology or teaching style, think about how you will know if learning has taken place (Shelton, 2010). By answering this question you will find greater clarity in selecting the most appropriate mode of delivery and/or delivery technologies.

- **Determine the 'spine' of the blended learning and ensure that both 'live' and 'non-live' elements are designed to stimulate maximum and sustained participation and engagement**

This is quite a complicated one. Not surprisingly, participants, managers and, at times, facilitators are more focused on the live components of the blended learning. There is a temptation to re-teach content that was covered in self-directed or self-paced work, but this only reinforces the notion that non-live elements are optional. This is a sure fire way to derail the effectiveness of a blended approach to development (Hofmann, 2014a). A design error to avoid is to include too much self-paced content in too short a time period. The content and timing should realistically consider the target audience's work schedule and build in sufficient time for non-live elements to receive the amount of attention required. You may want to start the process with smaller and fewer self-paced elements but with a greater focus on designing more live components at the start of the programme.

It is also a good idea at this stage of the design to build in a tracking and managing process to help learners to navigate the self-paced content at the right pace. Providing a clear structure with support as part of the overall design will go a long way to ensure the successful implementation of the blend. If appropriate for your organisation, you may wish to include specific assessments of self-paced content, or be clear in the design whether or not progression to subsequent live or face-to-face elements will be dependent on successful completion of self-paced work or not.

Despite the live elements being perceived as the most important, this is not a guarantee that participants will remain engaged with any virtual live sessions you might include. Therefore, these need be designed actively to foster engagement, usually through interaction between participants. The sessions will be most effective if they focus on sharing understanding and exploring real-life applications and not on pure knowledge transfer. Introducing variety in activities and pace during virtual teaching sessions is even more important than in classroom sessions, and is needed to ensure that participants stay actively involved (Arbaugh, 2014). However, be careful to select an appropriate activity that will add value to the participants at that particular point in the session (such as small group discussions in virtual break-out rooms or a large-group plenary conversation), rather than introducing a formulaic approach of set pieces (such as polls or Q&A slides every three slides).

The purpose of interactive contributions should be to ensure that content is being processed and that application is being critically discussed and considered. Facilitators need sensitivity to recognise when new content can be introduced (Hofmann, 2014c).

- **Work according to a plan**

Because blended learning involves multiple elements spread out over time, it is good practice to create a design plan to manage the development of the blend (Hofmann, 2014c). More than just a Gant chart, you need to ensure that you include a variety of stakeholders in the design team, including non-subject experts to harness multiple perspectives and ideas.

Your plan should contain your approved learning outcomes, performance objectives and assessment techniques for each of the proposed learning methodologies. It would be good practice to also include a profile of the participants which also considers their technological landscape (Hofmann, 2014c).

Food for thought

How joined up is your organisation's approach to learning? What would help you to ensure a clear line of sight between business strategy and learning and development activity?

Planning and designing a programme like this can really help you to link your L&D strategy with overall organisational strategy.

4. Implementation challenges

A sustainable and successful blended learning experience really needs a dedicated implementation strategy involving the careful managing and monitoring of a range of issues. There's a long list! It includes: coordination within the design and development team, internal and external marketing of the blended learning, coordination of global cohorts, logistical scheduling, resource scheduling, technical training and support for delivery team and participants, administrative support for managing queries, monitoring attendance and feedback, and proving follow-through support. As you can imagine, it is not uncommon for successful blended learning implementation to rely on a dedicated project manager. This section provides a number of further recommendations to support successful implementation.

- **Provide a clear road map to the blended learning experience**

Communication, communication, communication! Participants will really appreciate a visual programme map clearly indicating all the various elements, including the dates and times of the live elements. In addition, participants welcome guidance on how to approach the self-directed elements of the programme. This can vary in detail depending on your audience but often provides a suggested schedule, order of tackling the required work and the approximate amounts of time involved. This is where the learning platform you have selected can play a useful role, in that some platforms are super structured, whilst others need to be designed in such a way as to guide participants through the relevant material.

In order to encourage reflective practice, it's really useful to include a series of structured open questions linked to the participants' journey through the self-directed and live content.

The blended programme's website or learning platform thus needs to contain clear signposting to the structure, the content and the process. The inclusion of easily accessible contact information for administrative, academic and technical support (including their office hours) and a comprehensive Q&A section is also considered best practice (Shelton, 2010).

Oh, and by the way, try to ensure that all email communication to participants is also duplicated on the learning platform in a central position so that participants know where to look for news or updates, and to ensure that they remain informed of any upcoming events or deadlines.

- **Create and implement an in-depth marketing strategy for your blended learning programme**

Anticipate that the news of your blended learning will spread like wild fire through your organisation and be prepared to control the messages that get communicated. Ensure that they are positive and consistently reinforced. Here are a few tips (Hofmann, 2014d):

Position the blended learning: Continue to present your blended learning as an integral part of the organisation's learning culture with regular communications and with clear messages around why blended learning is appropriate, what benefits it will bring, what it will entail and what success will look like. Remember that participants will need reassurance that blended learning is right for them and relevant to their role.

Create a shared, accessible language: Decide on simple terminology that works in your context and apply this consistently when explaining the complexity of the blend. For example, call all live and non-live elements 'sessions' or 'lectures' – don't differentiate between them, regardless of delivery mode. This simplification will help participants see the blended learning as one programme or course instead of disjointed activities.

Engage advocates: Find champions within the business who are respected and admired, who will be your brand ambassador and make your blended learning sexy. Share success stories widely and, if you do encounter and overcome problems, make sure you communicate how these have been used as valuable learning experiences.

- **Build in assessment and review of the blended learning**

Schedule regular reviews of the programme to ensure that all the content elements are current, particularly self-directed, non-live content (Shelton, 2010). Don't forget that, as a general rule, online (non-live) content requires longer timelines and greater budgets to change or update compared to live virtual or face-to-face teaching material.

5. Engagement challenges

Because of the nature of blended learning, sustained engagement for participants and facilitators needs to be worked at.

Both groups benefit if management is involved, particularly if the senior management is seen to be actively involved in supporting the programme by delivering contextual insight, hosting Q&A conversations, sponsoring projects and possibly also being responsible for the final programme evaluation. High levels of leadership engagement are often associated with the high impact of most successful learning programmes, and blended learning is no exception. It's worthwhile considering a dedicated launch event specifically for the senior leadership team(s) to highlight the alignment between the learning objectives of the programme and the corporate goals, particularly illustrating the links to external stakeholders such as customer and suppliers (Hofmann, 2014d).

As participants' motivation and their level of engagement in online discussion activities are closely correlated, it is key to ensure that participants experience a positive balance between workload and value added. Research suggests that the optimal online cohort size for useful, interactive discussions is twelve (Goldman, 2012), but the ideal cohort size for your organisation will need to be decided in the light of your organisational context, budget and learning objectives.

If you are planning on using members of the L&D team or the wider organisation to design and deliver your blended learning strategy, try the following suggestions to ensure continued engagement:

- Provide continued reminders of the validity and value of blended learning – walk the talk, do some yourself!

- Provide real support systems for those tasked with creating and delivering online activities. Assistance will be needed in designing online sessions and materials as these take more time and effort than traditional courses. Provide training on how to do this effectively.

- Provide support for instructional designers and ensure early on that there is collaboration between technical and content expert staff.

- Ensure that employees who have had a bad experience with using technology or multimedia are reassured and encouraged to try again.

- Find a way to recognise employee contributions to engaging with blended learning in your performance management system. According to research (Hollenbeck et al., 2005), the prestige of innovative teaching fades quickly and so more substantial rewards are needed to sustain enthusiasm among delivery teams.

Closing words

Blended learning is here to stay but not everyone will be equally successful in managing the different modes and methods of delivery. Any learning intervention designed to enhance management capability in today's business environment must mirror the complexity of that environment. Those who succeed will be those who understand the challenges as well as the opportunities offered by blended learning and who pay careful attention at the planning stage to each of the five areas we have discussed in this chapter.

References

Alavi, M., & Gallupe, R. (2003) Using Information Technology in Learning: Case Studies in Business and Management Education Programs. *Academy of Management Learning & Education*, 2(2), pp.139–53.

Arbaugh, J.B. (2014) What Might Online Delivery Teach Us About Blended Management Education? Prior Perspectives and Future Directions. *Journal of Management Education*, 38(6), pp.784–817.

Bocchi, J., Eastman, J.K., & Swift, C. (2004) Retaining the Online Learner: Profile of Students in an Online MBA Programme and Implications for Teaching Them. *Journal of Education for Business*, 79(4), pp.245–53.

Bucciarelli, E., Muratore, F., & Odoardi, I. (2010) Consolidation processes of human capital in modern economic growth dynamics: an estimate based on the role of European corporate e-learning activities. In H. Keser, Z. Ozcinar & S. Kanbul (eds), *World Conference on Learning, Teaching and Administration Papers*, Vol. 9 (Amsterdam: Elsevier Science B.V.).

City & Guilds Kineo (2014) Blended Learning Today: Designing in the new learning architecture – 10 tips for blend design. *Designing Blended Learning Guide* [online PDF], <http://www.oxford-group.com/pdf/blended-learning-today-2014.pdf> accessed 27 January 2015.

Čonková, M. (2013) Analysis of Perceptions of Conventional and E-Learning Education in Corporate Training. *Journal of Competitiveness*, 5(4), pp.73–93.

Duhaney, D.C. (2004) Blended learning in education, training, and development. *Performance Improvement*, 43(8), pp.35–8.

Endres, M.L., Chowdhury, S., Frye, C., & Hurtubis, C.A. (2009) The Multifaceted Nature of Online MBA Student Satisfaction and Impacts on Behavioral Intentions. *Journal of Education for Business*, 84(5), pp.304–12.

Goldman, Z. (2012) Online MBA Asynchronous Discussion Workload and Value Perceptions for Instructors and Learners: Working Toward an Integrated Educational Model for Professional Adults. [Online PDF] <http://jolt.merlot.org/vol8no3/goldman_0912.htm accessed 25 January 2015>.

Hofmann, J. (2011) Top 10 Challenges of Blended Learning. *Training*, [Online magazine] <http://www.insynctraining.com/assets/landing_fulfillment/Blended%20Learning%20Training%20Magazine%20March%20April%202011.pdf> accessed 29 January 2015.

Hofmann, J. (2014a) Solutions to the Top 10 Challenges of Blended Learning. *InSync Training*, p.5 [online white paper], <http://www.insynctraining.com> accessed 28 January 2014.

Hofmann, J. (2014b) Virtually There: 5 Best Practices for Designing Virtual and Blended Learning. *Training* [Online magazine], 24 October 2014, <http://www.trainingmag.com/virtually-there-5-best-practices-designing-virtual-and-blended-learning> accessed 30 January 2015.

Hofmann, J. (2014c) Virtually There: Best Practices for Developing Blended Content That Meets Your Learning Goals. *Training* [Online magazine], 21 November 2014, <http://www.trainingmag.com/

virtually-there-best-practices-developing-blended-content-meets-your-learning-goals> accessed 30 January 2015.

Hofmann, J. (2014d) Virtually There: Managing a Blended Learning Implementation. *Training* [Online magazine], 19 December 2014, <http://www.trainingmag.com/virtually-there-managing-blended-learning-implementation> accessed 29 January 2015.

Hollenbeck, C.R., Zinkhan, G.M., & French, W. (2005) Distance Learning Trends and Benchmarks: Lessons from an online MBA programme. *Marketing Education Review*, 15(2), pp.39–52.

Kaur, M. (2013) Blended learning – its challenges and future. *Procedia – Social and Behavioral Sciences*, 93, pp.612–17.

Mansour, M. (2009) *Employees' Perception and Satisfaction about e-Learning in the Workplace* (Reading: Academic Conferences Ltd).

Martins, L.L., & Kellermanns, F.W. (2004) A model of business school students' acceptance of a web-based course management system. *Academy of Management Learning and Education*, 3, pp.7–26.

Padilla-Melendez, A., Garrido-Moreno, A., & del Aguila Obra, A.R. (2008) Factors affecting e-collaboration technology use among management students. *Computers & Education*, 51, pp.609–23.

Shelton, K. (2010) A quality scorecard for the administration of online education programs: A Delphi Study. *Journal of Asynchronous Learning Networks*, 14(4), pp.36–62.

CHAPTER 8

Live Cases in Executive Education

Vicki Culpin

Over the past 10 to 15 years, the field of management education has led the way in a paradigm shift with learning pedagogy (Elam and Spotts, 2004). The traditional lecture-based delivery of information has been replaced by a much more student-centric and student-focused approach, with the student, or participant in the classroom, 'experiencing' the learning in an active way through facilitation and dialogue with the self, rather than the previous passive transmission of content from expert to student.

The effectiveness of the experiential learning approach has been recognised in educational organisations across the world and has dictated the pedagogy of a significant number of executive education providers. For example, accrediting organisations such as the Association to Advance Collegiate Schools of Business (AACSB) have reported that experiential learning activities are effective in enhancing the skills and knowledge of students attending their accredited business schools and they reinforce this message within their accreditation standards:

> The most effective learning takes place when students are involved in their educational experiences. Passive learning is ineffective and of short duration. Faculty members should develop techniques and styles that engage students and make students

> responsible for meeting learning goals… Faculty members should find such approaches that are suited to their subject matter, and should adopt active learning methodologies.
>
> (AACSB, 2003, p.52, cited in Elam and Spotts, 2004)

And in 2013, the Learning and Teaching standards required by AACSB institutions expected that:

> Curricula facilitate and encourage active student engagement in learning. In addition to time on tasks related to readings, course participation, knowledge development, projects, and assignments, students engage in experiential and active learning designed to improve skills and the application of knowledge in practice.
>
> (AACSB, 2013)

Gentry (1990) highlighted three approaches or methodologies that he felt successfully encapsulated the very essence of experiential learning. The three are:

- Internships – usually unpaid experience of working in an organisation

- 'Computer-assisted instruction' – the use of multimedia-enriched learning

- 'Live' cases – a structured experience for participants, working on a real organisational concern to offer insights or solutions to help the business address the issue.

This chapter will focus on the latter approach – live cases. We will evaluate their effectiveness, particularly when compared with the more traditional, retrospective case study employed by many traditional business schools.

Gentry (1990) argued that live cases are closest to the true nature of experiential learning and they are certainly the most recent development in the history of case methodology. However, the use of the traditional, retrospective case study has been the mainstay of business-school activity for a significant number of years. The traditional case method was first introduced to the classroom by Copeland in 1909 (Chiesl, 1990) and Roethlisberger (1977) noted that the case method was developed at this time to bridge the gap between straightforward educational pedagogy, using 'experts' to disseminate knowledge, and the highly pragmatic needs of managers and leaders within organisations.

Theroux and Kilbane (2004) provide a very good overview of the traditional case study. A 'case' typically presents a static snapshot of an individual company, frequently defining a specific issue that the company has grappled with or fallen foul of. Most cases are presented in a written format, of approximately 7-to-12 pages of text, and, according to Theroux and Kilbane (2004), can cost an average of $20,000 to produce, with at least a month of researcher time and approximately a year in production. Even the best and most contemporary traditional cases, therefore, are always going to be historical, due to the research and production time, and the retrospective nature of the concept.

The use and benefits of this conventional case methodology is very well documented, both with a student population and within executive education (e.g. Garvin, 2007). It does focus on real-world problems and as such is excellent for the development of critical reasoning (Christensen and Hansen, 1987). There is also a significant body of research that demonstrates how the highly relevant and practical nature of the material and the resultant discussions can achieve a number of learning goals including the development of application, analysis, synthesis, evaluation and organisational skills, along with the development of real-world decision-making skills. The Dean of Harvard Business School, the institution that is synonymous with the use of the traditional case methodology, states that HBS uses the traditional case method in all of its business courses because "it produces graduates who are comfortable making decisions".

In support of this view, Weil and colleagues (2004) found that when using a traditional written case approach, students perceived the major benefit to be an improvement in their ability to evaluate situations rationally from more than one perspective. They felt more able to consider alternative solutions to problems. Confirmation of other outcomes has been provided by Hassall and colleagues (1998), who found that students perceived an improvement in transferable skills such as group working and presentation skills after discussing a written case. In addition, Weil and colleagues (2001) surveyed the perceptions of students on the use of written case studies and concluded that students believed that key benefits were their increased ability to deal with real-world complexity and, in particular, their decision-making capability.

Whilst there is certainly a significant body of literature examining students' *perceptions* of the benefits of using traditional case methods, there are fewer that focus on the skills and abilities that actually *do* improve or change as a result of utilising this methodology. Whilst this is not a disadvantage of the method per se, it does make evaluation of the effectiveness of this approach more difficult. It may well be that perceptions of benefits and actual benefits are closely correlated, but this may also not be as true as we might hope. Within the executive education literature, the research base on the effectiveness of the use of traditional cases is extremely sparse.

To consider the downsides, there are some obvious disadvantages to using the traditional case-study approach:

- By definition, a case study is historical and retrospective. Therefore, the students or participants are often in an external 'observer' role, responding to historic facts provided by a disconnected party.

- The pedagogy is customarily less than dynamic. Andrews and Noel (1986) and Bailey and colleagues (2005) note that the traditional written case method is very passive in nature. There is an inevitable separation between the student, or participant in the classroom, and the organisation being discussed. Therefore, the method is disconnected from the reality and the complexity of the organisational setting, including the prevalent organisational culture.

So, whilst the case method may have been devised to bridge the gap between the theoretical content delivered by academics and the real-world experience demanded by business, it does not seem to tick all the boxes for effective management education. As the pressure increases from organisations for executive education providers to ensure a strong return on investment (ROI) for executive education programmes and interventions, the focus on ensuring relevancy whilst creating a rich learning environment is critical. Within this learning environment, the development of 'live cases' has therefore been offered. This approach enables participants to work on a 'real' business issue facing an organisation whilst being immersed in the organisational physical environment, context and culture.

Live case studies have been widely used in management education for a number of years (Shapiro, 1984; Wines et al., 1994). They are claimed to be one of the best techniques for developing a wide range of generic skills such as communication skills, written skills, interpersonal skills, judgement and analytical skills (Ballantine & McCourt Larres, 2004). Live cases are also perceived as being successful by both students and businesses (Elam & Spotts, 2004; Farazmand et al., 2010) and of course they also, according to many researchers, including Schulman (1992), provide a proxy for the most direct form of experiential learning.

Live cases offer a radically different approach to traditional case studies. The model invites a host organisation to offer a real business issue with which they would like some consultancy help. They are more realistic, therefore, usually including participation by key decision makers within the organisation, although this may be at varying levels. The business issue is often current and 'live' (Markulis, 1985), which means that history cannot provide a solution. There is no correct answer: the answer is emergent and in real time. Gentry (1990) argues that the criteria for a successful live case should include:

1. That the issue to be addressed can be seen to be related to current business practice by both the organisational stakeholders and the participant

2. That there is active participation and interaction by both primary parties, and other stakeholders, in the process

3. That an issue of real concern is addressed, where the resolution is unclear.

Despite such clear criteria, the literature on live case studies reveals a wide portfolio of 'live' case examples. There is little consistency between them in terms of approach, population and location. There are differences in presentation style: some of the live cases are written and some are based on dialogue with the CEO of the organisation. There are differences in location, some are classroom-based and some are delivered within the host organisation, and there are differences in the learner population with some being pre-experience-student centric and some using executive education participants.

To navigate through this wide variety of pedagogies, all captured under the term 'live case studies', and to show the relationship between live cases and the traditional case methodology, Figure 1 offers a clarifying model. This identifies two factors which seem to be critical in the design case methodology:

-   The involvement of the client organisation

-   The timely nature of the topic (historic or current).

Figure 1

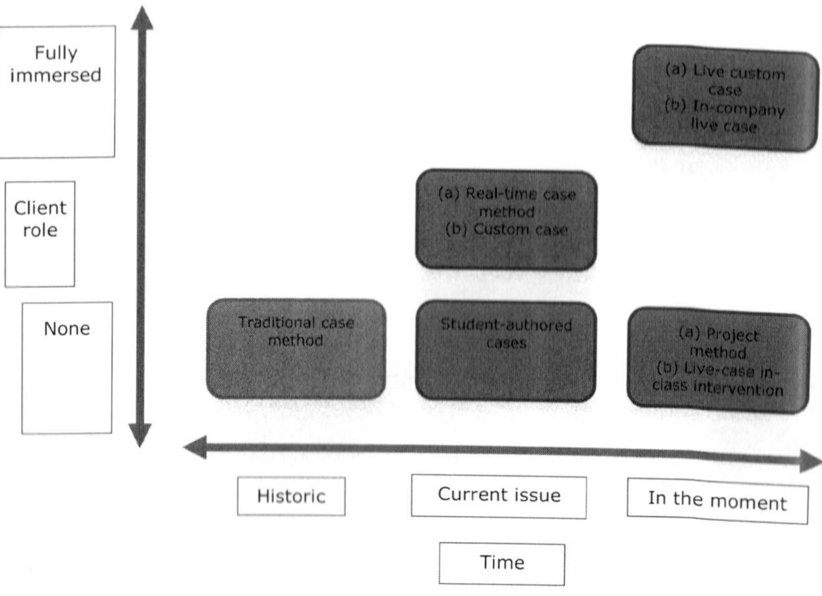

Table 1 provides a summary of the variations of live cases that have been described in the literature to date.

This chapter will evaluate the use of the in-company live case (ICLC), the final category identified in Table 1.

Table 1

Approach	Population	Time	Client Role	Participant Relationship to Organisation	Location	Presentation Method
Traditional Case	Students and executive education	Historic	None	None	Classroom	Written
Student-authored Case (e.g. Lincoln, 2006)	Students	Current	None	None	Classroom	Written
Real-time Case Method (Theroux & Kilbane, 2004)	Students	Live	Relevant individual from the organisation available at set times for virtual Q&A	None	Classroom	Written, virtual and discussion based
Project Method (Green & Farazmand, 2012)	Students	Live	Relevant individual from the organisation available one day/week during project and for consultation and final group presentations	None	Classroom (Semester Long)	Discussion based
Live-case In-class Intervention (Rashford & Figueiredo, 2011)	Students	Live	CEO or senior leader present during the entire exercise	None	Classroom	Publically available written material and discussion based
Custom Case (Dover, Perkins & Wylie, 2009)	Executive education	Current	CEO/senior team contributes to writing the material only	Within own company	Classroom	Written
'Live' Custom Case (Urban & Keys, 1994)	Executive education	Live	CEO and/or senior team available during the entire exercise	Within own company	Classroom	Written material and discussion based
In-company 'Live' Case (Culpin & Scott, 2011)	Executive education	Live	CEO provides the brief, hosts the day, listens to final presentation and provides feedback to participants	None	In-Company	Written brief provided prior to start, written material obtained during the course of the day from the CEO or other leaders in the organisation, and discussion based

The in-company live case (ICLC) methodology

The methodology underpinning this category was devised to ensure that the skills and knowledge developed during a management development programme were transferred to a real situation (i.e. the live-case event). In addition to the relationship between the host organisation and the learners, Christensen (1991) has offered four fundamental principles of effective learning when using the case methodology:

1. The case method is a partnership in learning and teaching between the facilitator/lecturer and the students/participants

2. The group of individuals in the classroom or in the organisational environment should transform from a collection of students/participants into a learning community

3. The facilitator or lecturer should be instrumental in helping the students/participants understand the material

4. The facilitator/lecturer is responsible for managing the process as well as the content.

Generally speaking, literature and practitioner experience indicates that the ICLC has a number of defining characteristics which enhance the learning experience and embed the theoretical parts of the programme. The first of these is that, often, the live case occurs following a classroom- or 'input'-based module. It is designed to allow participants to 'practice' the tools and skills to which they have been introduced previously and it is important that a relatively safe, yet 'real', organisational environment should be provided to extend the learning. The live case should address an issue with which the organisation is currently grappling and should be relevant to an issue that allows the participants to use the tools and techniques introduced in the earlier part of the module.

A host organisation is clearly necessary for an ICLC to take place and should ideally meet two criteria. Firstly, the industry should be sufficiently different from that of the participants' own organisation(s) to allow cultural differences to emerge and be acknowledged. Whilst it is possible for delegates to work on issues in their own companies, these tend to be termed 'projects' and offer different learning outcomes from those of an ICLC. Secondly, and very practically, the host organisation should be located somewhere to which participants are able to travel during their module. The live case usually involves a visit to the client organisation (participants are transported to the client location), offering an immersion experience which lasts for one or two days. The CEO of the organisation (or at least a senior member of the leadership team) must be available during the live case, and must be part of the client team that listens to the participant presentations at the end of the process. It is important that the client provides feedback on both process and content regarding the participants' work.

In terms of setting expectations, participants must be aware that a live case will take place and they must be given background information on the client organisation (publically available information) prior to the start of the class-room-based module. However, they should not be given the live-case brief until, at the earliest, the night before the live case. This is to prevent over-preparation and an undue emphasis on the task – it is equally important that participants address the process issues involved in working together to deliver a result on the live-case issue. The most effective groups will be of less than ten participants. For larger class sizes, the groups can be split into two, each with a different brief, but within the same client organisation.

As with all effective adult education, reflection and assimilation are key. The final day of the module (the day after the end of the live case) should be given over to feedback (on both process and content): from the facilitators of the live case, from participant colleagues and from the client(s).

The rest of this chapter reports on a study designed to evaluate the effec-tiveness of these principles in increasing the transfer of learning back in the organisation.

An evaluation of an ICLC

In 2011, research was conducted (Culpin & Scott, 2011) to understand the effectiveness of an ICLC on a specific executive education programme. As indicated earlier in this chapter, research on the evaluation of live cases has largely focused on the development of soft or 'transferable' skills such as communication skills, written skills and interpersonal skills (Ballantine & McCourt Larres, 2004). Culpin and Scott (2011), however, sought to examine whether 'hard', more technical skills, such as strategy, could also be devel-oped by using the live-case approach.

The study in question was conducted with 19 participants drawn from a single UK-based building materials organisation. They took part in a one-week, classroom-based taught module which covered key concepts, tools and techniques concerning:

- Devising strategy

- Structuring a process to solve a strategic problem

- Using strategy tools effectively

- Making a flat team effective

- Personal effectiveness

- Analysing and devising distribution strategy, and

- Analysing and devising Internet strategy.

Following this taught component, participants travelled from the UK to Sweden to take part in the live case. The client organisation, the host of the live case, was a large travel company, headquartered in Sweden. Participants were given no prior warning as to the nature of the challenge and were thus unable to do any preparatory work until the night before the challenge was set. Prior to the start of the case, each participant was provided with a briefing pack which detailed:

1. The objectives of the exercise – i.e. the objectives of embedding and applying the learning from the taught module.

2. Strong recommendations for participants to attend to the process and to their ways of working as well as to the actual task or content during the experience. This reflected input they had received during the taught module.

3. The roles of the facilitators – facilitators would only intervene to facilitate a process review and would not provide direction on content.

On arrival in Sweden, participants were briefed on the nature of the project by a senior manager from the host organisation. This briefing outlined, in detail, the real challenge facing the organisation, around which the organisation was seeking help and advice. Participants were then divided into two groups (a group of nine and a group of ten), with each group being given a different organisational issue to focus on during the two-and-a-half days they had to complete the task. Access to databases, the Internet, phones, staff, customers and suppliers were provided by the host, and participants were expected to provide feedback to the client, the senior manager of the organisation, during the afternoon of the third day. This presentation and feedback was also followed by more detailed facilitator feedback and peer review.

To allow a review and evaluation of the learning gained through this live case, participants were asked to complete and submit two identical questionnaires, one immediately before the start of the live case, one immediately after the final debrief and feedback session. These featured a range of questions asking participants to rate (on a ten-point Likert scale) their understanding and knowledge in the seven key areas of business that had been addressed in the taught module.

The subsequent statistical analysis of the data collected clearly indicated that the use of a live case is a successful method for learning new skills and techniques including, specifically, 'hard' technical skills. Participants rated a significant improvement in understanding, post live case study, of all of the strategy-related topics and abilities. A surprising result, however, was that softer skills (such as personal effectiveness) showed no similar increase in understanding after the case study. This is obviously contrary to other research in this area.

A possible explanation may be that this study was conducted with mature executive education participants who may have already reached their natural level of effectiveness and development in interpersonal or 'soft' skills. They had been successful leaders of people for a number of years, whereas the majority of other work in this area reflects student populations that have yet to develop these skills fully. It may also be that soft skills require reflection, and therefore time, to ensure they are embedded, which may mean that development may not feature in an immediate post-programme questionnaire.

The in-company live case challenges

Anecdotal evidence from this study indicates that, whilst there are clear benefits of using live cases, and in particular the ICLC, it is also important to be cognisant of a number of challenges that developing and delivering a successful ICLC can bring:

1. Finding the right client organisation – specifically one that is located within travelling distance of the participants in the classroom – is critical. This means finding an organisation that has challenges that can be tackled by the use of the skills, strategies and techniques that have

been introduced in the classroom-based element of the programme. This really means answering 'Yes' to the question "Do the learning objectives of the module match the client needs?"

2. It is also important to ensure that the client's issue is of the right size: that is, not too small that it can be resolved within a short time frame, and not so vast that the task becomes overwhelming and the participants feel that they will certainly fail. The client issue needs to be able to be sufficiently understood and potential solutions developed within an 8-to-16-hour time frame. The nature of the problem should also be capable of explanation within a 30-to-60-minute brief.

3. Client expectations must be managed appropriately. Whilst the client may, understandably, perceive the live case as an opportunity to engage in a piece of 'free' consultancy, the learning needs of the participants are paramount and the client must remain aware of this, whilst ensuring that they too gain some valuable insights for their organisation. Here, the focus should be on excellent contracting with the client and the client organisation from the beginning. It is critical that the client understand the nature of the learning intervention, what their role is, what the facilitators' and participants' roles are, and what is acceptable and what unacceptable behaviour within the learning framework.

4. Creating an effective and safe feedback environment – the client may become defensive if the presentation session from the participants highlights issues and solutions not previously considered by the CEO or the organisation more widely. This can significantly diminish the effectiveness of the feedback from the client and reduce the safe learning environment. At the opposite end of the spectrum, the client may also be frustrated by a perceived lack of innovative and cutting-edge solutions from participants. The risk here is that, whilst the learning for the participants is likely to have been rich, the client may feel the exercise, from their perspective, has been a waste of their time. This needs to be managed carefully, partially through the contracting stage, and partially in the moment. It is critical that these potentially damaging perceptions from the client do not contaminate the learning environment of the participants. Of course, the lack of novel solutions is an important learning point and should not be ignored. It is the process, rather than the content, of this feedback that is fundamental.

Best practice in using ICLCs

In summary, to ensure that the energy and effort involved in setting up and running a successful live case event are best utilised, educators and facilitators must be sure that:

1. The issue to be addressed can be easily related to current business practice for the participants – it must be relevant to their own management practice and/or their learning objectives.

2. There is active participation in the process – anything which potentially reduces the ability of participants to be fully active and present in the process is a risk to the event.

3. Interactivity is critical (with other participants, key internal and external stakeholders in the organisation and the senior management within the organisation). The interactivity is also a key aspect of the ICLC by the very nature of the design (high level of involvement by key stakeholders, location within the client organisation, feedback provided by internal and external stakeholders).

4. There is a real, relevant and significant situation to be addressed. Selecting the right issue(s) for the participant group whilst protecting the learning objectives, within a dynamic environment, is paramount to the success of any ICLC. If the issue is too complex, you are setting your participants up to fail; if it is too trivial, you are undermining the learning potential.

Conclusion

Live cases that are active, problem based and 'just in time', involving real clients with real issues, provide a rich atmosphere for learning. The live environment allows the learner to engage with the urgency of the issue and thus increases their motivation to learn; and the end stage of the live case, the reflection and feedback, provides a key part of the learning experience (Frontczak & Kelley, 2000). Finally, the ICLC, which puts the participants in an unfamiliar organisational landscape, requires individuals to address an issue that is relevant to them, but is sufficiently distanced to require them to engage in the process rather than leap to preconceive notions drawn from past experience. The ability of a live case study to develop and enhance a range of skills, tools and techniques, not just in the student population but also for participants on executive education programmes, is very exciting.

ICLCs are engaging and relevant for their participants and an excellent way to deepen the learning of classroom-based concepts and tools.

References

AACSB: The Association to Advance Collegiate Schools of Business (2013) *Eligibility Procedures and Accreditation Standards for Business Accreditation* (Tampa, FL: AACSB).

Andrews, E., & Noel, J. (1986) Adding life to the case method. *Training and Development Journal*, 40, pp.28–9.

Bailey, J., Sass, M., Swiercz, P., Seal, C., & Kayes, C. (2005) Teaching with and through teams: Student-written, instructor-facilitated case writing and the signatory code. *Journal of Management Education*, 29, pp.39–59.

Ballantine, J., & McCourt Larres, P. (2004) A critical analysis of students' perceptions of the usefulness of the case study method in an advanced management accounting module: The impact of relevant work experience. *Accounting Education*, 13, pp.171–89.

Chiesl, N. (1990) Interactive real time simulations. In J. Gentry (ed.), *Guide to Business Gaming and Experiential Learning* (London: Nichols/GP Publishing).

Christensen, C. (1991) Premises and practices of discussion teaching. In C. Christensen, D. Garvin & A. Sweet (eds), *Education for Judgement: The Artistry of Discussion Leadership* (Boston, MA: Harvard Business School Press).

Christensen, C., & Hansen, A. (1987) *Teaching and the Case Method* (Boston: Harvard Business School Press).

Culpin, V., & Scott, H. (2011) The effectiveness of a live case study approach: Increasing knowledge and understanding of 'hard' versus 'soft' skills in executive education. *Management Learning*, 43, pp.565–77.

Dover, P., Perkins, S., & Wylie, D. (2009) The role of customer case materials in action-based executive education programmes. *Journal of Management Development*, 28(4), pp.285–300.

Elam, E., & Spotts, H. (2004) Achieving marketing curriculum integration: A live case study approach. *Journal of Marketing Education*, 26, pp.50–65.

Farazmand, F., Green, R., & Miller, P. (2010) Creating lifelong learning through service-learning. *Business Education and Accreditation*, 2, pp.1–14.

Frontczak, N., & Kelley, C. (2000) The Editors Corner: Special issue on experiential learning in marketing education. *Journal of Marketing Education*, 22, pp.3–4.

Garvin, D. (2007) Teaching executives and teaching MBAs: Reflections on the case method. *Academy of Management Learning and Education*, 6, pp.364–74.

Gentry, J. (1990) What is experiential learning? In J. Gentry (ed.), *Guide to Business Gaming and Experiential Learning* (London: Nichols/GP Publishing).

Green, R., & Farazmand, F. (2012) Experiential learning: The internship and live case study relationship. *Business Education and Accreditation*, 4(1), pp.13–23.

Hassall, T., Lewis, S., & Broadbent, M. (1998) Teaching and learning using case studies: A teaching note. *Accounting Education*, 7, pp.325–34.

Kolb, D. (1984) *Experiential Learning: Experience as the Source of Learning and Development* (Englewood Cliffs, NJ: Prentice Hall).

Lincoln, D. (2006) Student authored cases: Combining benefits of traditional and live case methods of instruction. *Marketing Education Review*, 16, pp.1–7.

Maher, R., & Hughner, R. (2005) Experiential marketing projects: Student perceptions of live case and simulation methods. *Journal for Advancement of Marketing Education*, 7, pp.1–10.

Markulis, P. (1985) The live case study: Filling the gap between the case study and the experiential exercise. In J. Gentry & A. Burns (eds), *Developments in Business Simulation and Experiential Exercises* (Orlando, FL: Association for Business Simulation and Experiential Learning).

Mulligan, J., & Griffin, C. (1992) *Empowerment through Experiential Learning* (London: Kogan Page).

Rashford, N., & Neivade Figueiredo, J. (2011) The live in-class CEO intervention: A capstone experiential technique for leadership development. *Journal of Management Education*, 35(5), pp.620–47.

Roethlisberger, F. (1977) *The Elusive Phenomena* (Boston, MA: Harvard University Press).

Schulman, J. (1992) *Case Methods in Teacher Evaluation* (New York: Teachers College Press).

Shapiro, B. (1984) *Hints for Case Teaching* (Boston, MA: Harvard Business School Publishing Division).

Theroux, J. (2009) Real-time case method: Analysis of a second implementation. *Journal of Education for Business*, pp.367–73.

Theroux, J., & Kilbane, C. (2004) The real-time case method: A new approach to an old tradition. *Journal of Education for Business*, 79, pp.163–7.

Urban, T., & Keys, J. (1994) The live case method of creating the learning organisation. *Journal of Management Development*, 13, pp.44–9.

Weil, S., Oyelere, P., & Rainsburg, E. (2004) The usefulness of case studies in developing core competencies in a professional accounting programme: A New Zealand case study. *Accounting Education*, 13, pp.139–69.

Weil, S., Oyelere, P., Yeoh, J., & Firer, C. (2001) A study of students' perceptions of the usefulness of case studies for the development of finance and accounting-related skills and knowledge. *Accounting Education: An International Journal*, 10, pp.123–46.

Wines, G., Carnegie, G., Boyce, G., & Gibson, R. (1994) *Using Case Studies in the Teaching of Accounting* (Melbourne: Australian Society of CPAs).

CHAPTER 9

Learning to Take the Right Risk: A Framework for Leaders

Jamie MacAlister

Introduction

Risk, it turns out, is a curious subject. It is something we all think we understand, yet it appears to mean different things in different contexts. In organisations, it is often parked in processes and committees designed to 'drive it out', but then it pops up in discussions about strategy, culture or personality as something virtuous to be 'taken'. As leaders, we deal with risk daily on a personal as well as on an organisational level, but we don't often talk about it. Unfortunately, it can come back and bite us if we ignore it.

In this chapter, we explore this ambiguous subject, drawing on research we have conducted on how leaders work with risk. We describe a framework designed to help managers and leaders to work more effectively with risk by disconnecting a personal bias for or against riskiness from a perception of what the 'right' thing to do is. We also consider how, before leaders can work effectively with risk, the necessary skills can be developed in a business school environment.

Firstly, what are we talking about? We're using the word 'risk' when we add hypotheses about the consequences of actions to our (knowledge-based) concept of uncertainty. So when considering risk in leadership terms, we are evaluating the actions leaders may take to reduce or manage uncertainty, and the consequences of those actions. But we discover that the notion of risk is a complex one: the word can be used as a verb, as a noun, as a process, as a result, as a science and even as a way of life. When thinking of how individuals approach risk, it's often seen as having a binary quality. For some it has negative connotations, being seen as a danger; for others, it is a positive opportunity. Whatever a leader's view of risk, we could argue that it will be involved in almost all the dilemmas and decisions that he or she faces. How a leader frames the risks associated with his or her decisions or dilemmas is often key to how he or she deals with them. It must follow then that management development must help managers to manage risk. But what constitutes a risk for a particular person? Here we must introduce the concept of values, of ethics, of what is perceived as acceptable in the pursuit of personal and organisational goals.

This chapter outlines the Right Risk Model, which leaders can use to think about how to frame dilemmas involving risk. We also describe the research that paved the way for this concept. And we conclude with a discussion on how we might bring risk into the classroom, to help leaders experience, reflect and learn.

But before all that, let us examine why it is important to learn about working with risk.

Some background

In 2012, research was conducted (West et al., 2014) to examine *how* organisational leaders work with risk. We knew that leaders were interested in the topic, but they told us that what business schools offered was insufficient to help them deal with the dilemmas they encountered daily.

For example, a CEO of a large NHS trust hospital in London said: "If you want to make progress, because you can't control everything, you need to be aware of risk… [R]isk is the core skill of leadership".

There is plenty of business literature on the subject of risk. Attempts to quantify risk were made as early as 1685 by Bernouilli (1685) and Blaise Pascal (Ross,

2004). However, there is relatively little research on the practicalities of how leaders work with risk on a day-to-day basis.

There seems to be a paradox here. Many leaders say that risk management is a key part of their job. Yet in most of today's organisations, risk is the domain of the finance department, overseen by a risk committee consisting mainly of non-executive directors – or a specialised risk department. It may be delegated to special processes and documentation – risk assessments and risk registers. Or even outsourced to specialist organisations – insurers, regulators – sometimes supported by sophisticated mathematical models.

Advice for leaders seems to collude with a need for simplicity and certainty in order to 'drive out risk'. In reality, risk is a complex phenomenon which appears to defy definition. Though many attempts have been made, a clear definition of risk which captures its complexity remains elusive. The problem with definitions for complex concepts like risk is that they are in danger of saying all and nothing at the same time, touching on specific aspects of risk but perhaps unable to capture how the concept of risk resonates with managers working with risk every day.

Ethical aspects of risk

During our study, we noted that many of the senior executives we interviewed felt that, in the daily risk-related decisions they take, they are guided by their personal values. For example, the CEO of the NHS trust mentioned earlier articulated his priorities as a combination of the absolute pre-eminence of patient safety, combined with a commitment to change things for the better. He gave a particular example of a high-risk decision to discontinue a contract with a local supplier – politically a very unpopular decision, potentially with negative personal consequences for the executive. However, he stood by his decision, regardless of political pragmatism, because he was convinced that this supplier was adding risk to patient safety, and therefore to terminate the relationship was the right and ethical thing to do.

The management of risk is at the heart of banking practice and the financial services industry uses a scientific model to do this. In 2008, the Financial Services Authority (FSA) in the UK had developed a highly sophisticated computer-based model for assessing and measuring risk. It is now generally accepted that this model failed to anticipate the banking crisis – or in other words, it failed to manage the risk effectively. But some commentators argue that the real failure was the questionable nature of the underpinning values prevalent in the industry, combined with a lack of challenge to the widespread risk-taking practices which were regarded as acceptable by many working in the sector.

In his book *The End of Ethics – and a Way Back*, Malloch (2013) lists a number of ethical failures in the financial services industry, both before and after the crisis. He quotes a speech given by Kevin Rudd, the Australian Prime Minister, titled 'The children of Gordon Gekko':

> Beneath the financial jargon and dramatic stock market events, the sub-prime crisis has also reflected a fundamental failure of values. We have seen the triumph of greed over integrity; the triumph of speculation over value creation; the triumph of the short-term over the long-term sustainable growth…

The 'ethical shortcomings' that appear to have contributed at least in part to the banking crisis don't seem to have stopped. They have continued to happen in guises such as LIBOR rate fixing, money laundering and tax avoidance, to name but a few. The ongoing failings in financial services and other sectors seem to confirm there is a bigger issue than just having a big sophisticated computer system for managing risk.

The disastrous consequences of the global recession for countries and businesses demand that we find a new paradigm for dealing with ethical issues. To protect national economies and to ensure that businesses thrive within them, we must acknowledge that ethics is increasingly on the agenda for business, and thus for business leaders, and thus for business schools. Research conducted by CarringtonCrisp, a research company specialising in business education (2013) found that clients of business schools saw the most important role of business schools was to "develop business leaders with strong ethical behaviours".

So, the attitude and approach that leaders take to risk can relate to their personal values and approach to ethics. It's a key issue which was identified in *The Tone from the Top* (Muir, 2013), which reported research conducted in 2013 with the chairmen of thirty UK organisations. The research inquired into how boards provide ethical leadership to their organisations. This report develops the idea that boards can set ethical tone by their own behaviour, and by how they signal ethical priorities: for example, in what kind of person is either recruited, or promoted, or by how information is shared. The report links this back to organisational risk, arguing that a board's approach to ethical issues has a direct bearing on 'ethical risk', which is effectively the 'reputational risk' of non-ethical behaviour among managers.

Our research approach

There is relatively little in the literature about how leaders actually work with risk on a day-to-day basis. The research described in this chapter goes some way to addressing that void. It builds on the earlier report discussed above, through conducting semi-structured interviews with managers, and asking the research question: "How do senior managers think about and work with risk?"

Thirty-four managers participated in the study. They were risk specialists and/ or organisational leaders from a comprehensive range of industry sectors, including healthcare, finance, law, manufacturing, technology, housing, insurance and IT.

The interviews had five sections:

- You and your role

- How you think about risk, in principle

- How you work with risk, in practice

- What stories do you have about working with risk, both good and bad?

- What better would look like (in terms of thinking about and working with risk)?

All interviews were transcribed and analysed to identify common themes. From these themes, it was possible to identify the different ways that risk is dealt with in principle and in practice, as well as the challenges these bring. The implications for managers in general were developed following this analysis.

The two dimensions of risk: formal and informal

A key finding from the research supports an argument put forward by Preston Cline in a fascinating paper, *The Etymology of Risk* (Cline, 2004). In essence, the idea is that there is no consistent definition of risk. As a concept, it is unstable and its meaning has evolved over time. Historically, it is shrouded in mythology, associated with philosophy and religion – "the domain of the gods". At one point, the character of the risk-taker was considered more important than the outcome. Taking risk was often considered a virtue and associated with courage. Only in more recent times has the avoidance of risk, encapsulated in the word 'prudence', also been seen as a virtue. The concept seems to be two-sided, with one side statistical and the other based on personal principles and belief.

Our research picked up on this duality by identifying polarised approaches to risk which we summarised as 'formal risk' and 'informal risk'. Formal risk calls on processes which are objective and evidence based. Informal risk draws on intuition and experience. Both can work independently of each other, or they can overlap and inform one another.

Through discussion with our interviewees, we identified metaphors to encapsulate each of these types. One of our respondents talked about two teams that worked in parallel to achieve the effective global launch of a new product and technology. He referred to one team as the 'Elephants': wise, methodical, with long memories, creating momentum but slow. These were the formal risk workers who assessed risk using objective, quantifiable and evidence-based outputs. Often working in response to regulation (compliance, governance, legal, industry standardisation), their focus was on high visual sharpness, accuracy and timeliness in an attempt to reduce subjectivity.

The other team were the 'Tigers': fast, intuitive, flexible, creative but erratic – the informal risk workers. The emphasis was on breadth and was multi-dimensional, making use of wide channels of information, employing intangible and subjective processes. Informal risk workers used peripheral vision to scan the environment and to provide space for generating hypotheses. Sometimes referred to as instinct, gut feel or common sense, this requires an inherent ability to consider what is at stake by looking for threat or identifying opportunity. There is no one single focus of informal risk: we heard managers use the phrases 'three dimensional', 'entrepreneurial', 'holistic' and 'peripheral vision' when describing how informal risk perceivers scan their environment.

> We needed to manage the speed and still have control and manage the risk. We used the approach called 'Tigers and Elephants'. You can have one tiger in the one forest and he can manage, but if you have too many tigers, it will be chaos. We need elephants to deliver good basic policies and structure. But when you need to get something done fast or make something that is creative, then you need a tiger. The connotations for both words are good: the elephants are big, they are strong and they are long-timers with experience, wisdom and long memories. The tigers are flexible and driven by speed; they are hunters who deliver quickly and decisively.
>
> (Interviewee quote)

The research identified that both approaches comes with psychological traps, based on illusions. With formal risks, the illusion is that risk management is 'parked' with experts, or in formal processes or committees, and is thus somehow dealt with. On the other hand, informal risk is often covered by intuitive judgment calls by managers, often reflecting biases they may have from past experience, with limited objective evaluation. Much of the research on the psychological aspects of risk suggests that our individual risk-taking or risk-averse propensities are influenced by a wide range of factors, but are rarely rational.

Our hypothesis is that leaders and their organisations can tend to get stuck in one mode or the other. But neither is necessarily the right mode in which to operate.

The Right Risk Model

When we consider our two risk modes, the formal 'Elephant' mode and the informal 'Tiger' mode, we are in danger of colluding with framing the issue in this binary way, implying that our approach to risk can be one or the other, depending on preference. We know that organisational culture is often heavily influenced by its risk preference, which often comes from the leadership of the organisation. But we also know that when it comes to addressing dilemmas that involve risk, to get risk management 'right', we need to look at more than a personal or cultural preference. We need a 'rightness' dimension.

It is not always right to avoid risk for formal reasons; nor is it always right to take risk for informal reasons. One of the better-known exponents of ancient 'ethical' psychological thinking was Aristotle. He used as one of his concepts, courage, which represented the 'right' amount of risk, suggesting that too much risk was 'reckless' and too little was 'cowardly'. If we map this dimension onto our formal–informal continuum, we can create a two-by-two matrix, with one axis representing formal–informal approaches to risk and the other the 'rightness' of the risk (see Figure 1).

To meet the needs of our modern age of calculated probabilistic risk assessment, the model can be further extended. If we consider the diagonal aspects of our two-by-two, we can hypothesise four ways of evaluating dilemmas which involve different levels of risk. In looking at binary options (which a dilemma by definition involves), where one of the options is perceived to be of higher risk than the other, consider the diagonals of the model (the A diagonal and the B diagonal in Figure 1). The question to ask is whether the dilemma is represented more by the A diagonal or the B diagonal.

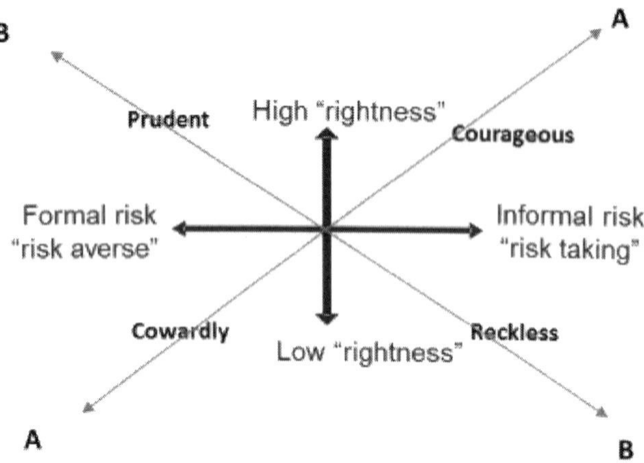

Figure 1 – Dimensions of Risk Taking

Let's try to expand our earlier animal metaphors to include this second dimension. We need a 'non-right' risk taker and a 'non-right' risk avoider. However, we accept that the idea of an unethical animal is a curious concept and ask you, the reader, to suspend your disbelief!

As regards a not-right risk taker, we need a 'reckless' animal. There are few of these, as most animal behaviour is determined by self-preservation. However, there is a species known as the Honey Badger which apparently has no fear of anything: it attacks and eats all kinds of animals including poisonous snakes, and in particular, because of its love of honey, will attack bee hives and get severely stung. It has tough loose skin and is not easily put off by bites and stings; but apparently, honey badgers occasionally overdo it and are stung to death. So the Honey Badger is our symbol of recklessness, of 'not-right' informal risk taking.

And we also need an overly cautious, risk-averse animal. We need a coward. After much debate, we have awarded this role to the "timorous wee" mouse. We also replace our diagonals with a compass needle image, to illustrate our desire to define direction in the face of risk and uncertainty.

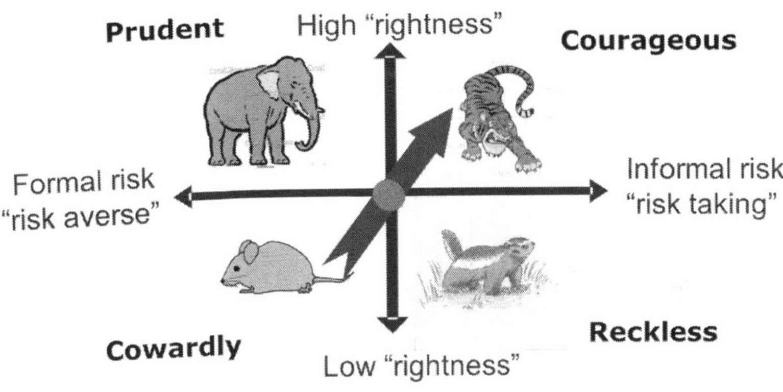

Figure 2 – Characterising the Dimensions

So, a manager facing a dilemma involving risk must question whether the issue is best approached through the Tiger or the Elephant option. The manager must also challenge himself on which approach his personal preference will steer him towards. This helps him or her to deal with the dilemma by diffusing, or at least acknowledging, any personal pre-disposition to either risk-taking or risk-avoidance, or formal versus informal risk, whichever may be closer to normal organisational or personal behaviour. The framework can provide a useful tool, as long as managers learn how to use it to manage risk optimally. We must consider how best to do that.

Let's look at a couple of examples. In the classic ethical case study 'Heinz steals the drug', from Lawrence Kohlberg's 'Stages of moral development' (Kohlberg, 1981), Heinz is a poor man whose wife is critically ill. He cannot afford to buy the drug she needs to make her well, so instead he steals it. Was he right to do this? He was faced with a dilemma which is shrouded with risk, but which also has an ethical dimension. How we frame the dilemma can lead in different directions. If we consider the right thing to do for Heinz is to steal the drug to make his wife well, then the risk is that he gets caught and goes to prison. However, the consequence of improved health for the wife is considered 'right' and the consequence of imprisonment is irrelevant. Once framed like this, the 'compass' points to the courageous Tiger, and away from the low-risk approach, that of the timorous Mouse, as shown in Figure 2. Thus, the decision is based on what the decider considers to be right, not on the level of risk involved.

On the other hand, let's look at the situation facing decision makers in banks in the period preceding the financial crisis. The potential prize of huge monetary gain for a few might have been seen to be worth high-risk, courageous and even reckless decisions. However, incorporating the 'rightness' dimension and projecting the potentially disastrous consequences of the global recession on the worlds' economies might have resulted in more prudent decisions being taken.

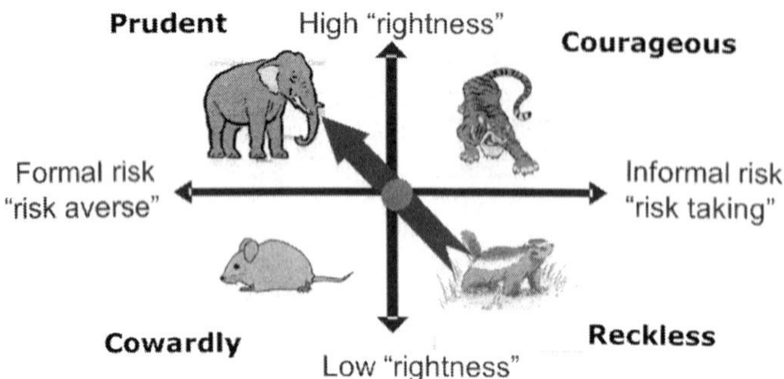

Figure 3 – The Compass Points to Prudence

As is often the case, this model doesn't necessarily give us answers, it just helps us to understand the questions in a different way. What we are doing is trying to take a potential propensity to a 'stuck' approach to risk out of the equation when considering what the right thing to do is. We think organisations need both Tigers and Elephants, and we think that managers need to be able to operate as both, depending on what the context requires. As a general rule, they need to be more like Tigers at some times and Elephants at others. And they need to try to avoid being Mice and Honey Badgers – neither are renowned for their leadership skills!

Bringing risk into learning

Asking the question "How do leaders work with risk?" begs the question "How do leaders learn how to work with risk?"

An executive education programme provides a number of opportunities for considering how to handle risk at an intellectual, 'thinking' level. We explore with participants the way financial risk can be assessed by broadening their understanding of financial reporting. We look at how management and governance processes work to manage risk, to take logical decisions which account for the risks involved, to take steps to mitigate risk or to develop contingency plans in the event of adverse outcomes. However, we find that even though much of this process theory is well documented and seems reasonably well learned, leaders often make important decisions without recourse to these processes which help them to evaluate risk explicitly.

We see this most significantly in discussions about strategy. This might seem unsurprising given that strategies, by definition, address an unknown future in which risk is implicit. Yet in our experience, risk is often an afterthought when top teams get together to discuss strategy. It's mentioned in passing, but rarely evaluated. If there is a strategic plan, evaluation of risk, if covered at all, is covered as an appendix or a sub-heading towards the end of the plan. And then, as is often the case, it is described as something which is 'taken care of' and is somehow delegated away to the appropriate management or governance process. It colludes with the idea that we can have processes which effectively drive out risk.

We suspect that one of the reasons for this is that most, if not all, members of some senior teams do not actually understand what risk is. Or rather, they do not have a common understanding. When senior leaders are asked what they understand risk to be, and whether this understanding was shared with their colleagues, a diversity of opinion is revealed. Some leaders describe risk in terms of dealing with danger, others as opportunity. Some see it as minimising the likelihood of an adverse outcome, others cite variability, with equivalent upside and downside potential. This latter view is the one typically promoted by the corporate finance world.

We believe that business schools must help managers and leaders to develop a common language and understanding of risk, particularly in the context of developing strategy. There is a gaping hole in the capabilities of top teams, not only to talk about risks in a mutually understandable way, but also to address misconceptions about the whole area of the measurable variability of possible outcomes (one possible definition of risk). Teams can benefit from coaching in understanding randomness and probability – decisions would probably be quite different with this understanding. Some risks may not be as risky as they appear to be; other decisions may actually be more risky than they appear. Developing an understanding of strategic risk is part of the solution to this issue. The way we do this, by improving the concepts and models that we teach, and the way that we experiment with and reflect on them, addresses to some extent what we call the 'formal' approach to risk. But this does little to address the 'informal' – the intuitive and sometimes emotion-based decision-making processes which can fly in the face of any kind of rational risk approach, and which are a critical aspect of managing risk effectively.

Those involved in the holistic development of managers and leaders must help their participants to understand both the formal and informal aspects of risk, and to use that understanding to make skilful choices in their working lives. The challenge is well acknowledged by the management development industry. In traditional teaching environments, away from the buzz of everyday working life, how do we replicate the real risks that leaders face, in the relatively safe environment of the classroom? The ideas of risk and safety seem contradictory. Conceptualising risk for learning purposes appears to have an anaesthetising impact on our actual experience of it. We may think our way through a case study involving risk in an abstract way, using suitable models to help us; but the emotional aspect of risk is generally missing in a safe environment. Virtually nothing we do or say in a classroom setting will put the company finances at risk, nor the health of our stakeholders, nor our own careers. To some extent, this is exactly why the classroom is designed to be a safe environment – it's confidential, it's safe. "What happens in the room stays in the room."

Indeed, the unique selling proposition for away-from-the-workplace learning is that it is a safe environment in which to experiment, in which to take some risks that participants wouldn't normally take in the workplace. These risks can be about exploring and articulating new ideas to colleagues, about having conversations that they wouldn't normally have, about interacting with others in a way that may not feel comfortable. So for some aspects of working with risk, the classroom offers an advantage, even if it may feel a little artificial or clinical.

But paradoxically, we are creating safety to work with risk. How can this be authentic?

We have successfully worked around this dilemma in our management-development practice by using simulations that generate the emotion of risk. These take the form either of team-based competitive decision making in a computerised market-place simulation over a series of rounds, or of working through specific artificial challenges working with professional actors, whose role it is to re-create some of the emotion of difficult, risky situations. Participants have also been asked to wear heart-rate monitors over one or two days, as they work together to resolve simulated problems which may be creating tensions between individuals. Participants are encouraged to experiment with roles which are different from those they would normally have, and with types of interventions which they would typically not employ. Their emotional responses are monitored and measured.

These programmes demonstrate that they can have a significant residual learning impact – meaning that this learning manifests itself after, not during, the experience of the programme. Participants start to apply certain aspects of what they have experimented with on the programme back at work and they are encouraged, post programme, to reflect and to continue learning from these reflections. They effectively build on the risk that they have already taken during the programme by applying the experiment in a real work environment. There is effectively a physiological stress memory, reflected in the heart-rate print-out, which gets replayed in the workplace. This has been called the development of emotional muscle memory, in the same way that a tennis player only really learns how to hit an effective tennis shot when he does it automatically without having to think about it (i.e. when he has developed muscle memory).

We believe that the simulations of the emotions associated with risk help participants to develop skill in the management of informal risk by allowing them to experience the emotions and the intuitions associated with them, to reflect and then to transfer that muscle memory to the workplace.

How might the Right Risk Model help managers and leaders learn about how to manage risk?

The Right Risk Model encourages leaders to consider that, while some risk may be useful, taking the risky option will not always be right; likewise, taking the low-risk option. When it's right and it's courageous, it's the 'Tiger' choice. When it's not right, it's the reckless 'Honey Badger' choice. Sometimes a more prudent, managed-risk 'Elephant' approach is what is needed. But you need to challenge yourself to be sure you are not employing the timid 'Mouse' approach.

So, how can managers determine the rightness of which approach to take? Or more specifically, where to locate their decision on the right–non-right axis? We suggest there are three key factors to take into consideration: logic, strategy and values.

- Firstly, does the risky option defy logic? Does the proposed solution to a dilemma seem irrational? Does the solution seem to come from a gut feeling, or a desire to experiment, or to have fun? Without wanting to diminish the importance of having fun, these kinds of risks can backfire. And whatever the outcome, they are unlikely to contribute meaningfully to either learning or dilemma solution if they are unlikely to be relevant to the workplace. So a risk that conflicted with logic, where a logical choice is available, could be reckless.

- Another guiding principle is strategy. The author has seen 'strategy' used most effectively to turn down higher-risk creative options at a multinational FMCG company where each brand had its own strategy statement. Where an agency presents the storyboard for a new creative piece of advertising, the first question the brand manager asks himself is: "Is this advertising consistent with the strategy?" If the answer is "No", it is rejected regardless of how good, humorous or creative the story. This can feel risky – there being a risk of undermining the relationship with the agency which has invested significantly in the idea being presented. In this instance, the brand manager is usually encouraged to take the courageous Tiger option.

- The third area that influences choice around risk is that of values. Values help to make the case for or against taking a risk. For example, a risky choice that might offend someone else may not be the right choice if it conflicts with a personal value that holds causing offence to be wrong. Sometimes values can, of course, argue for the taking of a risk. The risk may be whistle blowing, or coming to the support of someone in a group experiencing difficulty with intergroup relationships. It is obvious that when using values as a determinant of 'right risk' those values will differ between individuals, organisations and even national cultures. A real strength of a model such as the Right Risk framework is as a starting point for a productive conversation – for example, in a leadership team setting out to explore how different values in the group might impact on situations or dilemmas involving risk

Conclusion

Doing the right thing often means taking a risk, but taking a risk is not always right. Leaders need to manage personal and organisational risk in making decisions effectively when faced with strategic and ethical dilemmas.

Understanding risk is core to effective leadership, and to being able to work with difficult decisions, which we call dilemmas, particularly where doing what is 'right' requires some judgement.

Executive education must offer a place for leaders to explore these things. We can offer concepts which help develop meaning, through the way such dilemmas are framed. These concepts need credibility – the research and the model offered here help to provide that. They need to be memorable and engaging – we prioritise that.

And for true learning to take place, we actually need to experience risk, to reflect and learn from it, emotionally and intuitively. Business schools can shape participants' experiences in such a way that they can do this in a 'safe' environment and leverage the paradox that safety is essential for learning to manage risk.

References

Bernouilli, J. (1685) Some questions about interest, with a solution of a problem about games of chance. *Journal des Savants*.

CarringtonCrisp (2013) *See the Future 2013* (London: Carrington Crisp).

Cline, P.B. (2004) *The Etymology of Risk* (Portsmouth: Harvard).

Kohlberg, L. (1981) *The Philosophy of Moral Development: Moral Stages and the Idea of Justice.* Essays on Moral Development, Vol. 1.

Malloch, T.R. (2013) *The End of Ethics – and a Way Back* (London: Wiley).

Muir, I. (2013) *The Tone from the Top* (London: Ashridge Business School).

Ross, J. (2004) *Pascal's Legacy.* European Molecular Biology Organisation (EMBO) reports.

West, T., MacAlister, J., Mookherjee, D., & Brown, M. (2014) *Working with Risk: In practice and in principle: Lessons from the Field* (London: Ashridge Business School).

CHAPTER 10

Sustainable Development and the Changing Role of Business Leaders on the World Stage:

What Does this Mean for Executive Education and Leadership Development?

Matthew Gitsham, Ashridge Business School

A quiet change has been slowly progressing over the past decade: without attracting much attention, there has been a fundamental shift in the scope of the role business leaders are required to play for their businesses to survive and thrive in today's turbulent, uncertain and volatile times.

A new 'shared value' approach to purpose and strategy

Ever since Michael Porter and Mark Kramer published their seminal article on creating shared value in the *Harvard Business Review* in 2011 (Porter & Kramer, 2011), more and more organisations have been formulating goals In terms of the problems and needs they will help to address in society. Rather than articulating goals solely in terms of the financial value that will be created for shareholders, they have been instead defining goals in terms of the value they will create for their end consumers and wider stakeholders, which will allow them to create value for shareholders in the process. Perhaps the most famous example is the Unilever Sustainable Living Plan. Unilever's corporate strategy announced in 2010 that, in order to meet its aim to double the size of its business in ten years, it would focus on strategic goals including helping a billion people improve their hygiene, bringing safe drinking water to 500 million, and halving the greenhouse-gas impact of their products across their lifecycle.

More and more similar examples have appeared: Philips' strategic goal to improve the lives of 3bn people a year by 2025; GE's mission to build, move, power and cure the world; GSK's goal to improve the quality of human life by enabling people to do more, feel better and live longer. In 2014, Novozymes launched a new corporate strategy, 'Partnering for Impact', aiming to grow sales organically by 10 per cent by 2020 by catalysing public–private partnerships on sustainable agriculture and energy, and helping customers save 100m tonnes of CO_2 a year through using Novozymes products. While still only a minority, the number of companies framing their purpose and future activities in term of 'shared and sustainable value' is growing fast.

Two fundamental shifts in the business context

Although these kinds of strategic goals are a relatively recent phenomenon, what we're seeing is the outcome of two much longer-term trends.

On the one hand, we have seen the rise of complex interconnected global challenges that span national borders and require more than just action by national governments to tackle. A quick glance at the annual *Global Risks* reports produced in recent years by the World Economic Forum (World Economic Forum, 2015) highlights interconnected challenges including fiscal crises, unemployment and underemployment, severe income disparity, chronic disease, pandemics, malnutrition (both under- and over-nutrition), water stress, biodiversity loss, climate change, social and political instability, failing states, corruption and geopolitical conflict – ultimately all global governance failures. Global strategies to tackle these interconnected challenges are increasingly organised under the heading 'sustainable development' – organising human society and activity in such a ways as to enable people to meet their needs and lead fulfilling lives with dignity, at the same time as respecting planetary boundaries and enabling future generations to meet their own needs.

At the same time, there has been a radical shift in perceptions regarding which institutions in the world must play a role in responding to these kinds of challenge. In the 1970s and 1980s, the prevailing view was that governments and their leaders dealt with society's challenges. For business leaders, what it took to survive and thrive was to keep their eyes squarely focused on short-term profit. Broader societal issues were seen as none of their business – to get involved would only add cost and be a distraction. Forty years on, much has changed. A more globally integrated private sector has become increasingly influential on the world stage. In 1970, the world's biggest economic entities were all countries, but now, with globalisation, a sizeable number of them are global private companies (Global Trends, 2013). Now there is a widespread view that most of today's big interconnected global challenges are almost impossible for governments to address on their own, and that a much wider group of players needs to be at the table.

It is these two fundamental shifts that have been driving a shift in CEOs' thinking about fundamental business models and strategy. The 1980s saw business adopt the model of 'maximising shareholder value' as a way of fixing some of the problems of poor profitability in the 1970s (Dobbin & Jung, 2010). But as business leaders have seen first-hand, the weaknesses of this model became clearer in the past few years and many have begun experimenting with alternatives, like Michael Porter's 'creating shared value' model (Porter & Kramer, 2011). More and more business leaders are coming to the view that to survive and thrive in today's world they must develop strategies that focus primarily on creating value for their wider stakeholders to ensure they generate return for shareholders in the medium and long term as well as the next quarter.

All these shifts have had some pretty fundamental implications for the kind of leadership role senior executives are now finding themselves having to play.

A more collaborative leadership role at the heart of society

It can be argued that this greater economic influence of globally integrated businesses has thrust business, and therefore business leaders, into a far more overtly 'political' kind of role on the world stage.

There have been many business leaders over the past decade or so who failed to recognise how these forces had started to change the nature of their role. The consequences of this lack of vision landed them and their companies in trouble. Examples include former Nike CEO Phil Knight trying to defend sweatshop labour, former GSK CEO Jean-Pierre Garnier leading the pharma industry in suing Nelson Mandela's government over access to medicines, or Google CEO Eric Schmidt trying to defend tax avoidance. These leaders did not recognise how the balance of power, and hence perceptions of responsibility between government and business, has shifted and what that means for how they need to play their role.

But in the past few years, more and more business leaders are embracing this new scoping of the senior executive's role. Some leading examples include:

- Unilever CEO Paul Polman sitting on a UN High Level Panel with presidents, prime ministers and the UN Secretary General to help shape the UN Sustainable Development Goals.

- Kingfisher CEO Ian Cheshire chairing the UK Corporate Leaders Group on Climate Change, lobbying for stronger government policy on the low-carbon economy.

- Sainsbury's CEO Justin King speaking out on tax avoidance, challenging his peers in other industries to contribute a fair rate of tax in the countries where they benefit from investments in infrastructure and communities.

- GSK CEO Andrew Witty partnering with NGO Save the Children on innovation in child-friendly medicines and reinvesting 20 per cent of profits made in the world's least-developed countries back into projects which strengthen health-care infrastructure in those countries, primarily through training community health workers.

Playing this new kind of leadership role well is not some kind of personal vanity project. It has emerged in response to fundamental shifts in global geopolitics – and the ability for business leaders to play this role well has increasingly become a key variable in the success or failure of both their organisations and wider society. A vanguard of today's CEOs is now playing this role well. Others still need to learn, and learn fast.

What's required to be able to play this new role well?

A programme of research around the leadership skills needed to respond to these changes has been undertaken over the last few years. Using in-depth interviews, the researchers have talked to some of the CEOs who've been at the forefront of this trend – people like Paul Polman, CEO of Unilever; Neville Isdell, former Chairman & CEO of the Coca Cola Company; Paul Walsh, CEO of Diageo; John Brock, Chairman & CEO of Coca Cola Enterprises; Lord Browne, former CEO of BP; Sir Mark Moody Stuart, former Chairman of Shell and Anglo American; Peter Brabeck, Chairman of Nestlé; John Fallon, CEO of Pearson; Frederick Chavalit Tsao, Chairman of IMC Pan Asia Alliance Group; Carolyn McCall, CEO of EasyJet; and Mark Foster, former Group Chief Executive, Accenture. They have been asked to talk about how, in their experience, the role of a business leader is different now from in the past.

Analysis of the interviews shows that they believe the key differences can be grouped into three key themes: context, complexity and connectedness.

Context: understanding the strategic implications of societal trends and developing a broader view on the role of business leaders in society

What is clear from the leaders' experiences is that it is essential that business leaders today have a nuanced understanding of the major societal forces shaping the world and a genuine personal passion for running a profitable business by serving the interests of wider society; and that helping address societal challenges through their core business is the primary means by which they create value. This is a completely different view on the role of a business leader compared with the norm of a generation ago. Creating shared value is no longer seen as source of cost but of sustainability, and is at the very heart of their job description.

Mark Foster, former Group Chief Executive at Accenture, summed up how his thinking about his role had changed like this:

> The journey I'd been on was first of all an understanding that there was a world out there above and beyond the piece of

business you're in. The second thing is then a movement from business challenges to global challenges. And then you move into asking: "What's the role we're playing in participating in those challenges?" And then, "What can we do about it?" As a business, both in terms of the business opportunity and secondly, the broader ethical engagement with the world and what you see around you.

(Gitsham et al., 2012)

John Brock, Chairman and CEO of Coca Cola Enterprises argued:

In today's world I don't think you have a choice. If you're going to be an effective leader you've really got to be driving all aspects of sustainability as part of what you're doing, because it's the right thing to do and because it's the right thing to do for the business… If you're not personally persuaded then you've got a little bit of an issue, and maybe there are some people in that category, in which case I think leading – in some hypocritical sense – is quite hard to do. It helps a lot if you've got the personal passion and commitment.

(Gitsham et al., 2012)

Sir Stuart Rose, former CEO and Executive Chairman of Marks & Spencer, spoke about the significance of the changing balance of governments and companies:

The 100 largest financial entities in the world used to be governments. Now over 50 of them are businesses, so suddenly the whole scale in the world has changed, and businesses have become much more important than they used to be.

(Rose, 2012)

For Sir Stuart, the commercial implications of this and the case for acting differently were clear:

In 2007 I said Plan A wouldn't make any profit in the first five years. In the 2010 annual report, £50million of extra profit was attributable to doing the right thing. So there's the proof. Any chief executive that says: "I can't afford to do it, I haven't got the people, it's all too expensive, the consumers don't want it, they haven't asked me for it, it's the wrong thing to do and it's going to cost me money" is wrong, wrong, wrong, wrong and wrong.

(Gitsham et al., 2012)

The senior executives interviewed were also clear that doing this well means getting involved in activities that require a different skill set. Senior executives are now playing very specific roles in leading innovation and change within their own organisations. In addition, in order to drive the execution of shared value strategies, they're also now playing a much more significant leadership role in wider society too.

Complexity: a leader's role in leading change in organisations

For companies to pursue strategies that are primarily focused on creating 'shared value' in society means more than setting different kinds of strategic goals. It requires substantial changes in organisational culture. Organisations don't change because one individual says so; they are complex communities of relationships in which people's decisions and actions are guided by multiple influences. The chief executives in the study talked of seeing their own role in influencing change in their organisations in terms of opening up the space for others to behave differently. This meant clear articulation of new goals and the rationales they developed for pursuing them. It meant changing the stories and people they celebrated, the conversations they started, the questions they asked, what they were seen to spend their own time doing, and which individuals and groups got recognised and rewarded and for what.

Paul Walsh, CEO of Diageo, talked about the significance of the questions he asked in leading change:

> It's interesting how word gets around. I'm a great believer that if I want to focus the organization on X I just walk round the organization and I ask about X. And the word gets out.

(Gitsham et al., 2012)

For Mark Foster, the significance of how he was seen to spend his time was important:

> I would try and give a week a year to Accenture Development Partnerships for them to send me somewhere and engage with their programmes, as a very clear signal to the organisation that I thought this mattered.

> (Gitsham et al., 2012)

Carolyn McCall talked about the CEO's role in empowering more junior employees to play leadership roles in change, and challenging more senior leaders not to discourage them:

> I got younger people involved, I got champions in each of the divisions, and they started driving things rather than the more senior leaders. All I said to the senior leaders was "What I need is for you not to be an obstacle." I wanted them not to be blockers. I wanted them to also not roll their eyes, because a lot of it is body language.

> (Gitsham et al., 2012)

Lord Browne argued that to sustain the right kind of behaviours, people had to know that they would receive some kind of recognition, whether that be financial reward, a promotion, or just a sense of wellbeing that comes from being highly regarded by their peers:

> The biggest thing about getting anything done in an organisation of course is to really get to the point where everyone in the organisation owns the objective as if it's their own, and they recognise that by achieving the objective something good will happen to them. And these statements are as old as the hills but you must never ever forget them.

> (Gitsham et al., 2012)

Connectedness: a leader's role in leading change in wider society

A number of the interviewees also identified an important change in the scope of their work. More and more, they now see their role as leading beyond the traditional boundaries of their organisation. They believe they must proactively lead change in consumer and supplier behaviour, industry norms and government policy, for the benefit of both their organisations and wider society. Some are leading collaboratively with industry competitors, NGOs and governments where only collective, systemic solutions will do.

These new horizons for their role require leaders to demonstrate skills in areas that historically have not been a conventional part of the business leader's repertoire. Not only increased breadth is required in contributing to public debate with an informed point of view, proactively leading change in consumer and supplier behaviour, industry norms and government policy. Depth is also needed in relating well with multiple constituencies, engaging in dialogue to understand and empathise with groups and communities with perspectives contrary to one's own, and engaging in multi-stakeholder collaboration with unconventional partners.

John Brock, Chairman and CEO of Coca Cola Enterprises talked about the change like this:

> I think the role of a business leader today is much more challenging because you've got so many other constituencies out there that you didn't have before. Certainly the hierarchical approach – let's just lead from the top and if other people don't like it, that's their problem – that does not work anymore. You've got to engage with these multiple constituencies and make decisions in a more consensual way. And that requires a real skill. As the leading drinks manufacturer in several countries, and as a major player in the industry itself, we believe we have an important leadership role to try to figure out how to bring government, NGOs and industry all along. We as a company will invest a huge amount of time. And not just me, our whole leadership team.

(Gitsham, 2012)

What does this mean for talent management, executive education and leadership development?

Getting this new leadership role right has become key to whether an organisation (and wider society too, for that matter) survives and thrives in today's turbulent, uncertain and volatile times. But the extent to which organisations actually have leaders that can do this well (or not) has really, so far, been more to do with luck, rather than design. As Paul Polman notes, few of today's generation of business leaders have been trained for this:

> I don't think our fiduciary duty is to put shareholders first. I say the opposite. What we firmly believe is that if we focus our company on improving the lives of the world's citizens and come up with genuine sustainable solutions, we are more in sync with consumers and society and ultimately this will result in good shareholder returns… It is an enormous learning curve as no-one has been trained for this…

> (Confino, 2012)

So, this new generation of business leaders has started to recognise that their organisations need to take a more systematic approach to the selection and development of the groups of people who will be handed the responsibility of executive decision making. Their organisations need deliberately to build the right kind of culture, with the right kind of leadership capability to be able to survive and thrive in this new context.

For a start, it is clear that today's business leaders need a much more thorough literacy in global issues and their business implications. They also need the motivation and commitment to put taking action on these issues at the heart of their work, as well as needing a different level of relational skill to lead change inside and beyond their organisations. But how do you achieve this? How come some business leaders get it and others don't?

What can we learn about how to develop this new skill set from today's pioneering business leaders?

We asked some of these leaders for their perspectives on how it was that they and some of their peers had grasped the need to lead in this kind of way while many of their other contemporaries were still operating from an out-of-date leadership blueprint.

While each individual's story was unique, the clear theme was that certain key first-hand experiences had been crucial in influencing and shifting perspectives. For some it was formative experiences around upbringing, university and business-school study. For others, it was influential mentors or first-hand experiences like engaging with people living in poverty, personal experience of challenges like water stress or the impacts of climate change, or personal first-hand experiences of the changing interests of key stakeholders.

Neville Isdell, the former CEO of the Coca Cola Company and an influential sociology professor, talked of his activism as a student and his training as a social worker in Cape Town's Cape Flats shanty towns. He described how the polarised atmosphere of 1960s South Africa was a potent influence that shaped the positions he took as a CEO on issues like human rights, climate change and water scarcity:

> I majored in sociology at university in South Africa and I qualified as a social worker. I was also involved in student politics and I stood for the Student Council on an anti-apartheid ticket. So I started out with a frame of reference which was a little different from your average business leader.
>
> (Gitsham et al., 2012)

Mark Foster talked about how Accenture's International Chair, Vernon Ellis, had influenced him:

> I became interested in these topics by being exposed to others who were fairly passionate about it. They made you think about things you hadn't previously thought about.
>
> (Gitsham et al., 2012)

Paul Walsh talked about the powerful impact of being exposed to the realities of people's daily lives in water-stressed parts of the world where Diageo does business:

> I remember opening a borehole project in Lagos, in one of the terrible slum areas, and seeing these children flick water at each other. It was almost as if they were playing with a Christmas gift. It was incredible. Just flicking it in each other's face and giggling.
>
> (Gitsham et al., 2012)

John Browne at BP argued that one of the key influences that shaped his thinking on human rights and climate change in the late 1990s and early 2000s was a specific class he had taken at Stanford Business School more than 15 years earlier:

> I think it is right to say that all these thoughts were put in my head when I went to Stanford – in 1980 I took a programme by Professor George Leland Bach on managing the total enterprise. I remember a case study on a company, Hooker Chemical, dumping toxic waste and then they built a bunch of schools and houses on top of it, and all the children got sick.
>
> (Gitsham et al., 2012)

The message seems clear – the development of leadership is influenced by powerful and meaningful learning experiences that speak in some way to individual values.

What can we learn from today's pioneering learning and development teams?

In a parallel programme of research, pioneering learning and development teams at leading organisations have been asked to explain what they have been learning from innovations in their leadership development work.

It is remarkable that the experiences of pioneering L&D professionals at companies like HSBC, IBM, EY, IMC Pan Asia Alliance, Interface, Lend Lease and Sky all point to similar conclusions. As with the stories from the senior business leaders, it was clear that general awareness raising about global challenges and new approaches to business was critically important. What seems crucial is first-hand experience: first-hand experiences of key global challenges and organisations working effectively to tackle them, as well as first-hand exposure to changing stakeholder expectations and senior business leaders who care about these global challenges and can articulate their business relevance.

However, it is essential to note that the results from the research suggest such first-hand experiences are a necessary but not sufficient condition for effective learning to take place. Successful leadership development interventions must combine first-hand experiential learning with four other vital ingredients:

- Opportunities that enable participants to relate these experiences back to the business (for example, through business-focused strategic projects)

- Direct senior management involvement in these learning programmes

- Excellent facilitation again to help with participant sense-making

- Structured ongoing support for participants after their learning experiences once they are back in their day-to-day roles.

The research examined the learning interventions offered by the businesses and found that some of the most impactful leadership development innovations combined experiential learning with strategic business project-based learning. For example, HSBC worked with Earthwatch to develop the Climate Champions programme where managers spent two weeks on a learning programme based at a climate-research station. During the day participants worked alongside climate scientists collecting data on the impacts of climate change, while evenings were spent with learning facilitators sense-making and relating these experiences back to the core business of HSBC. After the two-week experience, participants then spent a year on related strategic projects back in the business, illustrating that the strength of the learning intervention was not solely centred on the out-of-office experience.

IBM's Corporate Service Corps leadership programme involved a one-month immersion project in an emerging market supporting a non-governmental organisation or local government organisation working on social challenges, similarly combining first-hand exposure to social challenges with business-related project-based learning.

IMC Pan-Asia Alliance developed a two-week experiential leadership development programme in partnership with the Hong Kong-based Global Institute for Tomorrow which took a cohort of the organisation's high-potential future leaders to spend a week on one of the company's own palm-oil plantations in Indonesia. Over the course of the programme, participants engaged first hand with some of the social and environmental challenges involved in producing palm oil and were tasked with the project challenge of developing a strategy for the business consistent with the principles of sustainable development.

Broadcaster Sky created a leadership development programme in partnership with WWF which involved high-potential future leaders in business-focused project-based experiential learning in the state of Acre in the Amazon region of Brazil.

In all these cases, pioneers within these companies were trying to help respond to the challenge of building new leadership capabilities by combining unique learning experiences to open up new perspectives, with the capacity to deal with everyday business realities. As a project sponsor at IMC put it:

> The primary objective is to instil and educate the next generation of leadership about how the world is changing and what that means for the way we want to run our business… There are three elements of our leadership model that are very important to us. Firstly, we want leaders who have an open mind and a world view, who can see some of the changes going on in the world. Secondly, we want leaders who are able – after being able to see – leaders who are able and willing to make a change. And thirdly we need leaders who have the skill to be able to lead that change.

> (Gitsham et al., 2013)

Similarly, a key project sponsor at Sky told us:

> I think for people in general senior leadership positions, the objective is just to send a signal to say "Actually this stuff about sustainability matters. You should take it seriously. We will hold you to it if you don't take it seriously." The leadership development programmes are a good space for having the conversations about why this is important and why we're doing what we're doing as a business. It's

not that every single senior manager should be a deep expert in sustainability. The fact is, though, they need to realise why and how it's really important to the success of the business.

(Gitsham et al., 2013)

And a regional coordinator for the HSBC programme talked about creating the mind-set where senior executives at the organisation understood the logic of what the organisation was trying to achieve through its sustainable development policies:

> Take the example of someone working in our credit-risk programme. There are many people from this kind of role coming on the Climate Champion programme. These people are saying 'yes' or 'no' on lending decisions. These people have to make decisions paying attention to our policies around responsible lending. Coming on the Climate Champion programme is a really hands-on experience which helps them understand why we have these policies. They have to make these decisions anyway because of the policy, but the experience of the programme helps them understand the logic of what they're being asked to do.

(Malnick & Gitsham, 2010)

Across all the examples, the power of first-hand experience was cited as key to the impact of these leadership development interventions. One participant in the HSBC programme argued that the experiential nature of the learning was a key factor in transforming abstract general awareness into something much more powerfully felt and known:

> The whole sustainability and environmental awareness piece starts right in your own back yard… we can all read this stuff in the press, but the hands on stuff is the hook.

(Gitsham et al., 2013)

A participant from IBM whose programme took them to Nigeria made a similar argument:

> We all know about things like poverty in Africa and corruption and bribery, and how hard life can be, but it's really interesting to feel it, or feel something of it, it's really powerful, in terms of appreciating

just how hard life can be for people. This kind of experience really brings what we already know – from the news and TV – and other things to life, you really feel it.

(Gitsham et al., 2013)

The same participant gave examples of some specific moments that had contributed to this for him, talking about experiencing absence of adequate health care, and corruption around illegal logging:

There was a boy who'd been hurt in a playground, and he'd been taken to the clinic, but they refused to do anything until the people who brought him came back with the equivalent of £7, even though he had blood coming out of his head.

(Gitsham et al., 2013)

Corruption, oh my goodness. When you see the rainforest under such pressure. The field office had no power, they had no vehicle to patrol, and it's very difficult for them to do their job. At one point there was a truck carrying logs that came past the office out of the forest, and it was escorted by none other than the military, and you think, well there must have been some payment. And you think, how can they get through this? How can they possibly do their job? It's so hard for us to appreciate here.

(Gitsham et al., 2013)

Two participants on the Sky programme shared similar sentiments:

Now that I've been there, I mean once you've had an experience like that, you can't change that, and you can't take it away. You would have to be so cold-hearted to go to a place like that and meet those people and spend time in those communities… and it not make an impact on you. You come away with a more visceral understanding.

(Gitsham et al., 2013)

I think it was the immersive nature of the experience… We were actually going into the jungle and visiting these communities and talking with them through translators. It's only then that you really start understanding the challenges… For me it was these personal relationships. A conversation with a guy, he probably can't read but being able to hear his personal story, you really start to understand… meeting face to face with the actual producers – the real learning came from this personal connection.

(Gitsham et al., 2013)

Two participants on the IMC talked in particular about the impact of these kinds of direct personal connections that had been created through experiential learning:

I look differently because, to be very honest with you, before this programme I always looked at the workers on the plantation as workers. Now I look at them as a colleague, someone that their future, their wellbeing, is actually in the hands of the organisation, and so in this manner is actually one of my responsibilities as a director.

(Gitsham et al., 2013)

Before this, to me these people were just numbers on an HR spreadsheet. Now I've been in their home, seen their kids running around, those kids could have been my kids. I'm aware of them as human beings now.

(Gitsham et al., 2013)

A common theme among participants was that these kind of leadership development experiences spoke powerfully to personal values, and had strengthened the motivation and commitment to lead differently. One participant from Sky noted:

It's really intensified my focus on the green agenda, and I feel like it's put an additional burden of responsibility on my shoulders, made me feel I need to make a difference and apply this within Sky, and how can I influence Sky to make it better. It's not like I'm someone who didn't care about the green agenda and this experience influenced me so that now I am. But before it was a nice green and community thing. Now, it's driven me into thinking about how I can really influence within the business.

(Gitsham et al., 2013)

And another from IMC told us:

> After the two weeks of the programme I more firmly believe what I believe. Before the programme, I paid attention to this, but I was pretty passive, I didn't really do anything. But the programme helped me become more firm about it, it helped me look at the issue from a different angle, it made me more competent and more determined. The programme made me aware I can contribute in this way.
>
> (Gitsham et al., 2013)

Many participants talked about an additional developmental perspective – about the power of these experiences enabling them to act as more effective vocal champions and advocates for a new way of thinking and acting in their organisations. One participant from IBM noted, for example:

> I think the ability to be able to speak from direct experience has made a big difference to being able to speak with confidence – I can tell the story of what I saw with my own eyes happening.
>
> (Gitsham et al., 2013)

This US-based HSBC participant makes a similar point:

> Partnering with the Smithsonian was a real plus. It's a really prominent institution in the US that is held in some reverence… My perspective on the fieldwork is that… its real value is that it gives a sense of credibility when talking about the experience later, when being – for example – able to talk about the science behind the arguments. So if I'm having conversations with older people, or people in a position of influence, or if I'm talking to younger people – for example, my children, who are college age. For both groups, when you say you spent a week studying climate change at the Smithsonian's field-research station, it makes for a different conversation… It gives you a different kind of credibility.
>
> (Gitsham et al., 2013)

A participant on the Sky programme argued:

> Does it change my everyday behaviour? In all honesty, probably not. But am I a better advocate of any organisation trying to make a difference? Absolutely… I've also been raising awareness with all the various people I work with across different teams, because it's easy to be flippant, and you get some people who question why we're doing this, and why it's important… So I guess I'm talking about it more, and if it comes up in conversation then I'm challenging people, or trying to help them see from a different view, if they're not so convinced this is important.

> (Gitsham et al., 2013)

Again the power of the first-hand experience is key, as the participant from Sky continued:

> There's something about having been there: you've had this unique experience, you understand things at a much more granular level, through your personal experience, and it gives you a different kind of authority when you're in that conversation and putting across your perspective.

> (Gitsham et al., 2013)

Selecting and developing today's and tomorrow's senior executives

These stories have important implications for how organisations think about talent management and executive education. They suggest that more is required than just briefings and lectures on global trends and their commercial implications. It seems that relationships and first-hand experiences are at the heart of what it takes for business leaders to build the emotional connection and commitment required to put this agenda at the front and in the centre of their work. However, it is unlikely to be sufficient simply to offer frameworks and models within which to develop effective interpersonal relationships. Therefore, in order to foster the right kind of leadership capability in organisations, a more radical approach is needed. In partnerships with learning and development professionals, business schools must begin to:

1. Understand the role of life experiences in effective learning and work creatively in partnership with HR and L&D professionals to integrate them in development and succession-planning interventions.

If personal, first-hand experience, such as engaging with people living in poverty, hands on knowledge of real water stress or the impacts of climate change, is key in stimulating the required kind of business leadership for the current era, then these kinds of experiences need to be planned, offered and facilitated. It appears that these are not simply 'nice-to-haves' that develop a more rounded individual but, because of the crucial contribution they make to developing a worldview, relational ability and organisational culture are now essential for organisations to survive and thrive.

This will require new skills on the part of learning and HR professionals and those in the management-development industry. When recruiting, for example, instead of selecting in an organisation's own image by hiring based on what worked in the past, this new understanding means deliberately looking for something and someone different, who has experienced and learnt out of the norm. New metrics and new measures of success will be needed.

2. Embed the opportunities to have these kinds of experiences in leadership development and executive education.

Our research with organisations like IBM, HSBC, Lend Lease, IMC Group and others (Gitsham et al., 2013) suggests that more and more organisations are structuring their leadership-development activities to create opportunities for their current and future senior leader to have precisely these kinds of personal, first-hand experiences, and make sense of them through business-focused strategic projects. To achieve this, they are employing powerful experiential learning that:

- Gives senior executives the opportunity actually to develop relationships with people experiencing some of the world's most pressing challenges, and also with the people working to help address these challenges.

- Gives them the opportunity to engage with new ideas to help make sense of the demands of the new business context. Concepts such as ecology, complexity, systems thinking and social constructionism are all of relevance. It is important, however, to offer facilitated support to help individuals understand how these ideas link with business realities and language through new concepts of 'shared value', 'brand substance', 'closed loop manufacturing' and 'integrated reporting'.

- Supports them to make their own sense of these experiences through expert facilitation by helping individuals to relate them to their organisational roles. Techniques that are valuable here include action learning, challenging strategic projects and exposure to individuals in their own organisations already modelling this way of leading.

- Develops and articulates executives' own authentically held views on the purpose of their work, and the value it creates for wider society, through meaningful reflection.

- Ensures that learning is supported and that organisations allow leadership to be different once participants return to their day jobs.

In summary

Feike Sijbesma, CEO of Dutch multi-national DSM, has made it his catchphrase to assert that "You can't call yourself a successful business leader in a failing world". Today's world is changing, and this is changing the role of business leaders and therefore also what is required of their leadership development. When designing development interventions, off-the-shelf solutions will no longer do. Unique and seminal experiences, elsewhere in this book described as 'crucible' experiences, must be created, offered and invested in, to bring about the sea change required in the leadership of those who must take their organisations forward to deal with ever more complicated, interrelated and acute challenges.

References

Confino, J. (2012) Unilever's Paul Polman: Challenging the status quo. *Guardian Sustainable Business*, 24 April, available from: http://www.theguardian.com/sustainable-business/paul-polman-unilever-sustainable-living-plan.

Dobbin, F., & Jung, J. (2010) The misapplication of Mr Michael Jensen: how agency theory brought down the economy and why it might again. *Research in the Sociology of Organizations*, Vol. 30B, pp.29–64.

Gitsham, M. (2012) The Changing Role of Global Leaders. *Harvard Business Review Insight Center*, 14 February, available from: http://blogs.hbr.org/2012/02/what-it-takes-now-to-lead-a-bu/.

Gitsham, M., et al. (2012) *Leadership in a Rapidly Changing World* (Ashridge and IBLF).

Gitsham, M., et al. (2013) *Building Leadership Capability for a Rapidly Changing World* (Ashridge).

Global Trends (2013) *Corporate Clout 2013: Time for Responsible Capitalism* (Global Trends).

Malnick, T., & Gitsham, M. (2010) *External HCP Earthwatch Learning Evaluation Final Report* (Ashridge).

Porter, M., & Kramer, M. (2011) Creating Shared Value: Redefining capitalism and the role of the corporation in society. *Harvard Business Review*, January 2011, Vol. 89, Issue 1/2, pp.62–77.

Rose, S. (2012) Sir Stuart Rose on the changing role of business leaders. *Guardian Sustainable Business*, 29 March, available from: http://www.theguardian.com/sustainable-business/sir-stuart-rose-changing-role-business-leaders.

World Economic Forum (2015) *Global Risks 2015* (Geneva:World Economic Forum).

CHAPTER 11

Exploring the Craft of Artful Knowing in Leadership and Organisation Development

Chris Nichols

Introduction

I hope this chapter will be a good read, and a provocative one too, because I'd like you to enjoy it enough to do something as a result of reading it. It's a practitioner chapter – I run workshops about the leadership we need for the creation of sustainable ways of living and working in the world. In this chapter, I want to show you how working artfully makes this work rich and powerful. I say 'show' deliberately – I don't think I can 'tell' you how it is. So the chapter is based around artful working and includes details of where you can see some film of the work in action because some of it just can't be put into writing.

It takes the view that we should all of us – practitioners, consultants, leaders – take extended epistemology seriously. By extended epistemology, I mean all the diverse and rich ways of knowing that are commonly overlooked in traditional organisational work and leadership: this might include drawing and painting, sculpture and making, story and poetry, music and sound-making and bodywork, and potentially much more.

The chapter is based around two stories:

- First, the story of an actual workshop that used a lot of artful knowing in its design and approach.

- Second, a fictional story of an encounter with a legendary craftsman. It takes the wisdom of craft seriously and applies the insights from the craftsman story in terms of its application to our work in organisational and leadership learning and development.

In this chapter, I suggest that the situations we all find ourselves in today call on us to see more deeply and richly than commonplace ways of working allow. It then goes on to consider the implications of this for how we think about management and organisational development and learning and development interventions in organisations, and how we frame our work as practitioners in such work and as buyers of it.

The chapter looks like this:

- The story of a weekend workshop on a cosmological window on leadership that relied heavily on 'artful knowing'

- A discussion of that workshop to draw out some reflections on why artful knowing matters

- 'The Craftsman': my short story, which uses an artful form (narrative) to explore some of the issues in developing the skill of artful practice, and in being an artful practitioner

- My reflections on my story.

I hope that by joining me in thinking about these issues through these two stories and my reflections on them, you will step into artful work yourself, or step in more deeply. And that if you are a buyer or a consumer of management development work or consulting in any way, you will come to look on artful forms of working as more than team-building, skill-building or ice-breaking activities. You will hopefully come away from engaging with this chapter with your own reflections on what artful practice is and why it matters – and hopefully much more as well.

Part 1 – Making the universe story personal: a weekend using artful knowing

I co-direct an MSc in Sustainability and Responsibility (Marshall et al., 2011), a two-year part-time postgraduate degree based on action research. I like to define action research quite simply as a way of being rigorous about learning from exploring and experimenting with others for worthwhile human ends.

I love my work on the Sustainability MSc because it is something that matters deeply: it is designed to develop leaders that the world needs desperately. These are leaders who are able to address the enormity of the planetary issues we now face. Almost all of our major life-support systems are strained. While much attention is paid to the climate change debate, the work of Johan Rockstrom and the Stockholm Resilience Centre (Steffan et al., 2015) shows compelling evidence that out of the nine inter-connected global processes that influence the liveability of this planet, four have already crossed the consensus danger points and risk catastrophic human-induced change (see Box 1)

BOX 1 – THE STOCKHOLM RESILIENCE CENTRE: PLANETARY BOUNDARIES

In 2009, an international team led by the Stockholm Resilience Centre published pioneering work that examined the nine processes and systems that regulate the stability and resilience of life on earth. The analytical work has been extended and a new version of the work published in *Science* in January–February 2015, which featured in a presentation at the Davos World Economic Forum meetings.

The nine planetary boundaries are:

1. Climate change

2. Change in biosphere integrity (biodiversity loss and species extinction)

3. Stratospheric ozone depletion

4. Ocean acidification

5. Biogeochemical flows (phosphorus and nitrogen cycles)

6. Land-system change (for example, deforestation)

7. Freshwater use

8. Atmospheric aerosol loading (microscopic particles in the atmosphere that affect climate and living organisms), and

9. Introduction of novel entities (e.g. organic pollutants, radioactive materials, nanomaterials and micro-plastics).

The researchers conclude that four of these nine boundaries have now been crossed. These are: climate change, loss of biosphere integrity, land-system use and altered biogeochemical cycles.

The paper retains a strand of optimism. The silver lining is that the work suggests a research-led definition of 'safe operating limits' to guide integrated policy frameworks for future economic and social activity consistent with maintaining life within the capacity of these inter-related planetary systems and processes.

More about this work can be found at: http://www.stockholmresilience.org/21/research/research-programmes/planetary-boundaries.html.

The good news is that Rockstrom's work also points to systems interventions that could maintain the integrity of our 'safe operating limits' in the biosphere; but it will take the right will and leadership to bring these about. The problem isn't therefore a lack of science about our inter-connected planetary crises, but a lack of attention to the changing role of organisations in addressing what to do in response. The challenge facing leaders in all forms of organisation – businesses, NGOs and governments – is immense.

In my experience, many leaders 'get it': from their own scanning of current affairs, they know what the science is telling us. Many, even most, leaders also want to do something actively and positively to address the challenges. But almost all of them run into the brick wall of trying to bring about change in organisations that are themselves deeply part of the problem we are all trying to address; indeed, we are all part of the problem together. That is the nature of the complex, super-wicked problem that we face in trying to act sustainably and responsibly in organisations that are constructed not to give heed to the very issues that are most central to our strategic future as a society and as a species.

So, very often, even the best leaders shut down, close their eyes and press on, putting sustainability into a technical unit, doing compliance work, taking the least-bad course – and effectively changing nothing. To make this possible, these leaders might adopt a different personality at work than at home: being a permaculture allotment gardener at the weekend; whilst building the world's largest coal-fired power plant in the week, trying to grow cigarettes sales in Africa or finding new ways to get more people to get into more cars.

So, I am always looking for ways to make deeper and more personal connections between people and the planet on which we live. At the heart of our difficulties is the myth of separateness: the belief that we humans, we business leaders, are in some way separate from the rest of the living system that we are working within – a theme rigorously explored by Giles Hutchins (2014). And it is exactly this myth of separateness that the Universe Story (Swimme & Berry, 1994) is so powerful in addressing.

This is why we gathered a group of twelve experienced and diverse practitioners at Hawkwood College* to explore our personal connection to the Universe Story and to imagine how we might each use it to strengthen our work.

It is worth saying a few words about what I mean by the Universe Story. We live in a miraculous time, where the science of astronomy and astrophysics is telling us more and more about the deep origins of our universe, our solar system and the place of our planet in the wider story of everything. We now have a robust scientific understanding of how our planet was formed and when, and how this relates to the wider cosmos. At the same time, we live on an earth that has been robbed of its creation stories one by one. As the supremacy of everything rational has grown, our capacity to believe our own stories of creation and connection has fallen away.

The Universe Story tells a scientifically robust story of how everything in our world came about and is connected: from the Big Bang almost 14 billion years ago, through the formation of galaxies including the Milky Way, to the Supernova explosion from which heavier elements arose, to the formation of our own solar system including the Earth, to the first emergence of bacterial life, through to the emerge of mammalian life, including humans. It is our shared story, shared indisputably with each other and with everything. Awareness of this story has the potential to allow us to transcend other creation stories, whilst still acknowledging and respecting them, and provides a tangible, credible story of the origins of the universe, stars, planets and life, that provides a narrative within which all other narratives sit.

---

* Hawkwood college, near Stroud, UK, webpage: www.hawkwoodcollege.co.uk

But stating the science is not the same as living a story. And this is where artful knowing comes in. If we are to work with the Universe Story as inhabitants and as practitioners, in L&D and OD, helping others to explore and work with the story, we need to experience it more fully than merely being aware of the science. So our workshop allowed for richer and more diverse ways of knowing and experiencing the story.

During the weekend, we spent time drinking in the story and letting it flow through us in as many ways as possible. These included:

- Walking the timeline: we walked a measured kilometre walk, in which every one hundred metres represents one billion years. We started a little way back from the Big Bang, in the time of the unknown, the unformed nothing before the universe. As we walked to the point of the Big Bang, someone in the group read out words about that stage of the story. We repeated this at each major development in the story as we walked the timeline.

- Embodying: at each major stage we also used body sculpture and improvisation to play out the group's embodied sense of 'being the Universe' at that stage and moment. In movement and sounds, we played out being the Universe at the moment of the Big Bang, in the process of galaxy formation and as life emerged on earth.

- Retelling the story in the first person: later, back in the workroom, we took time to retell the story of the walk, but this time in words, speaking in the first person, speaking 'as the Universe' becoming itself, noticing the different story and the feelings and images associated with each stage of the story.

- Grounded creativity of the story in music: we then used a spontaneous musical process that we call 'grounded creativity' (see video at www. groundedcreativity.com) to experience the story as a piece of music created spontaneously and collaboratively – the story of the Universe as a wave of sound.

- Responding in image and writing: we gave time for people in the group to respond to their experience of the story in words and pictures, writing free-fall stories, making collages, drawing – whatever was needed for their own exploration.

Some extracts of the writing and images are included in Figure 1. But it is in the nature of this work to resist description in words: as Isadora Duncan once said when asked to explain a dance, she replied "If I could explain it to you, I wouldn't need to dance it'"[*]. So it is with this work.

Image One: Examples of artful inquiry produced during the "Cosmology, Ecology and Action" workshop

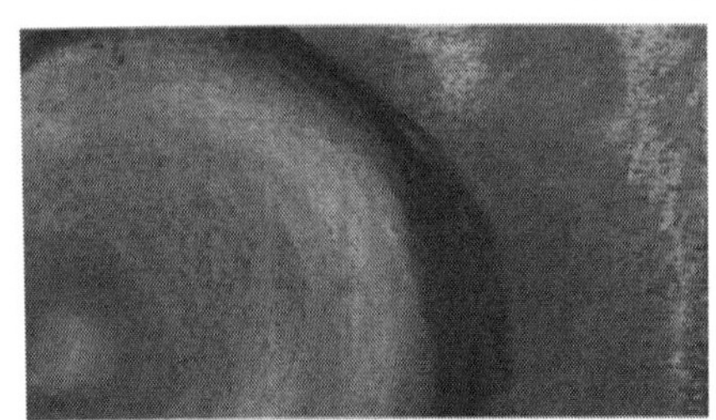

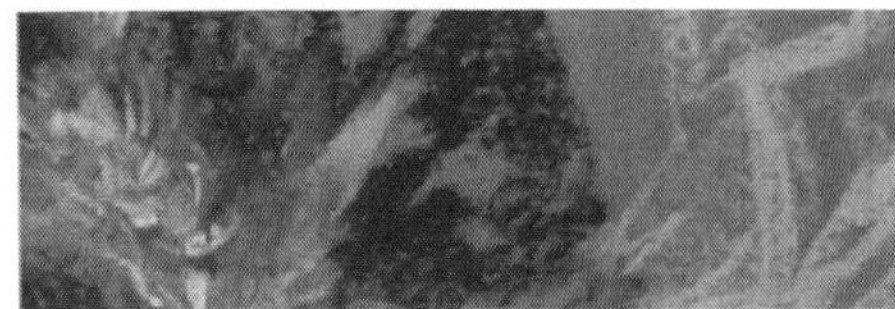

The surest way into the Universe
is through a forest clearing,
or through a smile,
in the fleeting kiss of a breeze
and
through the sound of rain,
or by your touch.

Lying at anchor,
five miles offshore: the night
alive with light, I meet
The Universe in my own breath
and heartbeat.

A very
local pulsar
echoing my part in this
single wave of energy
Forever dancing into new forms

Weavers and woven,
In one story

Poem written by Chris Nichols,
Extracts from artwork created by workshop participants
Hawkwood, January 31st 2015

To allow you to get closer to the work, we have created some films and soundtracks to accompany this article that can be located on the Internet.[†] These will provide a more complete insight into the work, although the point of the work is to experience the work itself.

Artful knowing stands at the heart of our MSc in Sustainability and Responsibility, as an essential and integral way of knowing. It is not an alternative to commonplace and conventional knowing, and it is not simply an ice-breaker or a team-building exercise, nor an illustration of ideas known in other ways. It is a legitimate way of knowing in itself.

Artful knowing embraces all expressive forms of art, including but not limited to stories, poems and other writing; drawing, painting and sculpture; music making, movement, drama, clowning, improvisation and more. In the literature of action research there is a strong tradition of legitimising 'extended epistemologies' – diverse and richer ways of knowing and seeing through modes of being that are generally excluded from academic knowing.

---

[*]   Sourced from the Cambridge University Contemporary Dance Workshop webpage at: http://www.societies.cam.ac.uk/dance/contemporarydance.htm
[†]   A short film of the Cosmos, Ecology and Action workshop is available on Vimeo at: https://vimeo.com/120239001.

Our contention is that the wholly rational, linear, analytical language of business and organisation is simply insufficient to address the challenges we face as leaders, as a society and as a species, and that accessing richer and broader insights from extended epistemologies (artful knowing) is essential if we are to address these issues fully and well.

The story of our cosmology workshop discussed above shows the following core practices in action.

Core practices of artful knowing

Sensuous encountering: We spend so much of our leadership and organisational lives in our heads that there is real value in making sure we pay attention to the data of our senses. Gestalt psychology asks you to 'lose your mind and come to your senses'. Part of the work of artful knowing is to become aware of the richer data from all around us. Stepping into the experience of being a living part of a messy creative planet is a vital part of the work. Intellectualising before experiencing guarantees a 'separation from' the messy living reality: we need leaders to step in to action with all their senses alert.

Suspending or 'holding our intellectual and rational breath': To allow the sensory experience to do its work, we must give it some time and space. Part of the work of artful knowing is to create experiences and exercises that temporarily derail the ever-present brainy mode of organisation and leadership. This is essential if we are to stop the rush from experience directly into expertise and problem solving based on old frames and existing ways of seeing. Suspending is a crucial stage in learning to appreciate what is going on before you leap in to fix it!

'Bodying forth': This means both paying attention to what our body is saying and doing in response to the previous two elements, and using our body to make sense of what we are encountering and experiencing. Throughout the cosmos work, we used bodily sensation as data and our bodies as ways of exploring and expressing – by movement, by sound and by using our bodies to draw or make music. All of these ways of knowing are normally shunned, indeed supressed, in organisational life. In our usual ways of being we legitimise only the brain and words expressed in a small range of organisationally legitimate codes of speaking and writing.

Being 'in-formed': This is a way of being that comes about when we allow our being to be informed by the messy, sensuous, embodied experiences of the other stages.

For me in my practice there is something rich and vital about respecting each of these stages in the design and facilitation of management and organisational development work, just as it was in the cosmos story workshop. Out of such richer and diverse work comes the opportunity to go beyond our common-space brain-only workings of the organisational world. There is a depth and a freshness that comes from experiencing something deeply, in the senses and in the body, that feeds the potential for profound learning – even more so if that experience is used to make visible the usually unstated assumptions and frames of the organisation, context or situation. It is my experience that the more deeply we allow our richly sensed and embodied experience to inform our questioning of the given frame, and to feed our creative re-framing of things, the bolder and more fruitful our work is likely to be.

In the case of our cosmology workshop, participants reported deep learning from the physical activity (the walk and the bodywork), from the art making, from the freefall writing and the music making. People in the group reported having a "renewed sense of connection" with the living planet and with the wider cosmic story, and felt inspired to bring this work into their practice using more and richer ways of interacting with teams. Some of the learning was of a profound spiritual nature, and some was very practical, about ways of exploring a subject with a team, of using multiple ways of knowing to making assumptions visible and to respond creatively to them. This is important because, whilst artful knowing is capable of producing spiritual insights, it is also a very practical and necessary way of working – bringing into the light sources of data and insight usually left invisible and untapped.

This section has drawn significantly on research by my colleagues Dr Chris Seeley and Ellen Thornhill. Seeley and Thornhill created a 'Manifesto for Artful Organisations', which I have reproduced in full here.

BOX 2 – A MANIFESTO FOR ARTFUL ORGANISATIONS

Artful organisations:

Cultivate knowing in many ways, in our hearts and guts as well as our minds and intellects

Allow people to cultivate their own imaginations and creative responses

Dare to challenge the deep underlying assumptions shaping how organisations act, artfully constructing new realities

Are courageous in showing vulnerability and unknowing

Expect, encourage and support their people in cultivating their own artful practices as a way of belonging and living

Welcome and value messy, inarticulate, heartfelt responses and explorations

Develop the courage to have fierce conversations

Dare to be guided by what is elegant and beautiful more than that which is efficient and expedient

Allow, expect and encourage people to dwell in and reflect on experience before making decisions

Value lived experience and practical knowing

Encourage multiple forms of expression, not just talking and writing

Operate more from the generative basis of love than the reactivity of fear

Will work persistently with artful knowing to provoke, question, disrupt and deepen thinking in preference to entertaining, decorating and soothing.

The 'Manifesto…' is, in my view, a necessary and bold proposition. For a fuller account of what artful knowing is and why it matters, see Seeley and Thornhill (2014).

How do you develop the practice and the skill to work in this way? Since there are few people working fully with artful knowing in organisational roles at present, it seems necessary to draw our insights from a parallel world. This is where I turn again to artful knowing, in my short story, 'The Craftsman'. It's based on a conversation I imagined having some time ago, with legendary craftsman and fine-furniture maker James Krenov (1920–2009). Krenov was a woodworker who wrote about the philosophy and practice of craft as a way of life, and taught at colleges and universities around the world. He established a school of woodworking in California which still operates today[*] and he inspired makers and thinkers about craft through his books. Although my story is fictional, it is based around quotes from one of James Krenov's books, *A Cabinetmaker's Notebook* (1991).

Part 2 – 'The Craftsman': A short fictional conversation with James Krenov, master craftsman

"Why do you do this work James?" I ask.

Late afternoon light filters through the summerhouse blind. James' eyebrows show he is thinking. I pour tea for myself, and top up James' water.

"I don't have a glib answer" he says. "I know it's not just a job or a profession, it's a very intimate thing… something matters to me in the relationship between the wood and my feelings, my intuition, my dreams."

"I think that's the same for me, when I'm working well", I offer. "At the best of times there is a real flow, almost a loss of myself, just being there."

James nods, understanding this, I sense.

"It's really important to find ways of working that lead to a sort of harmony" James says. "When you work in this way you are saying that this is the way you want to live, you are working in a way that you are prepared to live by."

I get what James is saying right away. Sitting up, I lean towards him. "And that's my difficulty", I say. "Sometimes I find myself doing work that doesn't have that harmony, it's not the way I want to live."

"Well", James nods, "for almost all of us at the outset, and maybe always, it's a condition of struggle and secret satisfactions. Sometimes you are not making anything like the money you need – but what keeps you going is that you are alive with your work, with the enjoyment of being with it."

I struggle a little with the implications of this. I think James is saying that you stick it out, just doing the work that makes sense to you, not taking on ill-judged, ill-fitting projects. "Isn't this a bit idealistic?" I say.

---

[*]   Krenov webpage: www.jameskrenov.com.

"There can be a vicious circle – you might become alarmed and saddened, even humiliated, by the inability to make ends meet. At this point something happens to many of us… a small compromise leads to another small compromise, and finally we end up doing something that we do not really love. It's a sneaky thing."

James seems to be speaking directly to my feelings about much of business life. I am about to speak when he continues…

"A craftsman lives in a condition where the size of his public is almost in inverse proportion to the quality of his work. He gives people something very personal: not very much of it, but very personal."

I am slowly nodding all the time as he speaks. This artist in wood has built his life and work around an idea that is slowly dawning for me – that if my work is valuable in the way I mean it to be, I need to do less. Not less by some exact quantity, but never more than allows me to pay full attention to it, and never doing work that lies on the slope that leads to compromise and work I don't love.

After a minute or two of quiet, James turns his gaze back from the garden, glimpsed through the window blind. He's worried that I've now gone off on some romantic notion about craft being all spiritual purity, and doing only the thing you love.

"Remember, this can be heavy work. People come and say, 'Well here you are! How does it feel to be an artist, to be doing artist's work?' Now, that's naïve, because I spend long hours moving those heavy planks all alone, working in the machine room. Maybe I'll have to work three or four days with very great discipline and concentration before I can finally do the fine sensitive side of the work. But first I have to discipline myself to do this other work."

That is interesting. It speaks directly to the parts of the work I dislike. I take a clear message from this – and it is a valuable realisation. That even with the projects I hand pick, with clients I really want to work with, I have to attend to parts of the work I like less: that these parts are integral to the craft. I share this with James, and he asks for an example – he is unfamiliar with the organisational world.

I explain how even though our work is explicit in its emphasis on a lack of prescription, on emergence and co-creation, very often we find ourselves in the bind where we are asked to predict specific details to win the work. Our philosophy of working makes this very dubious. Another example would be when a client wants us to work with a particular in-house change model or performance tool, insisting on pre-shaping our partnership. James wonders if this is a bit like craftsmen using drawings and machines, with which he seems to have an uneasy relationship, a combination of doubt and the sometimes necessary.

"I am not much for drawing: I can't say 'here's a working drawing, make the piece according to this.' My pieces are pieced together. All the little details, the way things add up, are unpredictable – or nearly so. It is a fingertip adventure."

This seems helpful to me. It echoes how I try to explain what I do to clients – and sometimes this approach isn't what they want. They want you to make it according to the drawing, exactly. James simply notes that maybe these are not the right clients for a craftsman like him. We work with a lot of uncertainty, he seems to be saying. His clients don't buy an exact reproduction of a drawing or image. They buy his skill in making something of beauty out of a shared idea. They buy his spirit, which he pours into his work. They buy his accumulated experience – it is this that builds the trust that means the uncertainty is not crippling.

James returns to my question about working with clients' 'pet' models – strategic models perhaps or 'The Balanced Scorecard', for example. It takes me a while to explain what this is – James listens, interested at this insight into another world. He sees this as the same challenge he has with power tools.

"Machines are treacherous and the real treachery is elusive. On the one hand they help the cabinetmaker greatly. On the other, they corrupt him. Somewhere between these two ways, there is a sensible and sensitive balance which our craftsman must try to find before it is too late."

He pauses, thinks, sipping his water.

"Each of us alone must determine the balance. Say to the machine, 'You and I have come this far together. Thank you machine and goodbye.' Because I have these beautiful tools. Because with them in my hands I know better what I want to say, and how to say it in my way, not yours."

"Tools?" I say. What distinction is he making between tools and machines? He means hand tools, often made by him, long worked with and loved, known as a friend. I know what he means. My tools are sometimes models, but they are usually handmade – my own or adapted by me. And even more, my tools are my informing perspectives – when I use complexity thinking, or emergence and co-creation, or expressive form, these are not machines with a predicted result. They are at best hand held, sensitive to the 'wood', used with purpose in mind. James echoes this and sees this deep relationship between hand, spirit and tool as a form of shared language.

"We are discovering the language of wood, which is the language of our craft. And just as with the best of our tools, when they become more than tools and turn into instruments of our innermost intentions, so with wood: one discovery leads to another."

The implication of this for developing our practice is profound – whether developing myself or developing others. At my best, this is how I feel. I am not wearing anyone else's clothing – I am not trying a philosophy on for size. In doing learning work as a craft, being centred comes from this spiritual alignment of purpose, way of acting, material and tools. James nods, noticing that this is learned the hard way, through experience, over years.

"The way you use the tools may not be according to the books; rather, it is the way your hands and body move when the work goes well that is the final interpretation of any knowledge. You are training still another part of you, perhaps the most important part of all – the centre which pulls it all together and gives it your meaning."

We sit quietly for a while. The sun is lower, and a wood pigeon is calling in the woods to our left. I sit in silence with James, reflecting on an extract from a poem hanging on his wall, about a woodcarver who made a bell stand so beautiful that people said he must be doing the work of the spirits. But the woodcarver said:

> I am only a workman:
> I have no secret.
> There is only this:
>
> My own collected thought
> Encountered the hidden potential of the wood:
> From this live encounter came the work
> Which you ascribe to the spirits…[*]

---

[*]   Extract from the poem 'The Woodcarver' from Merton (1965), referenced from Krenov (1991).

Taking this story seriously

As I reflect on this story, written in my journal many years ago, I notice how much of it speaks to my core beliefs about artful knowing, inquiry and artful organisations today. It also speaks to how we develop as practitioners, and about what we might aspire to in our practice.

The craftsman's journey is a lifelong one, and so it is with the learning and development profession and with leadership development in organisations. Whilst it is easy to aspire to quick solutions, to scalability, to guaranteed results and ROI, this is an aspiration that belongs to a machine mentality and gives machine solutions. Such solutions have their place – in training and in skill building – but they do not, and cannot, speak to the lifelong craft of becoming a leader or of supporting leaders and organisations in that journey.

The story speaks to me of the importance of blending internal and external awareness and actions, or inner and outer work. The story powerfully reminds us that skill building alone will never be enough to develop people. There is always a dance between the inner and outer arcs of development, and no classroom or on-line course will in itself deliver this dance. What it calls for instead is a practice and a discipline of attending to development as a lifelong 'fingertip adventure', in which the relationship of the maker, the tool and the wood moves and matures and responds to a changing world. I have in mind the wise words of theologian, Meister Eckhart (Fox, 1983): "The outer work will never be puny, if the inner work is great". The challenges we face call for nothing less than the synthesis of inner and outer attention that James Krenov sought to teach in his craft.

I have no doubt that more of this artful craft is needed in management and organisational development work, and indeed everywhere in organisations as we face this time of deep crisis and wonderful opportunity. We need a language big enough to allow us to see our problems differently and to develop responses from deep creativity outside the realm of everyday business language. We are starting to see some signs that globally people are awakening to the need for broader ways of seeing and knowing to address systems change. The mini example in Box 3 gives an example of the Global Bateson Initiative – an international collaboration founded to develop richer ways of knowing.

BOX 3 – BEYOND BIG DATA: TO RICH DATA AND WARM DATA

One of the 'foundational' thinkers about systems and systemic intervention was Gregory Bateson, whose work has influenced many fields from anthropology to cybernetics, systems change to ecology.

His daughter Nora Bateson, writer and film-maker, has made an award-winning documentary about the essential ideas of Gregory Bateson called *An Ecology of Mind*. (More about the film can be found at www.anecologyofmind.com.) Gregory Bateson lived a life fascinated by noticing and working with the patterns in systems and processes, and was a pioneer in seeing that art had a unique contribution to make in seeing and understanding systems.

More recently, Nora Bateson founded the International Bateson Institute, which takes forward this work, creating a field which she calls Transcontextual™ Research – which uses multi-faceted ways of knowing to address big questions in health, education and other systems in society. She calls the resulting data Warm-Data™. More about the IBI can be found on their website at www.internationalbatesoninstitute.org.

This has some similarity in common with the 'rich data' we see in artful knowing. Both approaches yield ways of seeing that go beyond the analytical crunching of 'big data' to produce integrated insights into systems problems and to create insight into new forms of thinking and action.

There is an important message, here. This work can be done by everybody – it is about artful practice, not about 'being an artist' – but it still takes discipline and effort to develop the practice, to develop the ways of seeing and doing that go beyond the lazy shorthand of the commonplace.

This work is risky – it isn't as predictable as using a formula or a template, and the results can vary because life varies. Believing that they need certainty and predictability in the development of their managers, organisations will find this approach challenging, although, I believe, ultimately liberating, catalytic and necessary. Working with these principles offers a journey in identity and purpose and needs practitioners and clients to challenge and confront their uniqueness, as well as their sameness. It is work with vulnerability in it, because it is human work.

There is no conflict between artful work and economics, technology or scale. Artful work can be done using MOOCs, virtual spaces and on large-scale events. The work certainly pays its way – indeed, paying its way is at the heart of the craft – it is about adding value to the client. But this is not work that seeks scale nor does it clamour for profit: it is work that needs to be done skilfully and sensitively at all times, and that is particularly true when it is done using virtual technologies in large projects. As the story says, it is fine to harness the technology to the artful craft; it is never fine to allow scale, speed or technology to undermine the integrity of the work. Learning to manage the balance calls for experience, judgement and the courage to stand your ground as a practitioner and a professional.

In concluding, I want to extend a warm invitation to anyone new to artful working to explore this field further. There is richness here for the quality of work we do and invest in, in all kinds of organisations. But more deeply, this work is valuable to our human spirit; it celebrates more of who we are and who we aspire to be. As Warren Bennis (2009) wrote, becoming a leader is synonymous with becoming yourself. It's that simple – and that difficult. The language of becoming our fully human living selves is not restricted to the everyday language of the business vocabulary. Global and organisational needs call for us to evoke the potential of our creative and vibrant fuller selves in the service of our clients and our organisational managers, who seek new ways of being and behaving. In doing so we make an adventure into artful knowing a leadership necessity to which everyone in the learning and development and organisational development communities, including business schools purporting to develop leaders, must respond.

References

Bennis, W. (2009) *On Becoming a Leader* (PA: Basic Books / Perseus Books Inc.).

Fox, M. (1983) *Meditations with Meister Eckhart* (Santa Fe, NM: Bear & Co).

Hutchins, G. (2014) *The Illusion of Separation* (UK: Floris Books).

Krenov, J. (1991) *A Cabinetmaker's Notebook* (USA: Sterling Publishing Company Inc.).

Marshall, J., Coleman, G., & Reason, P. (2011) *Leadership for Sustainability – An Action Research Approach* (UK: Greenleaf Publishing).

Merton, T. (1965) *The Way of Chuang Tzu* (USA: New Directions Publishing Corporation).

Seeley, C., & Thornhill, E. (2014) *Artful Organisation* (UK: Ashridge).

Steffan, W., et al. (2015) Planetary Boundaries: Guiding Human Development on a Changing Planet. *Science*, 13 February 2015, Vol. 347, No.6223.

Swimme, B., & Berry, T. (1994) *The Universe Story* (NY: Harper Collins).

SECTION 5 –
MAKING IT WORK NOW AND FOR THE FUTURE

Six Principles for an Effective Evaluation Strategy – Getting the Most from Executive Education

Ian Hayward

Introduction

Demand for executive education is unabated yet fewer studies are being published addressing its impact. Investment in executive education, and in leadership and management development in particular, has remained high in recent years even through the recession. It has represented something of a growth industry and is a top priority for many organisations. Estimates put the level of spend globally as high as over £30 billion and a research study addressing this subject in 2011 showed that three-quarters of respondents projected an increased emphasis on leadership development for the future.

When it comes to evidence that this investment is worthwhile and has impact though, the picture is somewhat different. The same energy directed towards evaluating how effective such programmes are, according to a number of commentators, is apparently lacking and has been for some time (see Cascio,

2000, Alimo-Metcalfe and Lawler, 2001, Burgoyne, Hirsh and Williams, 2004, Mabey, C, 2005). The challenge of evaluation is one that has both interested and frustrated management development professionals for many years.

Since the 1990s, there have been a number of research studies examining the link between Human Resource Management practices in general and organisational performance, conducted on both sides of the Atlantic (for example, Huselid, 1995, Gratton, 1999, Guest *et al*, 2000 and 2003, Hutchinson and Purcell, 2003). A landmark research study conducted by Huselid in 1995 examined the link between what he called "high performance work practices" (HPWPs) and organisational performance, as measured by employee turnover, productivity and corporate financial performance in over 1,000 firms. The HPWPs he looked at were:

- Comprehensive recruitment and selection practices

- Incentive compensation and performance management, and

- Employee involvement and training.

Results showed positive evidence that the existence of these HPWPs brought about increased organisational performance. Taking the research into HRM practices overall, most conclusions have been reasonably positive in terms of the link between high-quality HRM and increased organisational performance but there have been fewer studies published that have successfully isolated the contribution of specific HRM practices, including the provision of executive education.

What seems to be lacking is a body of literature reflecting small-scale evaluations of executive education in specific organisations. In the UK, public-sector studies have been undertaken and some results published, particularly for leadership development in the NHS (for example, Alimo-Metcalfe & Lawler, 2001; Edmonstone & Western, 2002; Blackler & Kennedy, 2004; Boaden, 2006). A number of meta analyses, integrating data and analysis from across a number of separate evaluation studies, have also been undertaken (for example, Burke & Day, 1986; Burgoyne, Hirsh & Williams, 2004) and a finding from the Burgoyne study, conducted for the DfES, was that too little research had been undertaken to examine the link between leadership and management development and changed behaviour in the workplace, let alone the link with organisational performance.

Doubtless, this situation is changing. The DfES study also noted that the number of small-scale studies of the behavioural impact of leadership and management development was increasing but that the results were rarely published. Key stakeholders, and specifically budget holders, are becoming more questioning about the return on the executive education investment and the indications are that interest in evaluation is broadening, away from simply proving the impact of executive education towards a more holistic understanding of what contributes to and prevents impact, in terms of behavioural change, in the workplace. Change has nonetheless been slow and a review of the literature on the subject, along with much anecdotal evidence, indicates that there are a number of factors that conspiring to prevent the need to evaluate being embraced as much as it should be.

Why is it that there is relatively little coverage of evaluation studies in the literature?

- Effective evaluation of training programmes can be difficult and there is often a perception that evaluation can be unnecessarily resource and time intensive, at a time when there are multiple pressures for those same resources to be used for what are seen as more pressing priorities. Of course, there is a counter argument in terms of costs. Given the trend for increased spend on executive education, it has been frequently suggested that the incremental spend on assessing the benefits accrued from those costs is relatively modest by comparison.

- Rigorous and robust evaluation is fuelled by data, either quantitative or qualitative, and often that data is difficult to come by. The reality of the 'organisational messiness' that pervades many organisations means that there are compromises needed over the quality of data which either may not exist at all or, as in the case of data for baseline comparisons, may be rendered incomparable due to changes to HR metrics or data-capture processes.

- The quality of programme goals and objectives, once illuminated in the glare of the need to evaluate, frequently prove to be too vague and woolly. Difficulties facing the need to evaluate also arise from different and sometimes clashing agendas of the different stakeholders, each with their own interests in the outcomes from executive education evaluation. This concept of evaluation 'purpose', together with the issue of whose purpose it is, will be returned to later.

In the past these factors have given rise to an 'avoidance tendency': it is simply easier not to do it and, in those organisations surrendering to that tendency, investment in executive education becomes an act of faith.

While it is sometimes avoided altogether, even where evaluation is attempted there has been an argument advanced in the literature that it is seldom done well (see, for example, Burgoyne, Hirsch and Williams, 2004, Mabey, 2005). As an example, one study of the impact of leadership development programmes found that evaluation in terms of on-the-job performance was undertaken in only 13 per cent of occasions. In the past, programme evaluation studies have been criticised, or even dismissed, for failing to match up to the requirements of the preferred research methods of the day, which are rooted in 'hard science'. In their meta-analysis of leadership and management development, Burgoyne and colleagues make the point that the paucity of evaluation studies in the literature may not be a reflection of the fact that little is going on but more the fact that evaluation findings are disappointing, either in terms of rigour or even a failure to demonstrate hoped-for outcomes. Publication is therefore unwarranted – or unwanted.

With this tricky background in mind, this article offers up six principles for an effective evaluation strategy for consideration in the field of executive education.

Six principles for an effective evaluation strategy

Principle One – Avoid evaluation 'afterthought'

With the practical pressures to get an executive education programme off the ground – which is, after all, the interesting bit – the requirement to evaluate can tend to be overlooked. Finalising programme design; addressing the programme logistics for trainers, materials, venues and equipment; building organisation-wide commitment to the programme; as well as constructing programme budgets – all can obscure the need to include evaluation in the overall plan. As a consequence, evaluation is tacked on at the end, by which time the opportunity to collect any base-line data, regarding performance levels, costs and so forth, is lost. Programme goals and objectives may be set and agreed, and yet later be shown to be inadequate as the basis for robust evaluation. Even when the need to evaluate is considered from the outset, critical factors associated with its effectiveness may just get lost amid the other pressures that are part of keeping a complex executive education programme on track.

To avoid this, evaluation needs to be part of the 'mainstream' thinking from the outset, integrated with other elements of the programme design and delivery and linked, in turn, to the overall business strategy. Easy words perhaps, but how can this avoidance of 'afterthought' be realised practically?

One solution is to develop right from the start a conceptual framework covering everything that needs to be taken into consideration for an effective evaluation strategy. Table 1, below, suggests one way of developing a conceptual approach that incorporates the following three key evaluation phases:

- Focusing the evaluation
- Designing and conducting the evaluation, and
- Communicating and using the findings.

Within each phase there are fundamental questions that need to be addressed in order for the evaluation strategy and approach to be well thought through from the start, thus guaranteeing that a robust evaluation process will be conducted. These criteria can be used to bench test the strength of an evaluation conceptual framework, addressing:

- Technical adequacy i.e. the likely validity, reliability and objectivity of proposed evaluation measures
- The relevance and importance of likely findings to evaluation audiences, i.e. do they address the matters that are of most concern to them
- Timeliness i.e. the timescales against which evaluation findings can be made available to ensure their usefulness to the organisation.

Table 1 – A Conceptual Framework for Executive Education Programme Evaluation

Evaluation Phase	Evaluation Activities
Focussing the evaluation	• Are key evaluation questions prioritised – i.e. are the evaluation purpose(s) clear? • Are key stakeholders identified, engaged early and their assumptions and expectations surfaced? • Is the evaluation planned in parallel with programme design? • Are programme outcomes specified at individual, group and organisational levels? • Are anticipated time periods for programme impacts specified? • Are the required resources identified?
Designing and conducting the evaluation	• Are multiple data-collection methods planned? • Will impact be assessed at different levels, i.e. individual, group and organisational? • Is impact measured over time? • Are time-series/control-group designs planned to isolate impacts? • Will impact be examined from the range of different stakeholder views? • Are data storage and treatment protocols identified to ensure confidentiality and anonymity?
Communicating and using findings	• How will results be communicated effectively? (i.e. using multiple methods for multiple audiences) • What specific courses of action have been identified as necessary? (i.e. to the supporting infrastructure and the initiative itself) • What is the detailed action plan for implementation? • How will action-plan implementation be monitored?

Based on Hannum & Martineau (2008)

Principle Two – Cherry pick from the toolkit

While coverage of evaluation studies in the literature may be limited, the same cannot be said of evaluation theories, methods and approaches. Since the mid-1960s, books and articles covering a host of methods and approaches have appeared, including Kirkpatrick's four-level framework for evaluation first published in 1967 and probably still the leading influence on those contemplating programme evaluation.

The evaluation approaches grid developed by Easterby-Smith (1986) is a useful framework within which to locate various approaches to evaluation, with one axis representing a 'scientific–naturalistic' scale and the other representing 'research–pragmatic' styles.

A scientific style is one in which the emphasis is on objective measurement and replication whereas, at the naturalistic end of the spectrum, the concern is more with unobtrusive observation of a phenomenon. A research style is guided by theory and characterised by rigour, independence and distance on the part of the evaluator, whereas a pragmatic style is characterised by minimisation of procedures and guidance by practical interests and operational decision-making requirements. The table below shows how these various approaches can be plotted on a grid.

Table 2 – A Range of Evaluation Approaches Plotted on Easterby-Smith's Grid

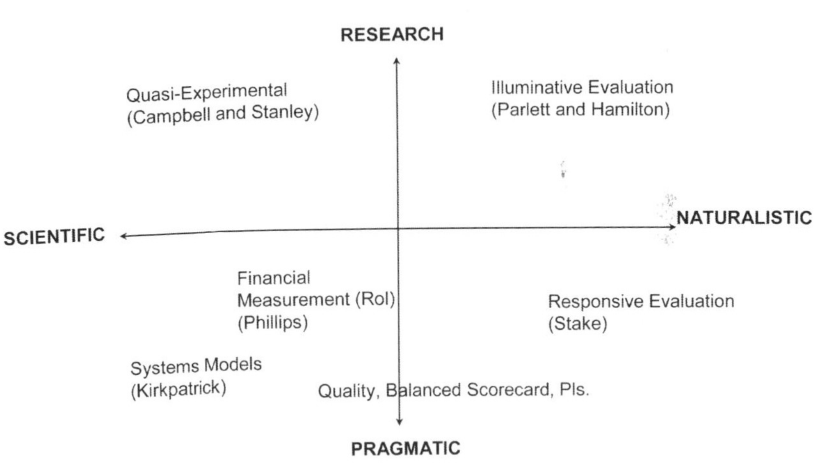

Based on Easterby-Smith (1986)

The following paragraphs have a look at all these approaches in some detail. It is worth remembering that none of these is the only correct or right way – they all have their uses in different situations.

Experimental research – the dominant paradigm in evaluation?

Early attempts at evaluation drew heavily on experimental research as the dominant approach and sit in the scientific–research quadrant of Easterby-Smith's grid. It was believed that only strict control and scientific rigour could provide measurable 'outcome effects', regarded as proof of programme effectiveness. The question asked was "Can the training programme be proved to be delivering desired behavioural change?"

Unfortunately, the results were unimpressive. In the 1960s, problems associated with proving cause-and-effect relationships and inadequacy of experimental design led to disillusionment with experimental research as an approach to evaluation. Over time, the dominance of the experimental research approach has been challenged and an alternative paradigm, less rooted in the natural sciences and more concerned with developing understanding of factors influenced by learning and development interventions, has been finding favour.

Quasi-experimental evaluation – 'softer' science

The need for measurement in evaluation, drawing on the principles of the scientific approach, has never gone away. However, in the light of the failure of experimental approaches to provide suitable evaluation, a range of 'quasi'-experimental research designs have been proposed (Campbell & Stanley, 1966) which recognise that, unlike in carefully controlled laboratory conditions, the realities of life will always intrude; thus making any inferred causal relationship unreliable.

These approaches offer a range of 'before and after' designs, using control groups with multiple measurements in time-series studies that helped restore some faith in the experiment as an evaluation methodology.

So whilst difficult to control and conduct, it is fair to say that if the purpose of evaluation is to demonstrate the effect of some particular event, such as a development programme, on a specific and measurable outcome, then quasi-experimental research, when done well, can come closer to achieving this than any other style or approach.

Illuminative evaluation – an alternative paradigm

The framework developed by Parlett and Hamilton (1976) called illuminative evaluation is an example of the alternative approach to evaluation. Adapted from mainstream education, the intention is to shine a light on the impact of a development programme.

So here, the focus is on description and interpretation rather than measurement and prediction. The questions asked by this approach include:

- How is the programme operated?

- How is it influenced by the organisational context within which it is run?

- What did people see as the programme's benefits and disadvantages?

- How did participants evaluate their experience?

This approach draws heavily on naturalistic and qualitative research methods and has become well established as a research-based, but practically focussed, method of evaluation. The main advantage over more experimental approaches is that, when done well, the outcomes are more likely to result in a more complete understanding of the development programme and its impact within the organisation. As a holistic approach, it is capable of enabling a degree of understanding around a number of evaluation purposes – including programme impact, requirements for programme improvement and individual learning of programme participants. However, to work well, the purpose and fit of the development interventions must be crystal clear, or the wrong inferences may be drawn.

The systems model – a 'hierarchical' approach to evaluation

The systems model has its origins in organisational research and has been widely used across different programmes and organisations. Its core components are the programme objectives, the identified programme outcomes and feedback from various stakeholders. One of the best-known exponents of the systems model is Kirkpatrick, who suggested four levels of evaluation:

- Level 1 – The reaction of the learners, usually immediately but often after a time lapse. Usually referred to as 'Happy Sheets'.

- Level 2 – Any evidence that learning has taken place, often knowledge based.

- Level 3 – Transfer of learning to on-the-job behaviour, usually results or behaviour based.

- Level 4 – The impact on work-unit results, perhaps financial or employee engagement figures.

A key feature of the systems model is the critical role provided by feedback. At all four levels, feedback is provided by and to a range of stakeholders, including the decision makers and budget holders who decide the future of any learning intervention, based on its ultimate value. Like any approach, this has its limitations. While feedback at the level of learner reaction is readily accessible, feedback at higher levels of impact on results is altogether more challenging and subjective. Setting objectives and specifying outcomes for all levels is rarely done well in organisations. Despite these limitations, this is the most widely used approach to evaluation in many organisations.

Responsive evaluation – a 'decision-oriented' approach

Responsive evaluation is a 'real-world' approach that trades off some measurement precision in order to increase the usefulness of findings to stakeholders. Developed by Stake (1973), this method sits directly opposite experimental research in Easterby-Smith's grid, within the naturalistic–pragmatic quadrant

Showing less concern with the formally stated criteria for a development programme, the emphasis here is on activities and measurement that are focused on the *value* created for participants and other stakeholders. So, what drives the decisions here is less the evaluation design and more the nature of the information required. This can only be achieved through clear definition of objectives beforehand.

The strength of this methodology is clearly a focus on the absolute relevance of findings. A pragmatic approach, it can also be less resource intensive than other methods and offers results that are usable in a cost-effective way. Compared to other approaches it is more dynamic, capable of flexing and adapting to changing circumstances and the need to pursue alternative directions as information comes to light through the evaluation process. As a downside, the ambiguity and lack of certainty involved is sometimes uncomfortable for an L&D professional procuring an evaluation services.

Return on investment (RoI) – a financial measurement

The pressure to develop economic or financial measures to evaluate development programme effectiveness continues to intensify. One of the key proponents of this approach is Jack Phillips (Phillips & Phillips, 2005; Phillips et al., 2001) who pointed out that 'return on investment' (RoI) could hardly be regarded as a fad, since it had been around and actively used in business since the 1920s. While RoI has been used effectively to measure the payoff from investments across a range of business activities, it is only relatively recently that attempts have been made to measure investment in HR activities and executive education programmes in particular.

Whilst not too difficult for 'hard' management skills such as accounting or logistics, applying RoI evaluation to 'soft-skills' programmes is notoriously problematic. Isolation of programme effects and the conversion of benefits to monetary values is challenging, particularly where the development goals for soft-skills programmes, such as leadership or team working, are often vague.

However, the approach asks the most fundamental question decision makers always ask: does the economic or financial benefit of a development programme justify its cost? It is therefore hugely relevant, and remains the holy grail of evaluation in the eyes of many organisational executives.

Other non-financial measures

The 1980s saw the concept of 'quality' as a strategic weapon generating a range of quality-measurement frameworks which required businesses to devise criteria for measuring the quality of their activities and outputs across the full range of their operations – including learning and development programmes.

For example, in the 1990s there was a surge of interest in measuring effectiveness through 'benchmarking' – comparing practices with those of other organisations. An earlier attempt to produce metrics allowing the benchmarking of HR practice had been undertaken in 1984, by the Saratoga Institute. The 250 metrics comprising the Institute's Human Capital Benchmark were still the HR benchmarking 'gold standard' some fifteen years later.

Subsequently, a range of approaches to mapping the processes to be bench-marked have been developed, most notably the McKinsey 5P approach and Kaplan and Norton's (1996) balanced business scorecard. The scorecard allows for a range of processes and practices to be measured (i.e. in addition to financial performance), with the focus on the customer, measuring how the business creates value and provides benefit in terms of encouraging innovation and applying learning.

All of these non-financial measures are 'utilisation focussed', offering the possibility of generating detailed information about performance against criteria developed specifically for the purpose. The question asked is "What information do we need to achieve our strategy?" However, this is resource intensive, particularly where regular measurement and analysis is required.

Summary of Principle Two

The above synopsis is not intended as an exhaustive list of every evaluation method, technique or approach, but rather to show the wide range available. The conundrum facing those trying to devise an effective evaluation plan for a particular programme of development is how to choose. The choice must be dictated by the purpose the evaluation is serving, the precise nature of the evaluation question being asked and the results that are needed.

Principle Three – Check the 'fit' for 'purpose'

Principle One touched on one aspect of 'fit for purpose' evaluation, that of ensuring that the evaluation approach and strategy is well thought through and planned against a range of effectiveness criteria. Here we are looking more closely at the question any evaluation is attempting to answer. The previous section offered a range of possible evaluation methods and, in each, the concept of evaluation 'purpose' was central. In reality, evaluation can serve a multiplicity of purposes.

Broadly, evaluation can be focussed on the need to appraise a training and development programme in order to judge its effectiveness. This has been termed 'summative' evaluation. Alternatively, it can be focussed on the need to identify what programme improvements or changes might be needed in order to further increase its effectiveness and this is called 'formative' evaluation. Simply put, this distinction is the difference between 'proving' and 'improving' the impact of any given programme.

In practice, this means that being clear about the primary purpose of evaluation is crucial to the identification of appropriate evaluation approaches and methods. If the primary purpose of evaluation is to establish proof of impact, a positive change brought about in a cause-and-effect relationship with the programme, then a more experimental research-based approach, as described in the previous section, is more fit for purpose. If on the other hand the primary purpose is to improve the overall quality of the learning experience, promoting greater understanding of what is going on for programme participants, then an evaluation approach more towards the naturalistic side of the grid in Table 2 might prove a better fit.

As well as this straightforward classification, we can consider other purposes evaluation can serve. For example, the promotion of learning has been suggested, where evaluation forms part of the learning process itself for participants. The reasoning is that posing evaluation questions to programme participants attunes them to desired learning outcomes and thus reinforces learning. Evaluation can also be an effective mechanism for use in monitoring and control behaviours as organisational needs change, as in the use of balanced scorecards, for example. There is also a more recent trend towards the evaluation of contextual factors surrounding a programme where the purpose is to promote greater social understanding of the factors that either help or hinder transfer of learning to the workplace.

So we're working with a complex evaluation system. There are the challenges of identifying the primary purpose for evaluation and then the appropriate methods and approaches. Then there is an additional confounding factor: we need to ask whose purpose we are talking about. It's an obvious but sometimes overlooked truth that 'things', such as executive education programmes and evaluation processes, don't have purposes but people do. Wherever it is applied, evaluation serves the needs of a wide range of stakeholders, each with their own agendas for evaluation. Stakeholder interests, and their importance to the programme in question, will differ according to whether they are budget-holding decision makers, programme managers, evaluation researchers or programme participants and all may have differing evaluation agendas.

Ensuring that evaluation is fit for purpose is therefore a function of being clear about both the fundamental evaluation questions: what is the primary purpose being served and whose purpose is it anyway?

Principle Four – Think multiplicity

Historically, the evaluation of training programmes was often confined to a single measure, the satisfaction of the programme participants with their experience of the programme (Level 1 evaluation within Kirkpatrick's systems mode). Notoriously unreliable in terms of learning, and really only reflecting how enjoyable a participant has found a programme, such 'happy sheets' are accused of encouraging an 'edutainment' approach to development. Contemporary views hold that a far broader and more extensive approach to evaluation is needed, one that makes use of multiple types of data from multiple audiences, using multiple methods at multiple points in time.

The roots of this principle lie in 'triangulation' – an established tenet in the field of traditional research. Here, in the interests of scientific rigour, data are collected from different sources of evidence along converging lines of enquiry. Avoiding over-dependency upon a single data source increases the likely validity of any findings. This same principle holds true in the evaluation of executive education, where, in attempting to assess the impact of a programme, drawing data potentially both quantitative and qualitative and from more than one source increases the robustness of any finding.

Kirkpatrick's four-level framework also highlights the need for multiple measures, particularly if evaluation is needed at all four levels. This brings us once again to the concept of evaluation purpose. Levels three and four can be seen as difficult and expensive to measure but, if the purpose of an evaluation strategy is to address questions relating to leadership behavioural change, as well as impact on business results, then clearly multiple measures are required – possibly drawing on a range of methods and approaches as mentioned in the previous section.

That data should be required from multiple audiences is also an important consideration. In planning the evaluation it is sometimes helpful to consider data collection at three levels: individual, group and organisation. By way of example, if programme impact is to be evaluated then a multiple-level approach might include 360° assessment for the individual level, use of control groups in a comparative study at the group level and staff survey results around leadership and culture for the organisation level.

Having data collected at multiple points in time can also add strength to the evaluation strategy, for example, time-series designs for the comparison of programme effects with data collected before, during and at different points after a programme are often effective. Data points at one, three and six months after a programme can be a clear indicator of whether the learning is 'sticking'.

While the case for avoiding reliance on single measures is strong, there is some potential risk in terms of ambiguous, or even conflicting, data, where multiple measures are used. In order to minimise this risk, the kind of care outlined in the conceptual framework earlier in this chapter is needed, where the evaluation is clearly focussed and the design and conduct of the evaluation well planned. The multi-faceted approach is a well-established research tool and represents an important principle for the conduct of executive education research.

Principle Five – *Weigh up perfection and practicality*

In their 2006 best-practice guide for corporate leadership development, Burgoyne and James drew a distinction between 'Mode1' and 'Mode 2' research, which they then applied to evaluation. Mode 1 research is essentially academic, taking place in a separate context, outside the organisation in question and usually university based. Whilst contributing to the development of a theoretical base for evaluation, the authors argued that such research had limited application potential in the real world of organisations.

Mode 2 research, on the other hand, represents more of a 'co-production' between researchers and organisational practitioners and, if rigorous as well as applicable, it can offer the possibility of more effective evaluation. One drawback here might be that involving practitioners in research brought a risk in terms of widening the range of expectations as to the outcomes needed from the research. There might also be potential limitations in terms of the 'special skills' required for pragmatic yet rigorous research. Further limitations include the realities of organisational constraints and cultures, such as limited access to required data and the compromises needed around conflicting stakeholder agendas. However, for Burgoyne and James the way forward is indisputably more systematic Mode 2 evaluation research.

The assumption often made that "what cannot be measured cannot be valuable" has often led to a pre-occupation with quantification and we have seen that this may not be the best route for evaluation. In some organisational cultures, methods such as RoI or the quasi-experiment might meet with 'tissue rejection' whereas a qualitative approach might resonate much more. Also, qualitative approaches, such as illuminative or responsive evaluation, are more in keeping with current evaluation preoccupations. It is important to consider where the dynamics of specific leadership programmes interact with their organisational contexts – what approach will 'land' in a particular organisation is an important factor to keep in mind.

Principle Six – Communicate, communicate, communicate – and apply and monitor

The final section of the conceptual framework in Table 1, and the third evaluation phase, concerns communicating and using findings. Sadly this is an often-overlooked part of the evaluation process. The best thought through, rigorous and robust evaluation strategy will fail to deliver value if findings are not effectively communicated to key stakeholders or followed up with appropriate action.

Where the evaluation strategy is multi-faceted, with different methods being used and therefore potentially different timescales for data collection and analysis, this can give rise to haphazard, piecemeal reporting of results, unless communication of the full range of findings is carefully planned. The consequence of this is that the evaluation strategy becomes fragmented and any impact diluted. Also, given the pace of organisational change, by the time results and findings are available stakeholder interest may have moved on to other issues, and evaluation studies and reports are consigned to the bottom drawer. It is important to find ways, as part of a clear communication plan, of maintaining stakeholder attention throughout this crucial third phase.

In addition to challenges with communication, there are also threats of evaluation findings being used inappropriately. Discussions of evaluation findings, by key stakeholder groups, can lead to programme changes that are costly, time and effort consuming and yet relatively small scale in impact, where there are no established rules agreed for using the data, either for validating it or deciding how best to use it.

Crucial to this third phase, therefore, are both a clear communication plan, with multiple communication methods for multiple evaluation audiences, and detailed action planning as to what activities are needed as follow on to a development programme, again using key stakeholders' expectations as a means of prioritising.

The first activity here is around communication of results and this involves both the frequency and manner of communication. For example, distributing interim reports to key stakeholders while data analysis is awaited is an effective way of keeping programme evaluation on agendas and specifying the links between the various evaluation activities that demonstrate an integrated evaluation strategy. For some stakeholders, face-to-face meetings with the evaluation team will be more effective as a communication method than circulation of a written report. The point here is to tailor the use of a range of communication methods to the specific needs of multiple evaluation audiences.

Alongside the communication of findings, there is a need to plan specific courses of action needed in response to findings. These actions represent changes needed, either to the programme itself or to its surrounding infrastructure (for example, to encourage increased transfer of learning). Since resources may be limited, actions need to be prioritised as part of this planning phase. Once specific courses of action have been identified, a detailed action plan is needed, specifying goals, accountabilities, barriers to action, sequencing and timetabling, and outcomes required, together with measures of success. The final activity is monitoring action-plan implementation, tracking progress made towards successful implementation and any need for corrective action where barriers are encountered.

Conclusion

As with all aspects of organisational life, the evaluation landscape is continually changing. Interest in this, arguably the most challenging aspect of executive education, is increasing. With the economic backdrop of recent years, the pressure to demonstrate the positive impact, as well as value for money, of executive education has never been greater. The focus of evaluation is nowadays more wide angle, zooming out from the executive education programme itself towards an examination of the contextual factors that either enable or inhibit transfer of learning to the workplace. On a more cautionary note, however, the practice of evaluation remains difficult and, on the basis of the literature, as well as from experience, the job is still seldom done well. The principles outlined in this chapter are offered not to guarantee perfection, but hopefully to help to avoid expensive disasters.

References

Abernathy, D.J. (1999) Thinking Outside the Evaluation Box. *Training and Development*, Alexandria VA, Vol. 53, Part 2, pp.18–23.

Abma, T.A., & Stake, R.E. (2001) Stake's Responsive Evaluation: Core Ideas and Evolution. *New Directions for Evaluation*, No. 92 (New York: John Wiley and Sons Inc.), pp.7–21.

Abt, C. (1979) Government Constraints on Evaluation Quality. In L. Datta & R. Perloff (eds), *Improving Evaluations* (Beverly Hills, CA and London: Sage).

Alimo-Metcalfe, B., & Alban-Metcalfe, J. (2005) The Crucial Role of Leadership in Meeting the Challenges of Change. *Vision – The Journal of Business Perspective*, Vol. 9, No. 2, April–June 2005, pp.27–39.

Alimo-Metcalfe, B., & Lawler, J. (2001) Leadership Development in UK Companies at the Beginning of the Twenty-First Century: Lessons for the NHS? *Journal of Management in Medicine*, Vol. 15, No. 5 (London: MCB University Press), pp.387–404.

Becker, B.E., Huselid, M.A., & Ulrich, D. (2001) *The HR Scorecard* (Boston, MA: Harvard Business School Press).

Blackler, F., & Kennedy, A. (2004) The Design and Evaluation of a Leadership Programme for Experienced Chief Executives from the Public Sector. *Management Learning*, Vol. 35, No. 2 (London, Thousand Oaks, CA and New Delhi: Sage Publications), pp.181–203.

Boaden, R.J. (2006) Leadership Development: Does It Make a Difference? *Leadership and Organisation Development Journal*, Vol. 27, No. 1 (London: Emerald Group Publishing Ltd), pp.5–27.

Burgoyne, J., Hirsh, W., & Williams, S. (2004) *The Development of Management and Leadership Capability and Its Contribution to Performance: The Evidence, the Prospects and the Research Need*. Research Report RR560 (Lancaster: Department for Education and Skills), pp.1–93.

Burgoyne, J., & James, K.T. (2006) Towards Best or Better Practice in Corporate Leadership Development: Operational Issues in Mode 2 and Design Science in Research. *British Journal of Management*, Vol. 17 (London: British Academy of Management), pp.303–16.

Burke, M.J., & Day, R.R. (1986) A Cumulative Study of the Effectiveness of Managerial Training. *Journal of Applied Psychology*, Vol. 71, No. 2, pp.232–45.

Campbell, D., & Stanley, J. (1966) *Experimental and Quasi Experimental Designs For Research*, 6th printing (Chicago, IL: Rand McNally).

Cappelli, P., & Neumark, D. (2001) Do 'High Performance' Work Practices Improve Establishment Level Outcomes? *Industrial and Labor Relations Review*, July, Vol. 54, No. 4 (New York: Cornell University), pp.737–73.

Capraro, R.M., & Thompson, B. (2008) The Educational Researcher Defined: What Will Future Researchers Be Trained to Do? *Journal of Educational Research*, Vol. 101, No. 4, pp.247–56.

Cascio, W.F. (2000) *Costing Human Resources: The Financial Impact of Behaviour in Organizations*, 4th Edition (Cincinnati, OH: South-Western College Publishing).

Charlton, K., & Osterweil, C. (2005) Measuring Return on Investment in Executive Education: A Quest to Meet Client Needs or Pursuit of the Holy Grail. *360°: The Ashridge Journal*, Autumn (Berkhamsted: Ashridge Publications), pp.1–8.

Cook, T., & Campbell, D. (1979) *Quasi Experimentation: Design and Analysis Issues for Field Settings* (Chicago, IL: Rand McNally).

Davidson, E.J., & Martineau, J.W. (2007) Strategic Uses of Evaluation. In K.M. Hannum, J.W. Martineau & C. Reinelt (eds), *The Handbook of Leadership Development Evaluation* (San Fransisco, CA: John Wiley and Sons Inc.).

Day, D.V. (2001) Leadership Development: A Review in Context. *Leadership Quarterly*, Vol. 11, No. 4 (New York: Elsevier Science Inc.), pp.581–613.

Dexter, B., & Prince, C. (2007) Evaluating the Impact of Leadership Development: A Case Study. *Journal of European Industrial Training*, Vol. 31, No. 8 (Emerald Group Publishing), pp.609–25.

Easterby-Smith, M. (1986) *Evaluation of Management Education, Training and Development* (Aldershot, Hants and Brookfield, VE: Gower).

Eccles, R. (1995) The Performance Measurement Manifesto. In J. Holloway, J. Lewis & G. Mallory (eds), *Performance Measurement and Evaluation* (London, Thousand Oaks CA, and New Delhi: Sage/Open University).

Edmonstone, J., & Western, J. (2002) Leadership Development in Health Care: What Do We Know? *Journal of Management in Medicine*, Vol. 16, No. 1 (London: MCB University Press), pp.34–47.

Fulmer, R.M., & Goldsmith, M. (2001) *The Leadership Investment* (New York: AMACOM).

Gratton, L. (1999) People Processes as a Source of Competitive Advantage. In *Strategic Human Resource Management: Corporate Rhetoric and Human Reality* (Oxford and New York: Oxford University Press).

Gratton, L. (2003) The HR Matrix Reloaded: A Multi-dimensional Look at the HR Function. *People Management*, June 2003, Vol. 9, No. 12 (London: Chartered Institute of Personnel and Development), p.21.

Gratton, L., Hope-Hailey, V., Stiles, P., & Truss, C. (1999) *Strategic Human Resource Management: Corporate Rhetoric and Human Reality* (Oxford and New York: Oxford University Press).

Guest, D.E., Michie, J., Conway, N., & Sheehan, M. (2003) Human Resource Management and Corporate Performance in the UK. *British Journal of Industrial Relations*, Vol. 41, No. 2, June (Oxford and Malden, MA: Blackwell Publishing Ltd.), pp.291–314.

Hannum, K.M., & Martineau, J.W. (2008) *Evaluating the Impact of Leadership Development* (San Fransisco, CA: Pfeiffer).

Houghton, J., Safferstone, T., Klippert, N., & Rhodes, C. (2001) *Exploring the Measurement Challenge: Results of a Membership Survey on HR Metrics*. HR Measurement Series, Vol. 2 (Washington, DC and London: Corporate Leadership Council).

Huselid, M.A. (1995) The Impact of Human Resource Management Practices on Turnover, Productivity and Corporate Financial Performance. *Academy of Management Journal*, Pace, Vol. 38, No. 3, pp.635–72.

Hutchinson, S., & Purcell, J. (2003) *Bringing Policies to Life: The Vital Role of Front Line Managers in People Management* (London: Chartered Institute of Personnel and Development).

James, K.T., & Burgoyne, J. (2001) *Leadership Development: Best Practice Guide for Organisations* (London: Crown Copyright).

Kaplan, R.S., & Norton, D.P. (1996) *The Balanced Scorecard: Translating Strategy into Action* (Boston, MA: Harvard Business School Press).

Kaplan, R.S., & Norton, D.P. (2001) *The Strategy Focused Organization: How Balanced Scorecard Companies Thrive in the New Business Environment* (Boston, MA: Harvard Business School Press).

Kirkpatrick, D.L. (1987) Evaluation. In R.L. Craig (ed.), *ASTD Training and Development Handbook*, 3rd edition (New York, London, Paris and Tokyo: McGraw-Hill).

Kirkpatrick, J. (2007) The Hidden Power of Kirkpatrick's Four Levels. *Training and Development*, August 2007 (Alexandria, VA), pp.34–7.

Leskiw, S., & Singh, P. (2007) Leadership Development: Learning from Best Practice. *Leadership and Organisational Development Journal*, Vol. 28, No. 5 (Emerald Group Publishing), pp.444–61.

Mabey, C. (2005) *Management Development Works: The Evidence*. Achieving Management Excellence Research Series 1996–2005, January (London: Chartered Management Institute).

Mayo, A. (2002) A Thorough Evaluation. In *People Management*, Vol. 8, No. 7 (London: Chartered Institute of Personnel and Development), pp.36–9.

Neathey, F., & Suff, P. (1997) Measuring Performance. In *Industrial Relations Services Management Review*, Issue 5 (London: Industrial Relations Services).

Patton, M.Q. (1978) *Utilization Focused Evaluation* (Beverley Hills and London: Sage publications).

Pfeffer, J. (1997) Pitfalls on the Road to Measurement: The Dangerous Liaison of Human Resources with the Ideas of Accounting and Finance. *Human Resource Management*, Vol. 36, No. 3 (New York: John Wiley and Sons Inc.), pp.357–65.

Phillips, J.J., & Phillips, P.P. (2005) *RoI at Work: Best Practice Case Studies from the Real World* (Alexandria, VA: American Society for Training and Development).

Phillips, J.J., Stone, R.D., & Phillips, P.P. (2001) *The Human Resources Scorecard: Measuring the Return on Investment* (Woburn, MA: Butterworth-Heinemann).

Pulley, M.L. (1994) Navigating the Evaluation Rapids. *Training and Development*, Training 101 (Alexandria, VA), pp.19–24.

Ready, D.A., & Conger, J.A. (2003) Why Leadership Development Efforts Fail. *MIT Sloan Management Review*, Spring, Reprint 44311 (Boston, MA: Massachusetts Institute of Technology), pp.83–8.

Russ-Eft, D., & Preskill, H. (2008) Improving the Quality of Evaluation Participation: A Meta-Evaluation. *Human Resource Development International*, Routledge, Vol. 11, No. 1, pp.35–50.

Sappal, P. (2004) Custom Dictates: Tailored Executive Education May Not Be a New Phenomenon, But With Growing Pressure to Deliver Results, Business Schools Have Been Forced to Shift Their Approach to Customisation up a Gear.

People Management, September, Vol. 10, No. 18 (London: Chartered Institute of Personnel and Development), pp.48–9.

Schwartz, R., & Mayne, J. (2005) Assuring the Quality of Evaluative Information: Theory and Practice. *Evaluation and Program Planning*, Vol. 28, Issue 1, pp.1–14.

Smith, P. (1995) Outcome Related Performance Indicators and Organisational Control in the Public Sector. In J. Holloway, J. Lewis & G. Mallory (eds), *Performance Measurement and Evaluation* (London, Thousand Oaks, CA and New Delhi: Sage/Open University).

Stake, R.E. (1973) Program Evaluation: Particularly Responsive Evaluation. Keynote presentation in *New Trends in Evaluation*, Institute of Education, Goteburg, Goteburg University, pp.1–15.

Stake, R.E. (1985) Responsive Evaluation. In T. Husen & T.N. Postlethwaite (eds), *The International Encyclopaedia of Education Research and Studies*, Vol. 7 (Oxford and New York: Pergamon).

Stake, R.E. (1987) Evaluation Design, Instrumentation, Data Collection and Analysis of Data. In Worthen, B., & Sanders, J. (eds), *Educational Evaluation: Theory and Practice* (Worthington, OH, Charles A. Jones).

Truss, C. (1999) Soft and Hard Models of Human Resource Management. In L. Gratton, V. Hope-Hailey, P. Stiles & C. Truss (eds), *Strategic Human Resource Management: Corporate Rhetoric and Human Reality* (Oxford and New York: Oxford University Press).

Tsui, A.S., Pearce, J.L., Porter, L.W., & Tripoli, A.M. (1997) Alternative Approaches to the Employee–Organization Relationship: Does Investment in Employees Pay Off? *Academy of Management Journal*, Pace, Vol. 40, No. 5, pp.1,089–121.

Tyson, S., & Ward, P. (2004) The Use of 360 Degree Feedback Technique in the Evaluation of Management Development. *Management Learning*, Vol. 35, No. 2 (London, Thousand Oaks, CA and New Delhi: Sage Publications), pp.205–23.

Ulrich, D., & Lake, D. (1990) *Organizational Capability: Competing From the Inside Out* (New York, Chichester, Brisbane, Toronto and Singapore: John Wiley and Sons Inc.).

Ulrich, D., & Smallwood, N. (2005) HR's New Rol: Return on Intangibles. *Human Resource Management*, Vol. 44, No. 2 (New York: John Wiley and Sons Inc.), pp.137–42.

Vollmer Le May, N., & Ellis, A. (2007) Evaluating Leadership Development and Organisational Performance. In K.M. Hannum, J.W. Martineau & C. Reinelt, *The Handbook of Leadership Development Evaluation* (New York: John Wiley & Sons Inc.).

Wang, G.G., Zhengxia, D., & Ning, L. (2002) A Systems Approach to Measuring Return on Investment for HRD Interventions. *Human Resource Development Quarterly*, Vol. 13, Issue 2 (New York: John Wiley & Sons Inc.), pp.203–24.

Wang, M.C., & Walberg, H.J. (1983) Evaluating Educational Programs: An Integrative Causal Approach. *Educational Evaluation and Policy Analysis*, Vol. 5, No. 3, p.347–66.

Warech, M., & Tracey, J.B. (2003) *Evaluating the Impact of HR: Identifying What Really Matters*, Working Paper Series No. 10-22-03 (New York: Center for Hospitality Research – Cornell University), pp.1–20.

Webb, E., Campbell, D., Schwartz, R., & Secrest, L. (1966) *Unobtrusive Measures: Non Reactive Research in the Social Sciences* (Chicago, IL: Rand McNally).

Wurzburg, G. (1979) What Limits the Impact of Evaluations in Federal Policy. In L. Datta & R. Perloff (eds), *Improving Evaluations* (Beverly Hills, CA and London: Sage).

CHAPTER 13

The Art and Craft of Sticky Learning: Learning that Transfers to the Workplace

Lee Waller

Introduction

In the past decade the world of work has changed greatly. As technological advances break down geographical borders and reduce manufacturing and operating costs, even the smallest organisations have greater access to larger markets and cheaper suppliers. In this fast-moving and competitive climate, companies are challenged to develop a real differentiating, competitive edge, which for many lies in their intellectual capital, specifically their human resource (Adler & Kwon, 2002). In recent years this need has intensified: the unstable economic climate necessitates the development of strong and competent leaders; a rapidly changing market place requires responsive and adaptable managers; and the approaching wave of baby-boomer retirements means organisations need to create a pool of talent to take their place (Lloyd & Newkirk, 2011).

As such, an increased emphasis and significant investment is being made in the development of employees' competences and work-related skills.

Estimates put annual global spending on leadership development at more than £30 billion (Reade & Thomas, 2004). And the recent economic uncertainty does not appear to have impacted this spending. In 2009, even as the recession bit, there were reports that found that companies intended to place greater emphasis on leadership and executive development (Duke, 2009), a commitment which seems to have been translated into actual learning and development activity, particularly in the higher levels of the organisational hierarchy, with reported increases in executive development for senior managers and vice presidents (Hagemann & Mattone, 2011).

However, the research literature concerning the transfer of learning from this investment is rife with statistics suggesting that as little as 10-to-20 per cent of the learning gained from management development is actually applied on the job (Curry et al., 1994; Saks & Haccoun, 2007). This is a poor return on investment in anyone's book. These, however, are just the statistics that are readily available. Despite these disappointing figures, it appears that few organisations are even assessing whether or not they are getting a return on their investment.

This chapter aims to develop this understanding by exploring what influences the transfer of learning and what those involved in the process of learning, including the individual, the programme designers and organisations, can do to ensure that learning is applied in the workplace.

One of the most widely used models for assessing learning impact is Kirkpatrick's Four Levels of Learning model which classifies learning into four areas, as detailed in Figure 1 (Kirkpatrick & Kirkpatrick, 2009). Such is the predominance of this framework in learning evaluation, it is also referred to elsewhere in this book, but is outlined again here for ease of reference.

- Level 1, *reaction*, includes participants' immediate reactions to the programme such as whether it met their expectations or whether they would recommend it to others.

- Level 2, *learning*, is concerned with whether participants have developed the skills and competences the programme was designed to enhance.

- Level 3, *behaviour*, is about whether, as a result of the programme, individuals are changing their behaviours and using their learning.

- Level 4, *results*, is to do with whether or not the learning is impacting at an organisational level, such as improved P&L, employee engagement or customer satisfaction scores.

Whilst some amendments have been made to the model over the years, including the addition of a fifth level to capture economic or social benefit, or financial return on investment (Kaufman & Keller, 1994; Phillips, 2003), the four-level model is probably the most widely used by practitioners and is considered effective in capturing the important organisational factors that might impact learning outcomes (Watkins et al., 1998).

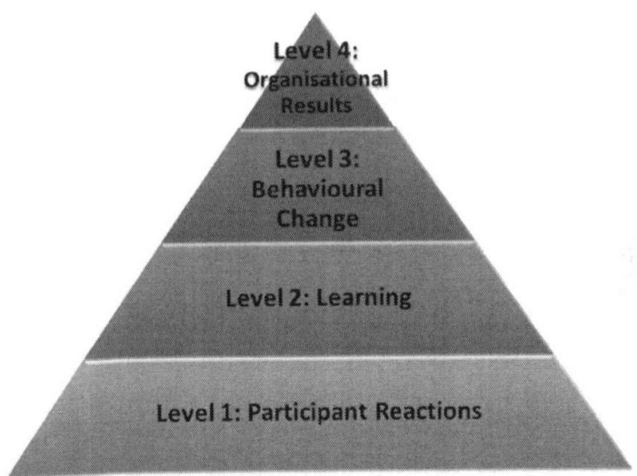

Figure 1 – Kirkpatrick's Four Levels of Learning Evaluation

(Kirkpatrick, 2009)

Learning transfer is concerned with Level 3, actual behaviour change, and it would appear from the research that few organisations are attempting to ascertain whether their investments are resulting in impact at this level, with less than 38 per cent of 39 organisations in one study assessing impact at Kirkpatrick's behaviour or results level, and nearly 40 per cent of 251 organisations in another having no formal measures for linking training to business impact (Rivera & Paradise, 2006; Balaguer et al., 2006). Similarly, reports have found that whilst anticipated reaction level and learning level evaluation had increased by 7 per cent and 19 per cent respectively between 2009 and 2011, anticipated evaluation at the behaviour and results level both decreased by 4 per cent and 18 per cent respectively.

Organisations are seemingly becoming more committed to conducting evaluations of their executive development programmes and are expressing an interest in learning outcomes as well as reactions, but appear less inclined to understand whether these programmes are having an impact in terms of behaviour change or results at an organisational level.

It would seem, therefore, that there is still more to be understood and communicated about how to ensure that development programmes have a tangible impact on individual and business performance.

The major influences on learning transfer

Leadership and management development is a complex business, and involves more than just learning new skills and acquiring new knowledge. To develop from junior to senior management, and to become a leader, individuals have to learn new behaviours and new ways of working, and change attitudes. As such, transferring this multifaceted cocktail of learning from the classroom into the workplace involves more than just memory. Indeed, it involves more than just the individual learner. In the context of leadership development, the ability to apply learning back at work involves a complicated interaction of a variety of factors. These factors can be categorised into three domains: individual characteristics, programme design and the work environment (Baldwin & Ford, 1988).

There have been changes in the areas of interest concerning how learning, say from a business school programme, can be made effective in the workplace. As well as shifts in the focus of the research, there have been shifts in the terminology to reflect evolving views of management education in general. Early research referred to the 'transfer of training', with the word 'training' indicating a model in which learning took place via knowledge being imparted by an 'expert' to a receptive learner. The word 'development' is now much more favoured, indicating awareness of the role the learner plays in acquiring and assimilating new skills and knowledge. Three key themes have dominated research into transfer of learning from programme, or other learning intervention, to the workplace:

- Individual characteristics of the learner, such as motivation and cognitive ability (Baumgartel & Jeanpierre, 1972; Hunter, 1986)

- The importance of the actual programme design and content

- Most recently, attention has turned to looking at the work environment to which the individual returns, where the opportunities are to be found for knowledge to be implemented and for skills to be used, practised and mastered (Tracey et al., 1995).

Let's have a look at each of those in turn.

Individual characteristics

Interest in the individual characteristics of learners has concentrated on whether individuals have the necessary knowledge, skills and attitudes to learn from development programmes and transfer that learning to the workplace. Unsurprisingly, cognitive ability is one such characteristic that strongly influences an individual's ability to transfer learning by helping learners both to acquire the skills being developed and to process and retain what they learn (Randel et al., 1992; Velada et al., 2007).

But whilst mental capacity, or one's cognitive ability to learn that which is being taught, is clearly a pre-requisite to learning and to transfer, what appears to be particularly critical to the transfer process is whether, when they arrive in the classroom, individuals are motivated to learn and to use their learning (Chiaburu & Marinova, 2005; Chiaburu & Tekleab, 2005). Motivation is a volitional drive to behave in a particular way, and individuals choose those behaviours according to what motivates them. So in this context, are they motivated to learn? Are they excited to be there, intrigued by whom they'll meet and what they'll learn? Do they consider themselves fortunate to be on the programme and proud of this recognition of their potential? Are they attentive, focused and engaged? No matter how well designed a programme may be or how supportive a work environment, if an individual has no motivation to learn what they are being taught or using what they've learned, then learning is unlikely to take place and so there will be nothing to transfer.

As well as motivation, self-efficacy has been shown to be critical in successful learning and transfer. In this context of learning, 'self-efficacy' refers to an individual's belief that they will be able to use what they've learned and change their performance. In layman's terms this is the degree of self-confidence that individuals have that their mastery of new knowledge will make a difference to their performance when they return to work (Saks & Haccoun, 2007; Velada et al., 2007). Greater self-efficacy leads to this – greater confidence in both applying what's been learned and enhancing motivation to learn in the first place (Cole & Latham, 1997; Chiaburu & Marinova, 2005; Colquitt et al., 2000). Essentially, those who are confident in their ability to use their learning are likely to be more motivated and able to use their new skills.

Programme design

The second area refers to the design of the development itself and it appears that there are four key areas that programme designers must incorporate into their thinking.

- The first of these is relevance – programmes must reflect the requirements of the individual's role to ensure that learners are both motivated to learn and will have opportunities to use what they've learned when they return to the office (Chiaburu & Marinova, 2005; Seyler et al., 1998). Before adult learners engage with programme content, they ask themselves if the content reflects the reality of their work environment: are the materials used, case studies, examples and simulations, representative of their industry; are the skills they are being taught those which they will need to fulfil their current or future roles? Relevance impacts transfer through two processes. Firstly, if the material is not relevant or useful this will influence participants' motivation to pay attention and engage in the learning experience, and if they haven't learned anything, what is there to apply? Secondly, even if an individual finds what they have learned fascinating and are especially motivated to use it, if it is not relevant to their role they won't have an opportunity to do so. If it's not used, it will soon be forgotten. Similarly, unless an individual can see that what they are learning will result in positive outcomes, such as improvements in their performance or enhancements to their career, they are equally unlikely to engage in the learning process or attempt to use what they've learned when they return to work (Devos et al., 2007).

- Secondly, as well as engaging and relevant material, programmes should also incorporate opportunities to practise new skills and behaviours, thus enhancing learners' confidence to use them in the workplace (Saks & Haccoun, 2007). This is particularly important for programmes which are designed to prepare participants for future roles, as an ability to practise back on the job may be limited until they are in post.

- A third element of a programme designed to enhance transfer of learning are the feedback processes which are incorporated at different stages of learning. These may constitute coaching sessions or peer-to-peer or facilitator feedback and provide information on progress, creating opportunities for individuals to adjust their behaviour, and as such also build confidence in the development and application of skills (Baldwin & Ford, 1988).

- Finally, for effective learning to take place, the importance of time for reflection is acknowledged to be essential. For new knowledge to be assimilated and accommodated into participants' cognitive processes, they need to be given the time to digest and consider it properly.

Work environment

The third and final area of influence on the transfer of learning from development programmes is the work environment to which a learner returns. Referred to by Baldwin and Ford as the 'transfer climate' (Baldwin & Ford, 1988), this area is crucial to transfer because the factors involved can have an influence on both an individual's motivation to transfer, and on their personal capacity to transfer (Watkins et al., 1998). As motivated as any participant may be to apply what they've learned back at work, if they don't have the time, energy, resources or mental space to do so, the learning is likely to be forgotten.

As one might expect, therefore, opportunities to use new skills and behaviours are also critical to the transfer of learning (Baldwin & Ford, 1988). Having the chance to lead new projects, accrue additional responsibilities, manage staff or mentor colleagues, for example, will help ensure that new skills are practised, developed and mastered. However, when practising new behaviours comes into conflict with pressing job requirements, manager support appears to be just as crucial, in terms of supporting the application of learned behaviour by identifying ways of using the learning, encouraging the application of learning, and being open to new approaches learned through training. Similarly, providing the autonomy that will allow individuals to create their own opportunities to use new skills will also help ensure learning is not lost (Randel et al., 1992; Velada et al., 2007). Managers can support their employees by providing an indication of how well new skills are being performed through feedback (Chiaburu & Marinova, 2005) but conversely, can also inhibit transfer though sanctions and resisting change (Phillips, 2003). Any negative response from a manager to the use of newly learned skills, such as disinterest, dismissal or refusal to accept the value of doing things differently, will obviously result in a disinclination on the part of the learner to attempt to apply what they've learned.

The importance of management support is well documented, and appears to be a significant influence on learning transfer. For example, research has found that only a third of learners in one study believed their training made a difference, and half of those considered this to be due to a lack of manager support in how to apply it (Rogers & Woodford, 1999). But it's not just managers who can facilitate the transfer of learning. Peers, direct reports and senior management can all influence an individual's motivation and ability to use what they have learned through their engagement and support of the use of new skills (Facteau et al., 1995).

An interesting finding from the participation literature adds further support to the importance of the transfer climate on transfer of learning, suggesting that individuals who receive no support for transfer from previous programmes are unlikely to participate or be motivated to transfer themselves from future programmes, and will in turn not support other's efforts to transfer (Saks & Haccoun, 2007). So a supportive environment can have an impact on learning transfer both now and in the future.

Which domain matters most to transfer?

In 2010, research was conducted which explored all three of these domains with the objective of determining whether any of them had a greater or lesser impact on the transfer of learning from business-school programmes to the workplace.

The research was conducted with 144 participants on eight 'customised' development programmes at a UK business school. Each programme was designed to develop leadership capability in one of eight separate organisations. As a first step, the researchers assessed the participants' perceptions of the three areas critical to learning transfer – individual characteristics, programme design and the work environment – then post-programme, asked them to report how well they had been able to use their learning, and what sort of things had helped or hindered them.

The results indicated that whilst all three areas had an impact on whether a participant would use what they had learned, what appeared to be most, and uniquely, influential were the characteristics of the individual. This was the only area to have a significant, unique influence on whether learning was transferred. What seemed most important was how prepared participants were to learn and how motivated they were to apply learning. This was much more significant to the transfer of learning than either the design of the programme or the support they received from the work environment to which they returned.

Domain	Correlation with transfer (r)	Significance value (p)	Unique influence on transfer (β)	Significance value (p)
Individual characteristics	0.53	<0.01	0.42	<0.01
Programme design	0.35	<0.01	0.04	=0.244
Work environment	0.40	<0.01	0.15	=0.24

Given this finding, it might naturally follow that interventions to enhance transfer should be focused on the individual. However, these individual characteristics are influenced by factors throughout the transfer system. Kirwan and Birchall's (2006) model illustrates this most effectively, and demonstrates the number of interactions between factors and mediating effects that exist (Kirwan & Birchall, 2006).

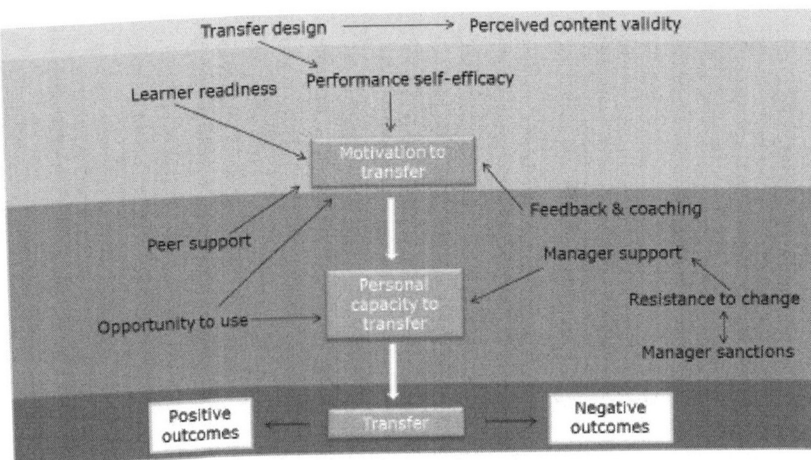

Figure 2 – **Kirwan & Birchall's Model of Learning Transfer**

This model reflects the factors that may impact the transfer of learning that have been discussed in the chapter and we can see that they can exert their influence in a number of ways. For example, the provision of opportunities to practise during learning will impact self-efficacy, the relevance of the material will impact opportunities to use new skills as well as pre-programme motivation, and support from managers will influence both opportunities to use learning and motivation to transfer.

Therefore, in considering how best to ensure that programmes are designed to enhance the transfer of learning from development programmes, it is necessary to consider all factors within the individual, the programme and the organisation.

Implications for practice

So what does this mean for those involved in the learning and transfer process? What is it that each stakeholder can do to ensure the transfer of a learning experience to the workplace? How can we ensure that they are engaged throughout; learning skills and behaviours that will be of value; and supported to use those skills and behaviours on return to the office? Let's look at how three key groups of stakeholders in this process can optimise the desired learning outcomes. The three groups are:

- The individual learners

- Programme designers

- Organisational colleagues.

The individual learners

The importance of individual characteristics, and the influence they have on learning and transfer, is notable, as is the fact that to a certain extent this is within the learner's sphere of control. So it is important that participants understand and have responsibility for the contribution they can make to enhance the impact of their learning. Preparing themselves prior to the start of the programme is just as critical as what they do whilst on a programme; and so before they have even stepped through the classroom door, they need to ensure that they are clear as to how the programme will benefit them. Clarity about the objectives of the programme – and the expected learning outcomes from programme designers, deliverers and organisational procurers – needs to be communicated strongly. Pre-programme activities such as webinars and pre-reading can also help to raise interest and engagement before participants embark on their programme.

Whilst on programmes, individuals should be helped to identify clear links to their role and career, and to think about ways in which they can apply the learning to their specific context. What, specifically, can they do differently when they walk back through the office door? Which current challenges might be helped by incorporating these new models? Once they return to work, they should be encouraged to reflect on what they've learned, to consider how, where and with whom they might use what they've learned, and then to take responsibility for using their new skills. Identifying and creating ways in which they can use their new skills, such as requesting new responsibilities, new projects, or involvement in decisions that might utilise their learning, will help ensure it is not lost. Continuing to seek feedback from peers, direct reports and managers will also help to build confidence in the development of their skills (Reber and Wallin, 1984). Simply scheduling meetings with their manager immediately after, then one and three months down the line will help to clarify expectations, identify opportunities to put the learning into practice, and afford them the chance to discuss any barriers they might be encountering in attempting to use their new skills. Similarly, sitting down with their team to discuss what they've learned and get their thoughts and input into how it might be beneficial to their performance as a group will help to get the buy-in of their peers and direct reports and secure their support for using the learning. How can we use this model? How can we incorporate this new process? How can we ensure as a group that we communicate effectively with one another?

The programme designers

In terms of programme design, as we saw earlier, the content should reflect the environment in which learning transfer will take place, allowing learners to gain experience with scenarios they may encounter back at work, as well as promote active engagement in learning (Salas et al., 2006; Burke & Hutchins, 2007). The implications of this are that the diagnostic phase in which educators learn about the real working environments of potential participants is critical and should not be skimped. This is rather easier for customised management education when a particular organisation can be explored in detail, but it is equally relevant for open programmes. The key here is to be crystal clear about who the programme is aimed at and what the expected learning outcomes are for those individuals. Conversations and interviews must take place with senior managers, line managers and future participants to ensure that the programme is designed to meet the objectives of the individuals as well as the organisation.

The part that the programme designers play is a continuing one and not confined to the duration of the programme. Whilst their first responsibility is to ensure that content is relevant to those who will attend (Chiaburu & Marinova, 2005), and indeed that content is professionally and expertly presented, this content focus is not sufficient. As mentioned above, the pre-programme phase is an important one for learner engagement. If this is effectively used, the face-to-face time with tutors and participants when they are on the programme can be maximised, with participants already familiar with key issues and areas. Programmes also need to be designed to provide opportunities for individuals to practise new skills, through experiential learning, simulations or role play. These types of activities are particularly effective in really engaging learners actively in the learning process and allowing them to practise their responses to different situations, helping to develop confidence in using these skills in the workplace.

Educators and facilitators should constantly ensure that participants are able to make clear links to their work and industry, to the responsibilities of the individuals and their roles, to the strategic objectives of their departments and functions, and the overall strategy of their organisations. They should help participants identify scenarios in which they might use what they've learned.

Coaching, feedback and time for reflection during programmes also offer opportunities for participants to identify in which scenarios they might use what they've learned, how they might apply their learning and overcome obstacles, and also help to build confidence by identifying strengths and areas for development (Baldwin & Ford, 1988). Programme designers should not be frightened of what appears to be 'white space' on a programme timetable. Space for reflection adds value to learning, and does not detract from it.

The role of the programme designers need not end when the participants leave the classroom. Follow-up sessions, coaching or simply touching base will help to continue the learning process into the workplace, and serve to prompt participants to use new skills rather than old and familiar ways of working.

Organisational colleagues

The role of other organisational members again begins long before the programme starts, influencing individuals' attitudes towards learning and their motivation to transfer this learning. The first step is the responsibility of managers, L&D professionals and senior executives to ensure that individuals will actually benefit from the development programme they are to attend, and that it is indeed relevant to their current or future role.

Appropriate selection and nomination processes are therefore key, to ensure that programmes are aligned to participants' jobs, objectives and core competences. Clear development plans can mitigate against the tendency to revert to type as learners become accountable to their line managers for using their learning. It's equally important that the benefits of the programmes are communicated clearly and development is positioned as a recognition of potential and vital to business need, if individuals are to be motivated to attend and to learn (Tracey et al., 1995). A demonstration by the organisation of their commitment to the programme will also encourage learners to attend, engage and apply what they've learned. Having senior executives launch an initiative can help to place the programme in the context of the organisation and demonstrate senior managers' support for the learning. Having senior managers attend presentations of work-based projects will have a similar impact, and make clear the value of what is being learned.

On return to the office, organisational support can take a variety of forms:

- The first is the actual ability to *use* their learning. Managers need to provide opportunities and space in their employees' workloads for them to practise new skills, increase their responsibility and offer stretching assignments (Bates et al., 2000). If, for example, leadership skills have been targeted, line managers should ensure learners have a chance to lead and, where this is not possible, perhaps offer opportunities to mentor.

- Identifying experiences that will help continue the development and allowing participants to use what they've learned is vital to ensuring that learning sticks.

- Similarly, continuing to develop clear action plans aligning learning to specific objectives and detailing how learning will be applied will help to ensure practical ways to use learning are identified, and barriers are overcome.

- Providing feedback, as well as developing self-efficacy and nurturing confidence, will also give learners the opportunity to talk about any issues they are encountering in using their learning. Perhaps they are not yet confident enough to try out what they've learned. Perhaps they simply cannot find the time to incorporate novel ways of working. A supportive manager can assist in overcoming such barriers.

In summary, involving line managers in communicating what their expectations are, ensuring the programme is right for the selected participants, and developing at this early stage a plan of action for implementation of the learning will encourage engagement in the learning from the outset and focus learners' thoughts on how their new skills can be employed (Chiaburu and Marinova, 2005).

Individuals also need to be confident that applying learning will bring positive results. It's important, therefore, that organisations demonstrate that learning and using new skills are valued, and support this through clear policies and rewards for development, such as recognition, stretching assignments or new responsibilities. This will encourage motivation to apply learning and promote a continuous learning culture so that learning is not regarded as something that stops once the individual leaves the classroom, and transfer becomes a natural part of the learning journey (Tracey et al., 1995).

Finally, attempting to introduce new ways of doing things can be quite some challenge, as the message can be construed as suggesting that the way things have been done before was wrong, or in some way inferior. Learners as such often encounter real resistance to doing things differently when they get back to the office. One means of overcoming this potential barrier is to share stories of success, incidents where new ways of working have been employed which have had a tangible and beneficial impact on performance. This will help to demonstrate the value of the new skills and behaviours, encourage buy in and reduce resistance.

In conclusion

It is difficult to overstate the importance of ensuring that individuals arrive in the classroom with the necessary knowledge, skills and attitudes to learn. This indeed may be the key to subsequently ensuring that the learning is applied back at work. However, our exploration of all the factors in the transfer system has shown that the development of these characteristics is very much a responsibility shared between individual learners, the programme designers and the organisations to which the individuals return. If one of these stakeholders fails to support transfer, the efforts of the others may be negated and it may have a serious impact on whether or not learning is applied.

Acknowledging and making explicit these inter-relationships could significantly increase the long-term impact of management and leadership development programmes. The holy grail of learning that transfers effectively and with impact from the classroom to the workplace would undoubtedly improve return on investment for organisations and individuals alike.

References

Adler, P.S., & Kwon, S.W. (2002) Social capital: prospects for a new concept. *Academy of Management Review*, 27(1), pp.17–40.

Balaguer, E., Cheese, P., & Marchetti, C. (2006) The High Performance Work Study 2006. Accenture. Available at: http://www.accenture.com/Global/Research_and_Insights/By_Subject/Human Resources_Mgmt/default.htm (accessed 25 January 2007).

Baldwin, T.T., & Ford, J.K. (1988) Transfer of training: a review and directions for future research. *Personnel Psychology*, 41, pp.63–105.

Bates, R.A., Holton III, E.F., Seyler, D.L., & Carvalho, M.A. (2000) The role of interpersonal factors in the application of computer-based training in an industrial setting. *Human Resource Development International*, 3, pp.19–42.

Baumgartel, H., & Jeanpierre, F. (1972) Applying new knowledge in the back-home setting: A study of Indian managers' adoptive efforts. *Journal of Applied Behavioural Science*, 8(6), pp.674–94.

Burke, L.A., & Hutchins, H.M. (2007) Training transfer: An integrative literature review. *Human Resource Development Review*, 6, pp.263–96.

Chiaburu, D.S., & Marinova, S.V. (2005) What predicts skill transfer? An exploratory study of goal orientation, training self-efficacy and organizational supports. *International Journal of Training and Development*, 9(2), pp.110–23.

Chiaburu, D.S., & Tekleab, A.G. (2005) Individual and contextual influences on multiple dimensions of training effectiveness. *Journal of European Industrial Training*, 29, pp.604–26.

Cole, N., & Latham, G. (1997) Effects of Training in Procedural Justice on Perceptions of Disciplinary Fairness by Unionized Employees and Disciplinary Subject Matter Experts. *Journal of Applied Psychology*, 82(5), pp.699–705.

Colquitt, J.A., LePine, J.A., & Noe, R.A. (2000) Toward an integrative theory of training motivation: a meta-analytic path analysis of 20 years of research. *Journal of Applied Psychology*, 85, pp.678–707.

Curry, D.H., Caplan, P., & Knuppel, J. (1994) Transfer of training and adult learning (TOTAL). *Journal of Continuing Social Work Education*, 6(1), pp.8–14.

Devos, C., Dumay, X., Bonami, M., Bates, R., & Holton III, E. (2007) The Learning Transfer System Inventory (LTSI) translated into French: internal structure and predictive validity. *International Journal of Training and Development*, 11(3), pp.181–99.

Duke CE (2009) *Learning and Development in 2011: A Focus on the Future*. Duke CE's Client Study (Duke Corporate Education).

Facteau, J.D., Dobbins, G.H., Russell, J.E.A., Ladd, R.T., & Kudisch, J.D. (1995) The influence of general perceptions of training environment on pre-training motivation and perceived training transfer. *Journal of Management*, 21(1), pp.1–25.

Hagemann, B., & Mattone, J. (2011) *2011/2021 Trends in Executive Education Development: A Benchmark Report* (Executive Education Associates Inc. and Pearson Education Inc.).

Hunter, J.E. (1986) Cognitive ability, cognitive aptitude, job knowledge, and job performance. *Journal of Vocational Behavior*, 29(3), pp.340–62.

Kaufman, R., & Keller, J. (1994) Levels of evaluation: Beyond Kirkpatrick. *Human Resource Development Quarterly*, 5(4), pp.371–80.

Kirkpatrick, D.L., & Kirkpatrick, J.D. (2009) *Evaluating Training Programs* (San Francisco, CA: Berret-Koehler Publishers).

Kirwan, C., & Birchall, D. (2006) Transfer of learning from management development programmes: testing the Holton model. *International Journal of Training & Development*, 10(4), pp.252–68.

Lloyd, F.R., & Newkirk, D. (2011) *University-based executive education market and trends* (International University Consortium for Executive Education).

Phillips, J.J. (2003) *Return on Investment in Training and Performance Improvement Programs*, 2nd edition (Burlington, MA: Butterworth-Heinemann).

Randel, J.M, Main, R.E., Seymour, G.E., & Morris, B.A. (1992) Relation of Study Factors to Performance in Navy Technical Schools. *Military Psychology*, 4(2), p.75.

Reade, Q., & Thomas, D. (2004) Critics question value of leadership training. *Personnel Today*, 12 October.

Reber, R.A., & Wallin, J.A. (1984) The effects of training, goal setting, and knowledge of results on safe behaviour: a component analysis. *Academy of Management Journal*, 27, pp.544–60.

Rivera, R.J., & Paradise, A. (2006) *State of the Industry in Leading Enterprises* (Alexandra, VA: ASTD Press).

Rogers, A., & Woodford, J. (1999) 'Training' supplement in Personnel Today, November 1999. In R. Buckley & J. Caple (2009) *The Theory and Practice of Training*, 6th edition (Kogan Page: London).

Saks, A.M., & Haccoun, R.R. (2007) *Managing Performance through Training and Development*, 3rd edition (Scarborough, ON: Nelson).

Salas, E., Wilson, K., Priest, H., & Guthrie, J. (2006) Design, delivery, and evaluation of training systems. *Handbook of human factors and ergonomics*, 3rd edition, pp.472–512.

Seyler, D., Holton III, E., Bates, R., Burnett, M., & Carvalho, M. (1998) Factors Affecting Motivation to Transfer Training. *International Journal of Training and Development*, 2(1), p.16.

Tracey, J.B., Tannenbaum, S.I., & Kavanagh, M.J. (1995) Applying trained skills on the job: the importance of the work environment. *Journal of Applied Psychology*, 80, pp.239–52.

Velada, R., Caetano, A., Michel, J.W., Lyons, B.D., & Kavanagh, M.J. (2007) The effects of training design, individual characteristics and work environment on transfer of training. *International Journal of Training and Development*, 11(4), pp.282–94.

Watkins, R., Leigh, D., Foshay, R., & Kaufman, R. (1998) Kirkpatrick plus: evaluation and continuous improvement with a community focus. *Educational Technology Research & Development*, 46(4), pp.90–6.

CHAPTER 14

The Future of Management Development: A Manifesto

Narendra Laljani and Kai Peters

The ability to learn faster than your rivals is the only sustainable competitive advantage of the future.

Arie de Geus

We are passionate advocates for education in general and management development in particular. When done well, management development has a transformational impact on both individuals and organisations. Numerous studies (Bradley et al., 2012; McBain et al., 2012) have recognised that effective leadership and management are a key asset in organisations. Strategy scholars, citing the resource-based view of the firm, suggest that superior profit can be earned by leveraging resources that are valuable, rare, imperfectly imitable and non-substitutable. Superior managerial skills meet these tests and there has been a widespread appreciation in organisations of the need to invest in the development of people. Indeed, as Arie de Geus (1988) suggested, learning is the only viable competitive advantage for the firm. As a result, management development has been a growth industry over the last few decades.

However, we are acutely aware that the industry has its critics. There is disquiet and debate about the effectiveness and impact of management and leadership development interventions, both in the lay media as well as in the research community. Some have argued that management development "does little to develop the capacity to learn how to understand the complexities of management practice" (Wilmott, 1994, p.110). Others lament the use of "pretentious American psycho-babble" in development interventions (Williams, 1996, p.3). The programmatic nature of many development activities is considered particularly problematic. Allio (2005, p.1,072) suggests that "organizations continue to embrace the myth that they can develop leaders by investing in leadership training programmers – in a day, week, or year". Similarly, Conger and Fulmer (2003, p.78) observe that traditional leadership development focuses on one-off events and "participants often return to the office energized and enthused, only to be stifled by the reality of corporate life". Similar scepticism is found within the client and practitioner community, with apparent post-programme behaviour changes often dismissed with the stereotypical comment "he must have been on a training programme: give him a few days, he'll be back to normal".

Elsewhere in this book it has been demonstrated that real value can be delivered through management development yet it is important to address the apparent contradiction of increasing investment for doubtful return. We suggest that closer attention needs to be paid to the relationship between the realities of the managerial world, which continue to change, and the management development industry, parts of which appears to be stuck in yesterday's paradigms.

In this essay, we reflect on the future of the management development industry. Our starting premise is that much traditional management development thinking, that of both clients and developers, is mired in the past, while the world around us is changing. While there is a human tendency to project the past onto the future (as someone has said, "generals always fight the last war"), it is our endeavour in this chapter to look with 'fresh eyes' at a number of issues. We consider, in turn, key trends which are already apparent and which will increasingly re-shape the context in which managers work; the skills and abilities managers and leaders will require in order to be able to cope with these challenges; and lastly, the rethinking required around education generally and management development specifically.

The future already exists. It is simply distributed unequally.

Michio Kaku

We are not futurologists, but it seems to us that some key societal trends have become apparent which are critical for organisations and their managers. Building on the research cited previously in this book, as well as the findings of influential think tanks (Dobbs et al., 2014), we offer a synthesis of five such trends. While each is significant in itself, they are also inter-related, creating what some have called a 'VUCA' world – one characterised by volatility, uncertainty, complexity and ambiguity.

1. Disruptive technology

While one can make a case that technological progress has been with us since the dawn of civilisation, or certainly since the beginnings of the industrial revolution, the speed of innovation has accelerated to the point where entire industries are being reinvented in periods of months and years rather than over decades. Aggregate computing capacity continues to surge exponentially. From an individual perspective, connectivity has brought billions of people across the world in touch with each other through mobile phones and other electronic devices, so that at present over two-thirds of the world's population have access. There are now more devices in circulation than there are people on the planet because many people have multiple devices. A recent report has suggested that by the year 2020, 80 per cent of the world's population will have a supercomputer in their pockets. Such dramatic increases in capability accompanied by reductions in cost are driving innovation and the emergence of new customers and markets, new competitors and new ways of doing business. This in turn makes it imperative to re-invent constantly. In this new world, 'success is never final'.

2. Globalisation

The centre of gravity of the world economy has been shifting. Thanks to liberalisation and industrialisation, growth in emerging markets has transformed the world economy. We expect this trend to amplify. McKinsey authors (Dobbs et al., 2014) suggest that "by 2025, emerging markets will have been the world's prime growth engine for more than 15 years, China will be home to more large companies than either the United States or Europe, and more than 45 per cent of the companies on Fortune magazine's list of the 500 largest corporations in the world, versus just 5 per cent in the year 2000." Within emerging markets, the population is shifting from a rural, often agricultural lifestyle to an urban, industrial life. The global urban population is growing by 65 million people a year at present, and with that growth comes income, the development of a consumer society and a revolution of rising aspirations, with old loyalties – to firms or to brands – often swept aside. This creates the need for a high degree of cultural as well as product-market adaptation for organisations, and multi-culturally skilled and adaptive managers.

3. Demographic dynamics

Demographic shifts have long preoccupied policy makers. In the West, rising health-care costs and a lack of growth in the tax base, thanks to an ageing population with increasing longevity, have challenged the economics of welfare as well as the role of the state. In emerging markets, with typically younger populations, higher birth rates have fuelled concerns about growth and job creation. Most organisations, however, will have a mix of ages in the workplace. This co-existence of different generations under one roof creates interesting challenges.

As Culpin and colleagues (2015) note, either because of legislative changes or, more prosaically, because savings rates are insufficient and pension plans inadequate for 25 years in retirement, individuals either need or choose to work more years than they previously expected to. From a workplace perspective, organisations thus face the challenge of both care for and utilisation of an aging workforce. In addition, partly as a consequence of longer lives, but also a consequence of changing working conditions which include the move away from life-long employment and the move to more varied career patterns, there is significantly more movement in the workforce than previously. Moving to the other end of the age spectrum, the younger workforce has incorporated this expectation of a portfolio career whilst simultaneously being native users of new technologies. Generation Y (those roughly born in the 1980s and 1990s) and Generation Z (the latter born around the turn of the millennium) have been found to have quite distinct ideas on how work works (and how work should work for them) and how lives should be lived. Organisations will need to adapt to multiple generations, each with a different set of expectations, needs, values, aspirations, skills and attitudes. Less predictable retirement ages, global working, a renewed focus on work and non-work balance as well as organisational well-being will all need to be managed within varying frames of reference. Leading and motivating people in such a context will inevitably become more challenging and require new skills.

4. The knowledge economy

The people challenge becomes further magnified with the increasing dominance of the knowledge economy, in which the key assets of the business are not on the balance sheets, but go home every night. Knowledge workers frequently combine expert knowledge with a high need for autonomy and a low regard for positional authority. Although innovation and collaboration are crucial, aligning organisational needs with the professional interests of knowledge workers is no easy task; indeed, 'herding cats' is the somewhat disparaging expression the authors have encountered frequently. While some work has been done on how to provide leadership for professional service firms, for the arts and for R&D, it is generally acknowledged that managing for creative output is much harder than managing a chimney and smokestack business. Further, it is genuinely impossible to know *a priori* if a creative knowledge worker will generate a subsequent great idea. One can consider an individual's track record and hope for the best, but, as they say in the investment industry, "past performance is no indicator of future performance".

5. New social contract

Over the last decade, a weak signal of future change appears to have grown and moved centre-stage into many boardrooms. Since the appearance of the Stern Review of the Economics of Climate Change (Stern, 2007), there has been an increasing preoccupation with issues of sustainability. Gitsham and colleagues (2008) suggest that at a macro level, an increase in extreme weather and the associated problems of agricultural failure, water scarcity, disease and mass migration will bring forth crises on a scale we have never before witnessed. The Stern report, for instance, extrapolated that climate change could swallow up to 20 per cent of the world's GDP. At a micro level, the shift to a low-carbon economy to offset climate change is something that business leaders consider a key factor in the coming years. Wider concerns relating to the sustainability of the natural environment – finite and increasingly scarce resources, energy, water, food, metals and minerals – also figure prominently.

The need to consider sustainable business models and create shared value (Porter and Kramer, 2011) means that organisations must consider not only their own product or service portfolio, but also the broader effect of their activities on consumers and on society. A key element of this mix is not only the sustainability of the approach, but also of the responsibility and ethical approach taken. In practice, this requires organisations to build and maintain trust within their value chain and with their stakeholder groups, all within a climate of ever-increasing scrutiny and transparency. Leaders will need to understand this changing business context and how their stakeholders

– regulators, customers, suppliers, investors and NGOs – factor social and environmental trends into their strategic decision making.

So where does this take us? Once upon a time, classic management textbooks suggested that the work of managers is to "plan, organise, direct, and control" (Koontz and O'Donnell, 1968). Such notions now seem antiquated and would be amusing were it not for the fact that there is a human tendency to seek simple answers. In a complex world, simplicity is seductive and simplification tools (which abound in the world of education) become dangerous when applied to strategic issues and problems because they apply a simple structure to an unstructured situation. What then are the implications for managers and management development?

"Complicate yourselves" is the battle cry offered by Weick (1979, p.261), suggesting that managers need to be able to see and understand organisational events and behaviours from several perspectives, rather than a single one. Having a narrow framework for understanding often results in ineffective managerial behaviour. More complicated understanding will result in better understanding of organisational problems, so that the manager is likely to be more effective in addressing them.

The need for multiple lenses and perspectives is recognised by CEOs. In a recent study (Gitsham et al., 2009) carried out with 200 CEO respondents from around the world, 76 per cent thought it important for senior leaders in their own organisations to have the mindset, skills and abilities to lead in a holistic manner, yet only 8 per cent believed that these skills were present at the moment. There is, therefore, a clear leadership deficit.

We suggest that in the future, managers will require capabilities in four clusters:

1. Contextual mastery

We believe that all management is deeply contextual. By context, we mean a unique configuration of external (for example, competitive setting and life cycle) and internal environments (for example, culture and systems). So, context is the situation wherein particular structures, relationships, processes and competitive settings can be found (Mintzberg and Quinn, 1996). There are a variety of important concepts of organisation – strategy, the leader, process, structure, systems, culture, power and style – which combine to form the contexts of organisations. It should be self-evident that what works in the cement industry may not work in the advertising industry, or that the leadership style that works in a chemical plant may not work in a hospital – although paradoxically, most management ideas are presented as generic and universally applicable. Understanding the context, and being sensitive to it, gives leaders credibility. However, understanding is not sufficient in itself; leaders must also challenge the context, and the paradigms and views which characterise it, and explore how it might be changed.

Every context presents both an interpretive and an inertial challenge. The interpretive challenge involves recognising the issues, trends, opportunities and threats that impact the organisation and its future performance in an environment that is ambiguous and noisy. A context also presents an inertial problem. Many organisations do not adapt effectively to changes in their environments, resulting in strategic drift. While this commitment to the status quo may occur for understandable reasons (such as legacy investments in specialised assets), there is all too often an unthinking allegiance to a recipe that has worked in the past, and an assumption that tomorrow will be like yesterday. We describe contextual mastery as the ability both to understand *and* to challenge the context, and also to overcome the interpretive and inertial challenges that abound in organisations.

2. Behavioural complexity

Responding to complex demands in an uncertain and volatile environment requires managers to perform a wide array of leadership functions in organisations. They must build trusted relationships with a diverse range of people at different levels, and mobilise, motivate, collaborate with and influence them. Being effective across a range of situations and time horizons requires of managers not only "the ability to perceive the needs and goals of a constituency but also the ability to adjust one's personal approach to group action accordingly" (Kenny and Zaccaro, 1983, p.678). Behavioural complexity reflects the idea that managers who have a broad 'bandwidth' – or who perform multiple leadership functions, discern what's appropriate when, and can tailor their style, message and behaviour to the demands of the task, situation and role – will be more effective than managers who are relatively inelastic. A key premise is that the more complex a manager's behavioural repertoire, the more likely it is that the manager can respond effectively to the challenges at hand. Behaviourally complex managers can be facilitative and supportive, but also authoritative and decisive when required – and in the process, they can be more effective than managers who know only one way to get things done.

3. Judgement

Making the right choices in the face of conflicting processes, contending opposites and incomplete information requires the exercise of judgement.

Paradoxes are a central feature of modern managerial life. Managers must deliver in the short term and in the long term. They must give autonomy, but also ensure alignment. They must lead change, but also provide stability and continuity. All these require conflicting actions. Paradoxes are not problems that must be solved, but rather opposing positions that must be held meaningfully at the same time. For example, Mintzberg and Quinn (1996) emphasise the need to reconcile change and continuity. The manager must be a "pattern recognizer", with the ability to sense when to exploit established strategies and when to encourage new strains to displace the old. Jonas and colleagues (1990, p.40) found that effective executives must "simultaneously embody the status quo and question it". As the custodian of the firm's history, the chief executive officer must act as a force for stability. However, the leader must also challenge norms, ask frame-breaking questions and play the maverick to stimulate innovation. Bourgeois and Eisenhardt (1988) uncovered similar combinations of paradoxical conditions in their study of strategic decision processes in 'high-velocity' environments. They found that executive leadership required not only the articulation of a broad vision and bold commitments of resources, but also the ability to maintain flexibility and empower people throughout the organisation to take risks and challenge the status quo. Effective executive leadership would therefore appear to require a range of skills which seem on the surface to be mutually exclusive: an ability to focus on broad visions for the future while also providing critical evaluation of present plans; to create a sense of excitement and challenge while also focusing on getting the job done today; to seek purposefully organisational alignment and to retain organisational agility; to maintain stability and to prepare for change; to have a deliberate strategy and to allow the emergence of strategies; to know the business and at the same time be able to examine it as an outsider; and to work within the context but also challenge the context. Strategic leaders must paradoxically be reflective yet adventurous; they must have good plans prepared but at the same time be ready to forego those plans (Cummings, 1995).

4. Self-efficacy

Leaders need high self-efficacy which can be defined as an individual's belief in his or her capability to organise and execute the courses of action required to attain desired performance. Psychologists suggest that this is an important variable that affects leader performance. Self-efficacy affects the thoughts, feelings and actions of individuals in several significant ways. According to Bandura's seminal work (1997), people with high self-efficacy approach difficult tasks as challenges to be mastered, rather than as threats to be avoided. They set themselves challenging goals and remain committed to them in the face of adversity and potential failure. They recover their sense of efficacy after setbacks, attributing them to a lack of adequate effort or to skills that need to be further developed. Such a worldview supports personal accomplishments and reduces stress. By contrast, people with low self-efficacy have low aspirations and are reluctant to take on difficult tasks. They demonstrate weak commitment to goals and are likely to abandon them if achievement proves difficult. They attribute unsatisfactory performance to personal deficiencies. As a result, it does not require much failure for them to lose faith in their capabilities and they may suffer from stress and depression.

So against this background, let's look at how management development really happens:

> The only thing that gets in the way of my learning is my education.
>
> Albert Einstein

At one level, the purpose of learning and development is to develop the cognitive and emotional maturity which allows an individual to be as aware and as thoughtful as possible about the consequences of their actions. According to Cook-Greuter (2004), there are two types of development: horizontal and vertical. Horizontal development, which refers to the acquisition of new skills and knowledge, is something 'normal' life contributes to. Most traditional development is horizontal. Vertical development, which is more potent, refers to a change in worldview and a transition to a higher level of maturity and sophistication. The former is largely triggered by external forces and comes to the individual, whereas the latter is sought by the individual and is largely driven internally through reflection.

Management development interventions, when well designed, provide a combination of horizontal and vertical development and are characterised by:

- Novelty – a prompt which encourages exploration and seeks to engender curiosity

- Reinforcement and repetition

- Reflection and sense-making – reflection is built in to the interventions through discussion and dialogue (Willis, 2007).

This approach, when specifically designed to engender management development rather than more general development, requires a learning design in which the horizontal 'novelty' factor is directly related to, or adjacent to, the strategic issues and challenges faced by the organisation. If one applies a neuroscientific lens to development, a number of conclusions can be drawn for both learning and change. Brain research shows that positive, novel learning inputs release dopamine and create a virtual cycle of positive feeling and memory activation. Too much novelty, however, causes an overload, an amygdala hijack, in which learning ceases and panic begins. Neurons and synapses are also critical to learning. The new needs to create new synaptic paths. Walking metaphorically through the bush is simply not enough to create a new path, never mind a new highway. Repetition and reinforcement are necessary. New information needs to progress from working memory into stored memory. If something is not reinforced, it does not make this journey (Peters, 2011).

Learning to do something differently is a far greater challenge than simply having to learn something new. Individuals already have a developed synaptic superhighway which causes certain types of knowledge analysis and behavioural reaction. The longer one has reinforced this particular worldview, whether correct or not, the harder it is to alter. A brand new path needs to be created, cultivated and developed so that it becomes the new highway and the old one grows over. This can be accomplished through really hard work, but it is indeed hard to teach an old dog new and different tricks.

Just creating novel learning experiences, whether in the classroom or through the convening of a group of interesting people, is not enough, on its own, to prompt vertical development. To encourage higher stages of maturity, structured reflective processes need to be built into any interventions. These processes can be discussions that take place within groups, or discussions with an individual mentor or coach, and are processes grounded in individual and group psychology.

Our research into influential development processes that lead to vertical development suggests that three important and interacting forces are at work. These may be visualised as follows:

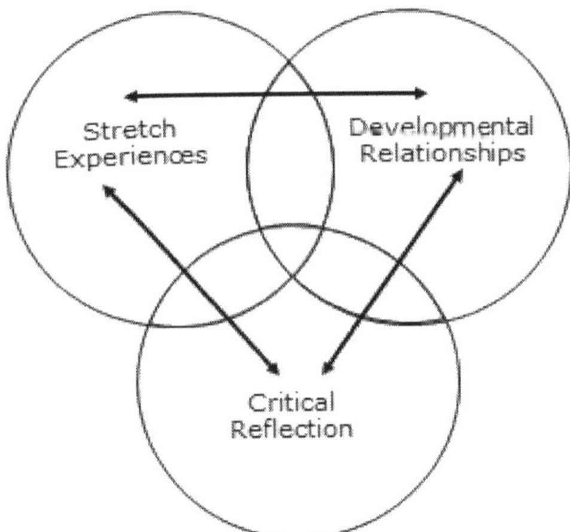

Figure 1 – Influential Development Processes: A Model

Source: Laljani, 2009

We will consider these in turn, starting with stretch experiences. This is an idea that has early support. Snell (1989) observed that most successful managers have been through the "school of hard knocks".

Thomas and Cheese (2005) found that a wide array of leaders (entrepreneurs, corporate executives, social activists and elected politicians) unanimously agreed that they had learned more about leading from challenging, real-world experiences than from formal leadership development. While formal programmes had helped them to gain technical competence, these had done little to help them learn the fundamental lessons of leadership.

Learning through real-life experiences can be called informal learning. It is powerful because it is determined and directed by learners themselves; it is an active, relevant process, arising in the setting where the skills are used (Leslie et al., 1998). However, such learning may remain intuitive and unrecognised. Managers may even find it difficult to articulate what they have learned or how, and may fail to understand and make full use of the learning opportunities that daily life offers.

While experience appears to be a key to the development of managers and leaders, the kinds of experiences that involve high degrees of stretch appear to be particularly potent. It appears that individuals often develop primarily through confrontation with novel situations and problems where their existing repertoires of behaviours are inadequate, and where they have to develop new ways of dealing with these situations. McCall and colleagues (1988) identify stretch experiences as a major source of the development of managerial skills and perspectives. Such assignments place the manager in dynamic settings full of problems to solve, and choices to make under conditions of risk and uncertainty, and these situations provide both the motivation and opportunity to learn rapidly. Such situations can surface shortcomings in current skills, frameworks or competencies and stimulate a desire to overcome these deficiencies.

Smith and Morphey (1994) observe that managers frequently refer to learning from experience in work situations and refer to difficulties, adversity, setbacks, failures and mistakes. The majority of these tough challenges come from significant job changes or changes in job content. Bennis and Thomas (2002) recount intense, often traumatic, always unplanned experiences that transform leaders and become the sources of their distinctive leadership abilities. They describe the transformative events that shape leaders as 'crucibles'. Crucible experiences are a trial and a test, points of deep reflection that force managers and leaders to question who they were and what matters to them. Crucibles require leaders to examine their values, question their assumptions and hone their judgement. Not all crucible experiences are traumatic: they can involve positive but challenging experiences such as having a demanding boss or mentor. Significant crucible experiences include adapting to a foreign territory, surviving disruption and loss, and enduring enforced reflection. Crucibles play a key role in building self-confidence and self-efficacy.

Secondly, developmental relationships are key factors in management development. There is considerable empirical and theoretical evidence that mentors make a significant contribution to the development of strategic leaders. Kram (1985) reports that mentoring greatly enhances the development of individuals in both early and middle career stages. Akin (1987) observes that some managers describe all of their learning experiences in terms of emulating a specific mentor. The mentor can offer a well-developed, coherent worldview; in effect, a system for 'putting it all together'. Kotter (1988) found that leaders in organisations reported they had learned a great deal about leadership from observing other managers and that such observation of role models positively impacted emotional and social development.

Mentors contribute to the development of others by enacting a variety of roles. They provide feedback, challenge and support. Clutterbuck (2004) describes mentoring as a multi-functional process that has four sub-roles: coach, offering job-related knowledge and guidance; counsellor, providing emotional support; guardian, acting for the protégé's well-being and interests; and networker or facilitator, providing access to networks and resources.

McCauley and Douglas (2004) report that in their narrative of significant learning experiences, managers often describe how they learnt from other people, with mentors being the most frequent influencers. Mentors provide psychological and social support; role modelling, in which the protégé takes cues and learns from the attitudes, values and behaviours displayed by the mentor; career development, in which the mentor coaches the protégé and insulates the protégé from adverse organisational pressures and forces, provides challenging assignments that stretch the capabilities of the protégé, sponsors career advancement of the protégé, and fosters positive organisational exposure and visibility for the protégé. In general, mentoring offers a private and protected relationship that enables protégés to test out new ideas and examine issues with a fresh perspective in a safe and non-threatening environment.

And thirdly, the role of critical reflection must be understood. While we all learn from experience, experience is a very slippery teacher: most of the time, we have experiences from which we never learn (Smith, 2001).

Reflection plays an important role in synthesising tacit learning from experience. By becoming 'reflective practitioners', managers can generate new insights and develop new ways of working in practice (Schön, 1983). As Boud and colleagues (1985) point out, the capacity to reflect is directly related to how effectively individuals can learn from their personal experiences. Reflection therefore provides a meaningful way for leaders to gain a deep understanding of their actions and environments. In other words, reflection helps to convert experience into "actionable knowledge" (Argyris, 1993). To paraphrase Smith's work on action learning, reflection seeks to cast a net around slippery experiences and capture them as learning (Smith, 2001). Conversely, the absence of reflection results in poor decisions, bad judgements and repetitions of previous mistakes (Brookfield, 1995).

However, reflection does not come naturally or easily to most managers and executives. This may be because of their task orientation or, as Conger (1990) suggests, leaders may avoid reflecting because such reflection might be discomforting and challenge their favourable perceptions of themselves.

Reflection is not by definition critical and 'simple' reflection, as in muse, think or consider, is not adequate. Smith (2001) observes that simply thinking back over what worked and what did not is not enough. Critical reflection involves becoming conscious of previously implicit assumptions, beliefs, templates and criteria, and critiquing them vigorously. So reflection should not simply be an 'improved understanding of experience' but should involve serious internal criticisms of it. According to Mezirow (1990, p.14), through critical reflection an individual becomes more open to the perspectives of others, less defensive and more able to accept new ideas, and all these elements contribute to "transformative learning". Through critical reflection, a manager can examine feelings, beliefs and actions, as well as the assumptions that underpin them.

Bearing in mind this framework, how can organisations best develop their best assets? We believe that in the future, management development must address seven key dilemmas, which in our experience support and underpin each other. This is our manifesto for the future of management development:

1. *Individual* and *organisation*

While much management development focuses on individuals, we believe this is necessary but not sufficient. We believe that individual change is inseparable from organisational change. All learning is by definition subversive; it encourages people to challenge the status quo. Helping the individual to change without paying any attention to the potentially unchanged environment into which the individual will return is a waste of development effort. Equally, an organisational change process that does not explicitly consider the implications for the development needs of the employees involved is unlikely to be sustainable over time. Indeed, management development is a potent vehicle for organisational change. Consequently, management development is most effective when it is accompanied by a process of organisational development. This twin focus on individual and organisation creates a symbiosis. It enables change that is directly linked to organisational needs, it helps embeds individual learning and also creates workplace impact.

2. *Cognitive* and *behavioural*

Knowing how to calculate the cost of capital, analysing market trends or designing a new product development process are rarely the biggest challenges that managers face. While these cognitive skills are important, and sense-making frameworks have an important role to play, getting things done requires working with people. New products, budgets or strategies do not succeed or fail. People succeed or fail. As a result, behavioural skills become critical. While this divide is often framed as 'hard' skills versus 'soft' skills, a senior executive has rightly observed that "the soft stuff is harder than the hard stuff".

3. *Action* and *reflection*

As Drucker (1974, p.128) has pointed out, "the best plan is only good intentions, until it degenerates into work". In other words, thinking must be translated into action. Organisations are generally designed for action and for getting things done, and are all too often characterised by an institutional bias against reflection, resulting in frequent 'fire-fighting'. At the other extreme, an excess of reflection and little action creates the trap of 'paralysis by analysis'. In the development of managers, both conditions of thinking and acting must be met. Thinking must be translated into action, and action must inform thinking. Reflection helps with the gaining of new insights, and converting implicit knowledge into actionable knowledge. In turn, patterns of action help create 'muscle memory', as discussed elsewhere in this book, so that new ways of thinking and behaving become seemingly effortless.

4. *Theory* and *practice*

Theory often gets a bad press with managers, and is often dismissed as irrelevant and impractical. Ironically, most managers do not realise that they are constant users of theory. Right or wrong, managerial actions are based on beliefs about which actions will lead to what consequences and why – in other words, an implicit theory. Good theory helps us to predict, as well as to understand (Christiansen and Raynor, 2003). Managers therefore need good theory. Indeed, it has even been suggested that "there is nothing so practical as a good theory" (Lewin, 1951). Recognising that theory can often be generic, managers should be helped to learn to explore, adapt and deploy it in their own unique context, in the most relevant manner.

5. *Teaching* and *facilitation*

Both teaching and facilitation are complex professions. Together they help make the learning experience sticky and impactful. Many of us have had the privilege of great teachers; we recall them vividly, years later. Good teachers provide authoritative expertise and distinctive points of view; they engage, challenge, stimulate, inspire and make learning fun. Teachers help make managers discerning consumers of management ideas. Good facilitators are skilled in group dynamics and can help groups of managers by organising their learning journey, providing individualised support and feedback. Facilitators work with groups to co-create the learning and orchestrate discovery, a role that should not be under-estimated given the wealth of experience that is frequently found in the learner side of the room. Effective management development therefore needs both the 'sage on stage' and the 'guide on side'.

6. *Intellectual* and *emotional experiences*

Well-crafted management development enables managers, while in a safe and supportive environment, to stretch outside their comfort zones and confront new challenges, as well as prepare for the unexpected, and learn to manage the anxieties, stresses and pressures of an uncertain and ambiguous world. While tidy classroom abstractions and intellectual debate have their value, visceral development experiences that represent an emotional stretch are a crucial driver of development.

7. *Formal* and *informal learning*

We recognise that profound and enduring development happens from experience. The workplace provides myriad opportunities for development. The informal learning that happens on the job is potent and immediately relevant to the individual's context – with apparently low direct costs. However, it can also be risky, inconsistent (and therefore inadvertently high cost), or inaccurate and unchallenged, and the learning may remain implicit. Also, a 'sink or swim' approach represents a surrender to the vagaries of circumstances. Formal learning through deliberately designed interventions, on the other hand, can mitigate some of the inefficiencies of informal learning. Formal learning is scalable and explicit, and lends itself to customisation. It provides opportunities for vicarious benchmarking, for reflection, for learning from peers, and for converting tacit knowledge into explicit knowledge ("now I know what I know"). However, formal learning withers away when detached from the 'day job'. Ideally, therefore, we need well-thought-through strategies to integrate informal and formal learning. This requires an acknowledgement that real learning is not a 'one-week fix', and a new perspective in which development is seen as beginning on the job well before a formal intervention commences, and continuing back on the job well after the formal intervention has ended. Crafting 'managed development experiences' is the challenge.

In conclusion, the world is developing around us and creating new challenges. Disruptive technology, globalisation, demographic dynamics, new social contracts and the knowledge economy are changing not only our ways of working, but also our entire lives. Coping with these developments, and effectively engaging with them, calls for the skills to accept ambiguity and complexity and to use humility and dialogue to guide judgement. An uncertain and volatile environment requires managers to perform a wide range of leadership functions. Developing these skills is not easy as one must balance a number of dilemmas without falling victim to indecision and inaction, and while embracing development processes that are influential, but go beyond traditional modes of delivery. We are sure that effective management development interventions can help create the individual skill sets and organisational capability needed to succeed in the decades ahead, and will be a crucial driver of sustained success.

References

Akin, G. (1987) Varieties of Managerial Learning. *Organizational Dynamics*, Vol. 16, No. 2, pp.36–48.

Allio, R.J. (2005) Leadership Development: Teaching Versus Learning. *Management Decision*, Vol. 43, No. 7/8, pp.1,071–7.

April, K., Kukard, J., & Peters, K. (2013) *Steward Leadership: A Maturational Perspective* (University of Cape Town Press).

Argyris, C. (1993) *Knowledge for Action: a Guide to Overcoming Barriers to Organizational Change* (San Francisco: Jossey-Bass).

Bandura, A. (1997) *Self-Efficacy: the Exercise of Control* (New York: W H Freeman).

Bennis, W.G., & Thomas, R.J. (2002) Crucibles of Leadership. *Harvard Business Review*, Vol. 80, No. 9, pp.39–45.

Boud, D., Keogh, R. and Walker, D. (1985), *Reflection: Turning Experience into Action*, Kogan Page, London.

Bourgeois, L.J., & Eisenhardt, K.M. (1988) Strategic Decision Processes in High Velocity Environments. *Management Science*, Vol. 34, No. 7, pp.816–35.

Bradley, M., Woodman, P., & Hutchings, P. (2012) *The value of management and leadership qualifications* (Chartered Management Institute).

Brookfield, S.D. (1995) *Becoming a Critically Reflective Teacher* (San Francisco: Jossey-Bass).

Christiansen, M.C., & Raynor, M.E. (2003) Why Hard-Nosed Executives Should Care About Management Theory. *Harvard Business Review*, September.

Clutterbuck, D. (2004) *Everyone Needs a Mentor: Fostering Talent in Your Organisation* (London: CIPD).

Conger, J. (1990) The Dark Side of Leadership. In G.R. Hickman (ed.), *Leading Organizations: Perspectives for a New Era* (London: Sage).

Conger, J., & Fulmer, R.M. (2003) Developing Your Leadership Pipeline. *Harvard Business Review*, Vol. 81, No. 12, p.76.

Cook-Greuter, S.R. (2004) Making the case for a developmental perspective. *Industrial and Commercial Training* 36(7), pp.1–10.

Culpin, V., Millar, C., & Peters, K. (2015) Multi-generational frames of reference: managerial challenges of four social generations in the organisation. *Journal of Managerial Psychology*, 30(1).

Cummings, S. (1995) Pericles of Athens – Drawing From the Essence of Strategic Leadership. *Business Horizons*, Vol. 28, No. 1, pp.22–9.

De Geus, A. (1988) Planning as Learning. *Harvard Business Review*, March.

Dobbs, R., Ramaswamy, S., Stephenson, E., & Viguerie, P. (2014) Management Intuition for the next 50 years. *McKinsey Quarterly*, September.

Drucker, P.F. (1974) *Management: Tasks, Responsibilities, Practices* (London: William Heinemann).

Gitsham, M., et al. (2008) Developing the Global Leader of Tomorrow, Ashridge Business School and European Academy of Business in Society Report.

Gitsham, M., et al. (2009) Developing the Global Leader of Tomorrow, Ashridge and ABIS for the UN Principles for Responsible Management Education.

Jonas, H., Fry, R., & Srivastava, S. (1990) The Office of the CEO: Understanding the Executive Experience. *Academy of Management Executive*, Vol. 4, No. 3, pp.36–48.

Kenny, D.A., & Zaccaro, S.J. (1983) An Estimate of Variance Due to Traits in Leadership. *Journal of Applied Psychology*, Vol. 68, No. 4, pp.678–85.

Koontz, H., & O'Donnell, C. (1968) Principles of Management: An Analysis of Managerial Functions, 4th edition (New York: McGraw-Hill).

Kotter, P. (1988) *The Leadership Factor* (New York: Free Press).

Kram, K.E. (1985) *Mentoring at Work: Developmental Relationships in Organizational Life* (Glenview: Scott Foresman).

Laljani, N. (2009) Making Strategic Leaders (London: Palgrave Macmillan).

Leslie, B., Aring, M.K., & Brand, B. (1998) Informal Learning: the New Frontier of Employee and Organizational Development. *Economic Development Review*, Vol. 15, No. 4, pp.12–18.

Lewin, K. (1951) *Field theory in social science: selected theoretical papers*. Edited by D. Cartwright (New York: Harper & Row).

McBain, R., Ghobadian, A., Switzer, J., Wilton, P., Woodman, P., & Pearson, G. (2012) The business benefits of management and leadership development, Chartered Management Institute.

McCall, M.W., Lombardo, M.M., & Morrison, A.M. (1988) *The Lessons of Experience* (Lexington: Lexington Books).

McCauley, C.D., & Douglas, C.A. (2004) Developmental Relationships. In C.D. McCauley & E.V. Velso (eds), *Handbook of Leadership Development* (San Francisco: Jossey-Bass), pp.85–115.

Mezirow, J. (1990) *Fostering Critical Reflection* (San Francisco: Jossey-Bass).

Mintzberg, H., & Quinn, J.B. (1996) *The Strategy Process: Concepts, Contexts, Cases*. 3rd edition (Englewood Cliffs: Prentice-Hall).

Peters, K. (2011) Neuroscience, Learning and Change. *360 – The Ashridge Journal*, pp.44–7.

Porter, M.E., & Kramer, M.R. (2011) Creating Shared Value. *Harvard Business Review*, January.

Schön, D. (1983) *The Reflective Practitioner: How Professionals Think in Action* (London: Maurice Temple Smith).

Smith, B., & Morphey, G. (1994) Tough Challenges: How Big a Learning Gap? *Journal of Management Development*, Vol. 13, No. 9, pp.5–3.

Smith, P.A.C. (2001) Action Learning and Reflective Practice in Phase Environments that are Related to Leadership Developments. *Management Learning*, Vol. 32, No. 1, pp.31–48.

Snell, R. (1989) Graduating From the School of Hard Knocks. *Journal of Management Development*, Vol. 8, No. 5, pp.23–30.

Stern, N. (2007) *The Economics of Climate Change: The Stern Review* (Cambridge: Cambridge University Press).

Thomas, R.J., & Cheese, P. (2005) Leadership: Experience is the Best Teacher. *Strategy and Leadership*, Vol. 33, No. 3, pp.24–9.

Weick, K.E. (1979) *The Social Psychology of Organizing* (Reading: Addison-Wesley).

Williams, S. (1996) A Balloon Waiting to be Burst? Pseudo-management Training, Research Report No. 22 (London: Social Affairs Unit).

Willis, J. (2007) The neuroscience of joyful education. *Engaging the Whole Child*, 64(9).

Wilmott, H. (1994) Management Education: Provocation to a Debate. *Management Learning*, Vol. 25, No. 1, pp.105–6.

Contributors

Angela Jowitt BSc (Hons) Psychol, MSc

Angela is a faculty member, executive coach and client director at Ashridge, as well a founder member of the Ashridge experiential learning team. She researches in the field of experiential and holistic approaches to learning, and has created a facilitation framework which encourages a balanced approach to reviewing experiential learning events between thinking, feeling and doing. Her teaching interest and expertise are in the field of team development and she has a growing interest in team coaching.

Angela's chapter brings together her understanding of a range of organisational cultures and her fascination with creative problem solving in leadership. She believes there is no better way for a leader to have a 'lightbulb learning moment' than to have an experience and reflect upon it, and she highlights the fact that while there is much diversity and difference, our commonalities can transcend more cultural barriers than we realise. Leaders all want the same thing: to be successful and to deliver excellent results. The fascinating bit is how they approach it.

Barbara Banda BA, MSc, MBA, DPhil (Oxon)

Barbara Banda is an expert in strategy, marketing, and the leadership and team-development skills required for effective strategy implementation. She works with organisations to align their people and enable them to meet the demands of their internal and external customers and markets. She has a particular interest in how faculty can work with groups in ways which enhance subsequent learning transfer. Barbara works with a number of high-profile

Ashridge clients including Continental, Astra Zeneca, Unilever, BBC, Philips, and the Foreign and Commonwealth Office.

Prior to joining Ashridge, Barbara worked in international sales and marketing in the pharmaceutical, healthcare and retailing industries, holding senior positions within Fisons Pharmaceuticals, Boots and BASF Pharma. She has a doctorate in education from the University of Oxford, and an MBA and MSc in training and performance management, while her first degree is in German and Russian. She is a visiting professor at a number of European Business Schools.

Chris Nichols BSc (Hons), MSC, MBA, DMS, FRSA

Chris is a passionate communicator who moves between the worlds of education, organisational life, arts and entrepreneurship. A writer, installation artist and poet, Chris lives on Dartmoor and divides his working time between Ashridge Executive Education (where he co-leads the MSc in sustainability and responsibility) and his arts and entrepreneurial ventures.

Chris has worked with senior leadership groups from almost every sector, and his work is highly international, taking him to over 50 countries in the past twenty-five years.

As a social entrepreneur, Chris works to form hubs of creative practitioners. His current activities include www.groundedcreativity.com, an approach to using music as a strategic leadership intervention, and www.gameshift. co.uk, helping organisations to spot limiting assumptions and to change their frames of reference.

Chris has written several articles which are available free of charge on his faculty page at www.ashridge.org.uk. He can be contacted via Twitter, Facebook, Linked In, or at chris.nichols@ashridge.hult.edu.

Dev Mookherjee BA (Hons), MSc, MBA, FCMI

Dev Mookherjee is a management consultant and member of faculty at Ashridge Executive Education who consults, teaches and researches on strategy engagement, organisation design and risk. Recent research projects include 'The activities of the strategist' and 'Working with risk', while he currently works on a project provisionally titled 'The lived experience of organisation design'.

Dev's work includes supporting executive teams on live organisational challenges and he has a firm belief in the power of relevance and action when learning about leadership. His chapter is based on the experience of applying this belief, and he continues to inquire into and develop the role of the facilitator in the process of development, using the 'live case' method. The holder of a master's degree in Japanese from Stirling, organisation consulting from Ashridge, and an MBA from Henley, Dev's most important roles are as husband to Yana and doting father to daughter Sasha.

Ian Hayward BSc, MA, DBA, FCIPD

Ian joined Ashridge Executive Education as a leadership faculty member in 2006, having previously held senior HRD positions at British Airways and the BBC. Drawing from this experience, and with a lengthy background in training and development, his areas of interest are leadership, culture, organisational change and strategic HRM.

Having first come across the work of Donald Kirkpatrick in the early 1980s, Ian has long held an interest in the challenge of evaluation, with a particular focus on why it is seldom given the attention it deserves.

Ian is also a Fellow of the Chartered Institute of Personnel and Development, and leads delivery of the flagship open programme, the Ashridge Leadership Process. In addition to a DBA from the University of Bradford School of Management, Ian has a BSc in Psychology from Southampton University, and an MA in Organisation Development from Loyola University of Chicago.

Ilze Zandvoort DC (USA), MBA (UK), MSc (RSA)

Ilze is a faculty member of Ashridge Executive Education where she specialises in assisting organisations in implementing strategy and change across hierarchies. She believes that every individual impacts the whole, and encourages processes that develop reflective self-awareness.

Ilze combines her consulting and facilitation skills to assist individuals and teams to become better equipped to lead in times of complexity, ambiguity and within globally dispersed teams, helping them improve strategic decision making and strategy implementation in organisations. Her experience spans working with boards and delivering leadership development for front-line managers, across cultures and continents. She is skilled in delivering virtual training, coaching and action learning, helping global leaders develop the necessary skills to manage and lead in the virtual world.

Ilze is currently completing her second doctorate (DBA) at the University of Liverpool. Her research interest is in the interface between different levels of leadership and its role in strategy implementation, as well as in the role of compassionate leadership in relationship building.

Jamie MacAlister MA (Hons), MBA (Hons)

Jamie is a member of faculty at Ashridge, specialising in risk in strategy and commercial management. An experienced commercial manager, strategist, facilitator and executive coach, he previously worked as commercial director at Ashridge, playing a key part in a significant change programme. He has developed his understanding of risk through research on 'How leaders work with risk' and has published 'Engaging with risky dilemmas', which describes a character profiler he developed to support strategic change initiatives.

Jamie has coached and facilitated senior management teams in strategic decision making for nearly 20 years. Prior to his time at Ashridge, he was a management consultant with Pricewaterhouse Coopers and held management roles with Procter & Gamble and Comco (a Swiss technology start-up). His main interest lies in the different ways business leaders engage with risk, both analytically and intuitively, and how this manifests in strategic decision making.

James Moncrieff MBA, MBIM

James works with boards and senior teams to develop their strategic thinking. He helps them develop their vision and strategy, and to translate it into meaningful and engaging objectives and action plans. James leads on programmes in strategic management, leadership and change at Ashridge Executive Education. His consulting background enables him to look beyond programme content, to support the business and organisational outcomes his clients are seeking. His programmes are pragmatic and grounded in reality, often using 'live cases' to anchor the learning in the workplace.

James has developed a unique organisational and behavioural perspective on strategy, which now underpins the way strategy is taught at Ashridge. Working with clients across the world in energy and engineering, financial services, food & beverage, FMCG, retail and the public sector, he often delivers programmes through simultaneous translation.

Kai Peters BA (Hons), MBA, CCMI

Kai has been chief executive of Ashridge since 2003 and in 2015 added chief academic officer of Hult International Business School to his remit. Between 1993 and 2003, he was dean, having previously been director of MBA programs, at the Rotterdam School of Management (RSM) of Erasmus University in the Netherlands.

Kai has served on the boards of a number of organisations in the technology and healthcare sectors, and currently serves in various capacities for educational associations including AACSB, EFMD, AMBA, ABS and GMAC. His chief interest is in the management challenges organisations face in the twenty-first century, and how to develop the appropriate responses. He writes on strategy, leadership, and education. Kai recently co-authored *Steward Leadership* (University of Cape Town Press, 2013). He has twice been selected for *HR* magazine's top 100 HR professionals in the UK.

Kai holds degrees from York University, Toronto, University of Quebec in Chicoutimi (Canada) and Erasmus University in the Netherlands.

Kathleen King MA, MBA, PGDip, PhD

Kathleen leads the MSc and doctorate in organisational change at Ashridge. Under her leadership, the programme has adopted 'action research' as the methodological orientation of choice. Bringing theory and reflection to bear on work issues, experimenting with new approaches and using this to inform further learning generates immediate benefits for participants and their sponsoring organisations.

Kathleen brings her action research expertise to her practices as an organisational consultant, coach and supervisor, and has extensive experience in personal, team and organisational development. Her clients include private, public, charitable and not-for-profit organisations.

Lee Waller BSc (Hons), MSc

Lee is a director of the Ashridge Centre for Research in Executive Development at Hult International Business School, which conducts and disseminates research around adult learning, including the science of learning, the process of learning transfer and evaluating impact. She also teaches in the areas of neuroscience and learning, developing a high-performing learning organisation and psychological safety.

Lee believes that the behavioural sciences, and in particular neuroscience, have valuable lessons to teach us about why we behave the way that we do. She is passionate about developing and sharing that knowledge both to improve methods of learning and development, and to help individuals rise to the challenges of leadership.

Lee is a psychologist and holds an honours degree in psychology and a master's degree in occupational psychology. She is also doctoral student exploring the experience within the workplace of 'feeling like an outsider', and the impact this can have on psychological wellbeing.

Matt Gitsham MA (Hons), MA

Matt is the director of the Ashridge Centre for Business and Sustainability at Hult International Business School. He teaches on a range of Ashridge programmes and works with colleagues across Ashridge to promote research on leadership, organisational change, leadership development and sustainability.

Matt's most recent research explores CEO perspectives on the implications of sustainability for leadership and leadership development, working with the CEOs of a number of blue-chip organisations. He also works closely with the United Nations Global Compact, the International Business Leaders Forum and Business in the Community.

Matt is a frequent contributor to industry and academic conferences and is widely published in the business and academic press. He was recently awarded a 'Rising Star' award by the Academy of Business in Society–Aspen Institute European Faculty Pioneer Awards, held annually to honour business school faculty who have demonstrated great vision and outstanding leadership in integrating the principles of sustainable development into research, education, student communities and corporate practice.

Megan Reitz PhD, MA (Cantab), MSc, MRes

Megan Reitz researches, teaches and consults in the areas of leadership, organisational change and personal development. She is a director on the Ashridge Open Programme Management Team and leads a number of programmes directly including *The Leadership Experience; Leading on the edge* and the newly launched *Leading on Purpose*. Before joining Ashridge Executive Education, she gained significant experience strategy consulting for various organisations and working within the internet industry.

Megan is particularly interested in exploring leadership capacities appropriate for the twenty-first century. This has led her to explore mindfulness and collaboration through dialogue in organisations, and she has recently published a book, *Dialogue in Organisations: Developing Relational Leadership*. Through her involvement on *The Leadership Experience*, she has also become interested in the neuroscience of leadership.

Megan's chapter, co-written with Lee Waller, examines the role that pressure plays in learning processes. It signals her passion for striving for relevant, useful, positive and transferable leadership development.

Narendra Laljani BA, MMS, DBA

Narendra Laljani is the dean of graduate studies at Ashridge, and has worked internationally in executive development for over twenty years. He teaches, consults and researches in the area of strategic innovation and execution, and is particularly interested in the development of leaders at the apex of organisations.

Narendra believes passionately that management development works, and makes a difference to individuals and organisations, but that not all development interventions are equal. His book, *Making Strategic Leaders* (Palgrave Macmillan, 2009) challenges much of the received wisdom of the leader-development industry and offers new approaches.

Narendra has degrees in economics and management, as well as a doctorate in leader development. Prior to joining Ashridge, he had an international general-management career in industry, and takes pride in the delivery of education that is academically well-grounded, but also engaging and relevant. He is currently working with colleagues to develop a new qualification in management development.

Patricia Hind BSc, MSc, PhD, CPsychol, AFBPS

Patricia is a director of the Ashridge Centre for Research in Executive Development at Hult International Business School. She works with a range of international clients from both public and private sectors, specialising in leadership, organisational behaviour and change management. Recent research includes the study of the principles underpinning effective management development, responsible leadership and its role in embedding sustainable business practices in diverse organisations.

As a leadership and organisational behaviour specialist, Patricia has worked on many Ashridge customised programmes with global clients around the world. She has worked closely on the design and delivery of programmes for organisations in sectors such as finance, oil and gas, construction, electronics and communications.

A visiting research fellow at the University of Stellenbosch, Patricia has a degree in psychology, an MSc in organisational psychology and a doctorate in managing without authority. A chartered psychologist, she has also been appointed an associate fellow of the BPS.

Roger Delves MA (Hons) Oxon, FRSA

Roger is director of the Ashridge MBA and master's in management programmes and head of the People and Leadership faculty. Previous career moves include time on the board of an international advertising agency and a spell at Cranfield School of Management.

Roger has always been fascinated to explore different ways to engage participants in learning about themselves, others and relationships. In workshops he establishes frameworks outside the world of business and asks participants to find parallels with their professional worlds, often using actors, storytelling, Shakespeare and tales from the world of exploration and adventure to add to the experience. This has worked with tailored and open programme groups, with multi-cultural groups and single ethnicity groups.

Until researching this chapter, Roger had never tried this technique with students studying for a third-level degree, and he relished the opportunity to discover whether or not they would embrace the experience.

Vicki Culpin BA (Hons), MSc, MPhil, PhD, CPsychol, FHEA

Vicki is global dean of research at Ashridge Executive Education, Hult International Business School. She works with a range of international clients from the public, private and cultural sectors, and delivers guest lectures around the world on a variety of psychological topics.

Vicki studied psychology at Manchester University, followed by an MPhil and PhD in psychology at Lancaster University and an MSc in applied forensic psychology at Leicester University. She is an associate fellow of the British Psychological Society, a chartered psychologist and a fellow of the Higher Education Academy.

Prior to becoming global dean of research, Vicki was the director of the Ashridge Centre for Research in Executive Development, enabling her to work with clients to understand the most effective ways of making the learning 'stick'. Vicki sees this transfer of learning as critical to the success of any adult executive learning intervention, and is passionate about creating environments to maximise this.